Careers for Horse Lovers

Careers for
HORSE LOVERS

Ronald Trahan

with photographs by
David O. Aronson

Houghton Mifflin Company Boston

For Marcia
The memory of Luther Allison
And the experience of Vermont

All of which have helped lead me to
My writer's identity

For information about permission to reproduce selections from this book, write to Permissions, Houghton Mifflin Company, 2 Park Street, Boston, Massachusetts 02108.

Library of Congress Cataloging in Publication Data
Trahan, Ronald.
Careers for horse lovers.
1. Horse industry—Vocational guidance.   2. Horse sports—Vocational guidance. I. Aronson, David O. II. Title.
   SF285.25.T7   636.1′0023   81-6402
   ISBN 0-395-31331-7   AACR2

Printed in the United States of America

VB 16 15 14 13 12 11 10 9 8 7 6

Contents

Acknowledgments

I APPROACH THE EXPRESSION of my indebtedness with much gratitude.

First, I wish to thank my editor at Houghton Mifflin Company, Mrs. Ruth Hapgood, for everything she has done to bring the book to publication.

I am indebted, too, to the great cooperation I received from the various professionals of the various careers explored herein, namely: Dr. Ann Williams and Dr. Richard Sheehan; jockey Jorge Vargas, valet Tom Baron, jockey's agent Robert "Iffy" Casselletto, Richard McLaughlin of The Jockeys' Guild, and Robert Varey, Public Relations Director at Suffolk Downs Racetrack; breeding farm managers Nancy Caisse of Townshend Farm in Bolton, Massachusetts, and Lynn Cashman of Our Goal Farm in Middleboro, Massachusetts; Dr. Edward L. Squires, Associate Professor of Equine Reproduction at Colorado State University; Ann Borton, Extension Specialist with the 4–H Program at the University of Massachusetts; riding instructor Melody Fryer; Lt. Col. Mark Daley, Director of Morven Park International Equestrian Institute; photographers David Aronson, Bill Haggis, and Henry Carfagna; farrier Garth Bodkin; stable managers Rusty Cameron and Carin

Zuchero; and trainers Bobby LaPergola, Jack and Jimmy Farrell, and Marc deChamplain.

I owe a very deep gratitude to equestrienne Ann Tracey and her magnificent Trakehner, Burlingeist. Without Ann's help, the book might not have been possible.

Finally, my thanks to fellow authors Gary Provost and Dr. Jeffrey Lant, whose ample encouragement during the planning stages of this adventure was invaluable.

Hold fast to dreams
for if dreams die,
   life is a broken
      winged bird that
         cannot fly.

— LANGSTON HUGHES

Careers for Horse Lovers

ONE

The Equine Practitioner

"I CAN'T FIGURE IT OUT, doc," said Bradstreet. "I mean, he seemed okay to me up until this morning."

The jockey-sized Bradstreet had recently moved to the East from California. His three-year-old Thoroughbred had been shipped across the country by a commercial van line. When the colt got off the van a week ago, he was in excellent shape, according to Bradstreet.

Now, he wasn't.

"You say he hasn't eaten anything all day?" asked Dr. Carson Digby. She looked much too young to have been a veterinarian for ten years — even in the twenty-five-watt light of dusk in November.

"Not a thing, doc. Not a blessed thing. And there's something else, too — as if that's not bad enough. He keeps going over to his water bucket, see. But all he does is suck in a couple of small sips and turn away, like he can hardly stand the taste of it. Yet he keeps coming back for more. *Weird,* isn't it, doc?"

"Perhaps not. Have you taken his temperature?"

"A hundred and two at six this morning. That's when I decided to call you. Was I right, doc? I'm sorry I called so early and all, but ——"

Photo by David O. Aronson

"Please, Mr. Bradstreet. It's quite all right. I meant, have you taken your colt's temp since then?"

"Well, no, doc. Was I supposed to?"

Bradstreet nad paid a handsome price for Redwillo. The thought of the colt being overcome by some mysterious disease, suffering for a while, and finally dying, had haunted the rookie horseman all day.

Carson understood his concern. She stood to one side and watched Bradstreet's nervous hands finally open the barn door, thinking that the sooner she made her diagnosis, the quicker she could relieve the poor man's anxiety.

Inside the barn there were six stalls. All were vacant for now — except one. Redwillo stood in it, his neck stretched to infinity and his head hung low, coughing like some three-pack-a-day chain smoker. Carson leaned against his stall door and observed the sick colt, noticing in particular the watery discharge that was seeping from his nostrils. In the manner of the classic Hollywood-movie sleuth, Carson would begin her investigation by looking for physical evidence like the coughing and nasal discharge, insisting on seeing, hearing, and feeling the victim's condition before jumping to a conclusion and accusing the wrong disease.

The colt finally stopped coughing. "Let's check his vital signs first," said Carson. It was quiet in the barn. The only sound came from the cat that Bradstreet had inherited when he bought the country property. She was meowing at irregular intervals two stalls away. Carson hardly noticed. Instead, she studied the sweep hand on her wristwatch, then removed the thermometer from Redwillo. "One hundred and . . . three," she announced. The calm in her voice gave no indication that there was cause for alarm.

Bradstreet, nonetheless, had to ask, "Isn't that kind of high, doc?"

"It's certainly not normal," said Carson. "But it's still a whole degree below the point where I'd start getting concerned.

A fever temp, for sure, Mr. Bradstreet, but nothing to be overly anxious about."

"What's causing it? Any ideas?"

"It's an infection."

"Like a cold or something?"

"Similar," said Carson.

"How can you tell?"

"There are the usual symptoms. Loss of appetite, for one. The elevated temp, for another." She removed a stethoscope from her instrument bag and eavesdropped first on Redwillo's heart, then his lungs. All the while, Bradstreet hovered over her like a doting father watching his daughter tie her shoe for the first time.

Carson was accustomed to hovering owners. She continued, therefore, with the examination, holding the stethoscope against the front of the colt's neck. Beneath the surface lay the trachea, a tunnel through which air was making its way to the lungs. "There's congestion in here, all right," she announced. She then placed her fingers around Redwillo's throat, gently feeling the larynx which lay beneath the skin. The colt coughed instantly, as soon as Carson pressed even slightly.

"Well," she said. "It's a respiratory infection, that's for sure. Let's see if we can pinpoint where the actual inflammation is."

Facing Redwillo, she held the nosepiece of his halter with her left hand and placed her right hand underneath the colt's chin. Her fingers explored the hot and swollen area. Even the most delicate probe, though, caused the colt to jerk his head back in obvious discomfort. "It's no wonder he's not drinking much water — or eating either," she said. "His throat's sore. Swollen, actually."

With her forefinger and middle finger pressed together, Carson tapped lightly on Redwillo's face just below and between his eyes. "No congestion in the sinuses yet. That's good. Means the infection is still in its early stages, that it's entrenched in just one place. For now, anyway."

"You mean he's not too bad off, doc?"

"Not really," said Carson.

"This infection, doc. Do you know what it is?"

"Strangles. It's caused by a bacteria ——"

"*Strangles?*" interrupted Bradstreet. He folded his arms, furrowed his eyebrows, and leaned against the stall wall. "That's pretty serious, isn't it, doc?"

"Not at the stage we've discovered it. Young horses like yours are quite susceptible to it, I'm afraid."

Bradstreet punched a fist into a palm. "I knew it!" he said. "I knew I shouldn't have shipped him cross-country by himself. I'll bet that's how he caught it. Right, doc? Am I right?"

"More than likely," said Carson. "Some people even call it *shipping fever.* But don't be angry with yourself, Mr. Bradstreet — or the shipping company. It's not travel that causes the infection. It's contact with an infected horse."

Bradstreet sighed. "Can you cure him, doc? I mean, strangles *sounds* pretty serious, you've got to admit. Doesn't it?"

"It can be. But not in your colt's case."

"Why not?"

"Because, first of all, the infection's in the early stage. His temperature and relatively mild congestion suggest that. In two, maybe three days, his sinuses will start filling up with mucus. Then an abscess — a buildup of *pus* — will start to form under the lower jaw, beneath the skin, where the inflammation is now."

"Where the inflammation is?"

"The *mandibular lymph nodes,* Mr. Bradstreet," said Carson. She smiled.

"Whew! That's a mouthful, doc."

"You asked for it," said Carson. "That's precisely where the infection is growing right this moment. It's not serious at this point. Only if it were to go untreated."

"Then what would happen?"

"Well," said Carson. "The bacteria would probably spread elsewhere in his body where they'd be more difficult to fight.

Or else the swelling in his throat would get so severe it would clog the air passages completely."

"It could actually choke him to death, you mean?"

"That's why it's called *strangles*," said Carson. She advised Bradstreet to keep his colt isolated from the other horses when they finally arrived. "It's an extremely contagious disease," she said. "Sterilize all the clothing and equipment he comes into contact with — yours and his."

Bradstreet suddenly looked puzzled. Carson, it appeared, was getting ready to leave. "Aren't you going to give him an injection or something?"

Carson grinned, more to herself than to Bradstreet. It seemed as if most of her clients were always giving her medical advice. Some were more subtle about it than Bradstreet, though.

"Not quite yet, Mr. Bradstreet. You see, right now the bacteria are isolated. They're all staying put in the area where the abscess is forming. They're very difficult to kill there. A shot of an antibiotic would only stop them temporarily. It wouldn't eliminate them altogether. Eventually they'd renew their attack the minute the antibiotic wore off. Or even worse, they'd hide out in the body for a few months, then show up in another, harder-to-reach spot. And that," she said, "might prove fatal."

Bradstreet swallowed with just a little bit of difficulty. "Sorry," he said. "Didn't mean to be telling you your business, doc."

"That's all right. I know you're concerned, that's all. There is something you can do for him, though. Check his temp three times a day. If it shoots above one-oh-four, call me immediately. Otherwise, just soak a wad of cotton in some hot water and hold it against the swelling under his jaw for about fifteen minutes every time you take the temp. The heat will draw the pus to the surface," she explained, picking up her instrument bag, "where I'll be able to get at it. I'll be back the day after tomorrow to drain it. Till then, don't worry. He's fine."

On her way out to her station wagon, Carson glanced at her wristwatch. She was always glancing at her wristwatch. It was five-ten. A Friday evening. In less than twelve hours another work day would begin.

Tomorrow, though, would be different. Tomorrow, Tatum Huxley would be making the rounds with her. It will be nice, Carson thought, to have company while I'm driving around all day — someone to talk to from one appointment to the next.

For a change.

*

Carson Digby is an equine practitioner — a veterinarian who specializes in treating horses. She possesses all the basic veterinary training and skills as well as special knowledge of horses gained after graduation from veterinary college.

In some ways, perhaps, her daily reality is even more engrossing than that of her counterpart in human medicine, because Carson's patients can't explain how they feel or where they hurt.

"It's like trying to communicate with someone from another planet," she admits. "Every case is a mystery, a challenge, to one degree or another. In order to solve a mystery you've got to look for clues. That's why there's never a dull moment in my job. There's always something different happening every day — some new mystery that has to be probed and solved."

Last week, for example, she had her arm up to her shoulder inside a mare's birth canal, helping the would-be mother overcome a breech-birth emergency. The next day saw her engaged in surgery to remove a golf-ball-sized cancer from an old stallion's nose, and then set the badly broken leg of a valuable foal. There have been days when she's sped to a farm where dozens of horses were stricken with a virulent and communicable disease, days when she's checked racehorses to see if they had been illegally drugged, and days when she's inspected an imported horse for possible infection. "The list of possibilities," says Carson, "is endless."

For all practical purposes, equine practitioners like Carson Digby were the country's first professional veterinarians — for good reason. Until recent times, the horse had always been the most versatile and valuable animal our society possessed. Consider, for example, that it literally took "horse power" to build America — millions of horses were needed to cultivate soil and haul cargoes, provide transportation and communication, work mines, clear timber, and render hundreds of other vital services.

Of necessity, then, veterinary practice remained essentially one of equine medicine until the period preceding World War I. Thereafter, the horse began to be rapidly replaced by machines, and its numbers dwindled fast, which meant, of course, that veterinarians specializing in equines had to turn to other animals — dogs, cats, cows, and swine, primarily — in order to make a living.

Since 1950 or so, however, there has been a steady revival of interest in horses to the point where, today, there are more horses in the country than there are college students. And every one of those horses, at one time or another, needs the attention of a professional like Carson Digby.

*

The first stop today would be Windrush Farm. The patient, Questor, was a four-year-old grade gelding that was pleasure ridden four or five times a week. He had been turned out to pasture for the last three months. Carson had last seen him when she wormed him in mid-August.

For the last three weeks Questor's owner, Bart Redhouse, had been noticing that the gelding just wasn't himself. He wasn't eating all his hay, for one thing; nor did he seem as energetic as usual. When Bart realized that Questor wasn't getting any better, he made the appointment with Carson.

Carson had picked up a young woman by the name of Tatum Huxley on her way over to Windrush Farm this morning. Tatum was hoping to become a veterinarian herself. She was taking a year off between college graduation and veterinary college for two reasons: first, to earn some money to help pay for any future education; and second, to get a down-to-earth view of the realities of the job. "To see if it's what I really want to do with my life," she told Carson.

Although Tatum had seen many horses in her twenty-one years, she was immediately puzzled when she saw Questor. His coat looked extremely dull, as if someone had rubbed car wax all over him and forgotten to follow up with a rag rub.

Rather than taking an interest in his visitors, Questor ignored Tatum and Carson and even his owner, choosing instead to stand at the rear of his stall and stare into the wood wall. The first thing Carson did was check his temperature. It was a shade above one hundred degrees, well within the normal range. Then she spread open Questor's right eyelid, exposing the inner surface called the *conjunctiva*.

"You've been around horses a lot," said Carson. "Does that look normal to you, Tatum?"

The young woman hesitated, maybe, for one second. "No," she replied, her voice firm and forceful. "It's a lot more pale than the pinkish color it should be."

All the while, Bart Redhouse leaned over the stall door, hands locked as if in prayer, observing. He said nothing, which, for him, was unusual.

"Okay," said Carson. "What have we got for clues so far?"

Tatum inhaled deeply and sighed before answering. "His coat's pretty dull, for one thing," she said. "And so is he, for another."

"True," agreed Carson. "So what might be running through your mind at this point?"

"Possibly an infection of some sort?"

"But what about ——"

"I know what you're going to say, doctor. His temperature is normal, so that rules out the infection theory."

"Exactly," said Carson. "We can be sure of that by analyzing his blood. Meantime, let's see if we can uncover a few more clues." She peeled back Questor's lip, exposing his teeth, and pressed her thumb against the horse's gum. When she removed it, a white circle remained for three or four seconds before it refilled with color, at which point Carson looked at Tatum. "What are you thinking?" she asked.

"It took an awful long time for the color to come back," Tatum replied.

"Very good," said Carson. "What do you think, Bart? Can I retire pretty soon and leave the horse world's well-being to Tatum here?"

Bart grinned a one-front-tooth-missing grin. "I'd say so, doc. Think what she'll be like with four years of vet school behind her. Whew!"

Tatum acknowledged this with a long-lasting smile.

"Now," said Carson, "here's where you'd earn your money if you were the vet. Think a minute before you answer me. Combine the observation you just made with what you noticed a minute ago — the paleness in the conjunctiva. What's it add up to, those clues? Any idea?"

Tatum stared at the straw at her feet and moved her head from side to side. "I'm lost now, doctor," she mumbled.

"Don't sound so disappointed. You're not a vet yet, you know. You haven't had the benefit of four years of professional training and another ten of specialized experience."

Tatum looked at Carson. "Sorry," she said. "Didn't realize I was being so serious."

"No problem," said Carson, pinching a fold of skin on Questor's neck. She pulled on the fold and then released. It remained creased for an instant before smoothing itself out — another clue. Next, she put on her stethoscope and listened to Questor's heart, lungs, and intestinal tract. Everything sounded normal. She took a blood sample, too, which she'd analyze tomorrow at her laboratory.

When she finished drawing the blood, Carson asked Bart Redhouse to take Questor outside and jog him lightly for a minute, after which she took another blood sample the instant Questor stopped moving. She listened once again to the horse's heart, too, reporting that the rate was definitely elevated this time.

"One thing's for sure," she explained as they returned to the barn. "His body is being stressed. My educated guess, Bart, is that he's got a red blood cell deficiency — he's *anemic.*"

Carson further explained that *hemoglobin,* one of the components of red blood cells, carries oxygen from place to place in the body. "Any reduction in those red blood cells," she said, "cuts down on the blood's capacity to feed the body the oxygen it needs."

"I get it," said Tatum. "Since he has fewer red blood cells than usual, his heart has to pump a lot harder to push around the ones he does have. Which is why his heartbeat was elevated after just a little bit of exercise."

"I do declare, young lady," said Bart. "If it weren't for the fact that it's my five-thousand-dollar animal you're talking about, I'd be really happy with that diagnosis of yours."

"Don't worry, Bart," said Carson. "It's not serious at this point."

"Think it's worms that's causin' the anemia?" Bart asked. He led Questor into his stall.

"Yes, I do," said Carson. "They attach themselves to the intestinal wall, then intercept and destroy the red blood cells as they leave the stomach full of nutrients." She collected a fecal sample from Questor's stall as she spoke. "The worms don't only destroy the red blood cells, though. They also rob the body of the nutrients it needs to make more red blood cells." The fecal sample she was packaging would confirm the presence of worms in Questor's body.

"Why take two blood samples?" asked Tatum.

Carson explained that when a horse is at rest — as was the case when the first blood sample was taken from Questor — he keeps a number of red blood cells stored in his spleen. A little bit of exercise — when Bart jogged Questor for a minute — is sufficient to stimulate the spleen to its normal level of activity. "Brings the stored cells out of hiding," she said. If the second blood sample, when compared to the first, still showed a deficiency of red blood cells, Carson could then be certain that Bart Redhouse's horse was anemic.

But something bothered her. Experience kept whispering to her, telling her that an infestation of *strongyle* worms might not be severe enough to be the sole criminal in Questor's case. There might be an accomplice.

"What have you been feeding him, Bart?" asked Carson.

"Four quarts of oats. Three sections of timothy hay. Plus all the pasture he can sink his teeth into," said Bart.

Carson told him that the oats and hay wouldn't supply enough of the nutrients — particularly iron — to manufacture enough red blood cells even under normal conditions. If worms were, in fact, diminishing the already small supply even further, it was no wonder the horse was anemic. The proof would lie in the laboratory analysis of Questor's blood and feces.

In the meantime, before she and Tatum departed, Carson outlined a new diet and vitamin supplement for Bart to give Questor. She announced that she would return in two or three days, as soon as the verdict was in, to tube-worm Questor if that was what he needed to set him on the road to recovery.

*

The next appointment would be at the Heffernans' ranch some miles away.

Tatum had been making the rounds with Carson for only three weekends, but already she most enjoyed the quiet time between clients — the time spent with Carson while traveling from one appointment to the next. It gave her the opportunity to discuss Carson's profession in general or to ask particular questions about the situation they'd just left.

The ride to the Heffernans' ranch would last nearly twenty minutes. Tatum locked the door and leaned her body against it. She wondered, as she looked at Carson and began to speak, how old the vet was . . . thirty-seven, maybe, she thought. "Anemia this morning, doctor. Strangles yesterday, you said. A torn shoulder muscle later on today . . ." Tatum paused. "Don't you ever get tired of the constant suspense?"

"What do you mean, *suspense?*"

"Well, I mean, starting every day not really sure of what you'll be running into next — isn't that rather difficult on your nerves?"

Carson chuckled. "That's one of the things I like best," she replied. "No two days are ever the same."

"But aren't you always putting yourself on the spot? I mean, it's like you have to know everything in the world about veterinary medicine."

"C'mon, Tatum. You're giving me too much credit. I'm no genius. Really."

"But you're always running into something new, aren't you?"

"Yes. And no," said Carson. "Even though one day is always different from the next, within that variety is a certain sameness. Horses get sick just as we do, and a lot of those sicknesses are common types of ailments like upset stomachs, sinus infections, respiratory infections — same as we get. After you've been around awhile, those things are not all that mysterious to diagnose."

Tatum was silent for a moment. "But what about emergencies? That can't be easy on you."

"No. You're right. There's been many a time when my phone's rung at three o'clock in the morning. I can't just roll over and go back to sleep when that happens. Being a vet's no nine-to-five job, Tatum. It's a way of life, it really is. Horses don't take weekends and nights off. You know that." There was more brief silence while they waited for the red light to change. Then, as Carson stepped on the accelerator, she spoke again. "As much as this might sound corny, there's more reward in my job than in a Brink's truck."

*

Reward.

Perhaps that's why the American Association of Equine Practitioners (AAEP) reports that the number of professionals like Carson Digby has increased dramatically in response to the demand for them over the last several decades.

In 1955, for example, there were fewer than one hundred full-time equine practitioners in the country. Today, however, because of the increased interest in the horse as a companion animal, there are more than three thousand. And when you consider that those specialists must serve more than nine million patients, you can understand why Carson is so optimistic about the prospects of someone like Tatum Huxley.

"I've got more work," says Carson, "than I can possibly handle. I simply can't take on new clients anymore. Keep in mind, too, that I've never once advertised my services, not once in the entire decade I've been practicing equine medicine."

It should come as no surprise, then, that the U.S. government predicts that employment opportunities for equine practitioners are expected to be favorable at least through the 1980's.

A recent survey of veterinary college graduates by the American Veterinary Medical Association (AVMA) reported that the majority of first-year equine practitioners earn between $14,000 and $16,000 — although some earn less, and a few considerably more. Earnings tend to increase as the equine practitioner gains additional skills and knowledge via experience. Many vets, for example, with five or more years of practice behind them are earning between $25,000 and $35,000 annually.

Because of the potential for even higher earnings, many outsiders mistakenly view the profession as downright glamorous. Most, however, don't take into account the fact that Carson's occupation is one of high risk. She travels thousands of miles annually, in sometimes treacherous driving conditions, to work with the most dangerous of all domesticated animals. Long hours and late-night and early-morning emergencies are also part of the equine practitioner's "glamorous" job.

"Sure," admits Carson. "The potential to make a lot of money sounds exciting. But let me tell you something. At the year's end there's no *written* guarantee that my final earnings will have been any greater than that of a forty-hour-per-week union worker on an assembly line.

"But the worst part of it all is the ingratitude I run into once in a while. Sometimes I'll spend hours and hours looking through medical texts, asking myself, 'Did I miss something in my diagnosis? Is there something I haven't thought about?' I can try all the procedures I'm supposed to, maybe even consult with a colleague or two. But every once in a blue moon I'll run into a case where there's just nothing I can do for the horse. The owner will never know how long I agonized over his animal. The only thing that matters to him is whether or not I cured his horse. If I didn't, I'm incompetent in his eyes.

"If a person can't learn to live with that kind of blame occasionally, I'd strongly advise not going into this profession. It's a mistaken notion to think, as I once did, 'Well, I like animals better than people, so I'll become a vet instead of a doctor.' My profession is as dependent on *human* relations as it is on *animal* relations. It's simple — the successful vet is as good with people as he or she is with animals. That," insists Carson, "is tough to do."

She's quick to add, however, that there's nothing else she'd rather be doing.

"I'm my own boss. That in itself is worth plenty to me — plus the challenge my career affords me every single day. Let's face it. No matter what's wrong, I'm the person on the spot . . . I'm the one who's supposed to have all the right answers.

The fact that my patients can't tell me how they feel or where they hurt makes it doubly challenging.

"As far as I'm concerned, one of the most fascinating jobs in the world is to be able to give a horse — or any animal, for that matter — a useful life after a serious illness or injury. It's a tremendous feeling to know I have the skills to do a lot of good for the world."

*

In order to practice equine medicine — or any kind of veterinary medicine — Carson needed two qualifications: first, a Doctor of Veterinary Medicine (D.V.M.) or Veterinary Medical Doctor (V.M.D.) degree, and, second, a license issued by the state in which she intended to practice.

To be considered for admission to one of the country's twenty-four veterinary colleges (for a list of these colleges, see Appendix I) in order to earn her degree, Carson had to meet certain requirements. First, she had to have completed the equivalent of at least three full academic years in an accredited college or university. "With me," she says, "that requirement was no problem. By the time I had decided on applying to vet school, I already had a bachelor's degree — in, of all things, English literature."

However, although her degree was not science-oriented, while majoring in English she had taken many biological science courses, which allowed her to meet the second admission requirement of her particular veterinary college: "preprofessional training."

"Most vet schools," Carson explains, "require that an applicant have taken certain science courses — like biology, inorganic chemistry, and organic chemistry — as well as courses in physics, calculus, and behavioral science, or they won't even consider your application."

Getting accepted by a veterinary college is no easy task. Most of the colleges, for example, give preference to state residents, first of all. Additionally, the veterinary colleges as a whole only have enough room to accommodate fifteen percent of all those who apply.

"Don't be discouraged," advises Carson. "Be smart. Put yourself in the position of a member of an admissions board. What would you — the admissions board official — want to know about you — the would-be veterinarian — before accepting or rejecting your application? Keep in mind you can only accept fifteen out of every hundred of you who apply.

"The first thing you'd be likely to consider is the applicant's grades in high school and college. Why? You'd want to be certain the applicant's academic skills are sufficient to carry him or her through the four years of intensive medical study ahead.

"In addition, you'd definitely want to know about the applicant's interest in — and experience with — animals.

"There's good reason for being so careful in your assessment of the applicant. The cost of the applicant's veterinary education will be far greater — by ten times or more! — than the amount of money actually paid in tuition and other fees. Who pays the difference? The taxpayers in the state where the school's located. Obviously, then, as a member of the admissions board, you have an obligation to make sure that the applicant's interest is sincere."

One way for an applicant to demonstrate that sincerity is to have shown a genuine interest in animals from an early age. In Carson's case, her parents owned a horse, and she competed with it in local 4-H Club competitions. She also worked with animals during her summer vacations, during which time she acquired firsthand information as to how animals are born, raised, and cared for — fundamental knowledge that any admissions board official would expect of a serious applicant.

"And don't forget," adds Carson, "that as an admissions board official you'd be interested in the references the applicant has had sent to you. Regardless of superior academic standing or extensive experience with animals, as a veterinarian the applicant will eventually deal with people, too. If the applicant has demonstrated the ability to get along with others, you'll be more favorably impressed."

*

The curriculum at a veterinary college is similar to that offered in medical schools. Only in the advanced courses do medical concepts and the application of those concepts begin to be more specifically confined to animals other than human.

Make no mistake about it: veterinary college courses are difficult. You must learn and remember hundreds of terms and all kinds of facts and theories about many kinds of animals and diseases. (Keep in mind that you won't be specializing in horses until after you graduate.) You also have to become skilled in surgical techniques, as well as laboratory and diagnostic procedures.

In general, the degree curriculum at most of the nation's vet colleges requires four academic years of study. The first year consists primarily of lectures and focuses on the basic medical sciences. During the first year, students usually also receive their initial exposure to clinical veterinary medicine. For example, students might study the functional parts of an animal's anatomy by relating structures dissected from the cadavers of laboratory animals to the structures observed in the lab animals' living counterparts. At the conclusion of the first year, there is usually an optional summer period of study during which students can take elective courses, work in a research or diagnostic laboratory, or even begin working on their thesis research project.

The second year continues on the base developed in the first, with emphasis, however, on the study of diseases that affect animals.

Third-year curriculum is usually designed to provide courses in those portions of clinical medicine not covered in the second year — that is, the diagnosis, prognosis, and treatment of the diseases studied in the second year.

The following is a typical four-year curriculum:

First Year

First Semester

Gross Anatomy
Developmental and Microscopic
  Anatomy
Vertebrate Biochemistry
Nutrition

Second Semester

Gross Anatomy
Microscopic Anatomy
Neuroanatomy
Physiology
Veterinary Medical Orientation

Second Year

Veterinary Immunology
Veterinary Bacteriology
Veterinary Mycology and
  Protozoology
Physiology
Veterinary Pathology I
Veterinary Parasitology
Clinical Methods

Veterinary Virology
Infectious and Zoonotic Diseases
Basic Pharmacology
Veterinary Pathology II
Principles of Epidemiology
Avian Diseases
Obstetrics and Reproductive
  Diseases
General Medicine

Third Year

Applied Anatomy
Preventive Medicine in Animal
  Health Management
Clinical Pharmacology
Introduction to Lab Animal
  Medicine
Obstetrics and Reproductive
  Diseases
Large Animal Medicine
Clinical Pathology
Small Animal Medicine and
  Surgery
General Surgery

Applied Anatomy
Large Animal Medicine
Large Animal Surgery
Radiology
Clinical Nutrition
Small Animal Medicine and
  Surgery
Small Animal Surgical Exercises

Fourth Year

Preventive Medicine in Animal
  Health Management
Seminar: Case Studies
Large Animal Clinic
Ambulatory Clinic
Ancillary Clinics
Small Animal Medicine Clinic
Small Animal Surgery Clinic

Seminar: Case Studies
Large Animal Surgical Clinic
Large Animal Medicine Clinic
Clinical Pathology Clinic
Necropsy Clinic
Anesthesia Clinic
Ophthalmology Clinic

By the fourth year, the lecture courses are completed and the student spends the final year gaining "hands-on" experience via small- and large-animal clinics. Under supervision, the student is given experience in recording the case history of an animal, carrying out the physical examination, performing diagnostic procedures, and being responsible for treatment and management of the animal.

How much will a veterinary education cost?

Plenty.

For example, the cost of education at Tufts University's School of Veterinary Medicine for the 1980–81 academic year was $16,800. Some $9,000 of that figure was defrayed by the state's taxpayers (for those students who were legal residents of Massachusetts, the state in which the college is located). The remaining $8,000 was the responsibility of the student. Keep in mind that the figure represents tuition only — not the cost of books, instruments, room and board, transportation, and other expenses — and for only *one* of the four years needed to earn the degree.

A veterinary education, then, is by far the most expensive of all the careers outlined in this book. Fortunately, financial aid is available. (See the last chapter, "How to Find Money for Your Education," for further information.)

*

One of the best ways to learn more about the career of an equine practitioner is to become acquainted with one. Most are usually willing and eager to discuss their careers. Their information can be invaluable: after all, they've successfully combated and surmounted all of the problems typically encountered.

To locate an equine practitioner in your area, write to the American Association of Equine Practitioners (AAEP), Route 5, 14 Hillcrest Circle, Golden, CO 80401. Ask that the association send you its *A.A.E.P. Directory*. This 125-page booklet lists every member equine practitioner by state and gives each vet's mailing address.

Once you have the name and address of the equine practitioner closest to you, write a letter explaining that you'd like to make an appointment to discuss the profession. Say that you'll be telephoning in a few days to confirm an appointment.

Assuming that you've conducted yourself well during the interview, that the vet likes you and you like him or her, and that you have experience already working with horses, you might want to ask if you could be of assistance to the practice after school or on weekends. There are many jobs you could probably perform that would be helpful to the vet, while affording you the opportunity to find out at first hand what the practice of equine medicine is all about.

"Suggest that you can bring the gear and instruments to and from the car, for example," Carson advises. "Some of that equipment will have to be cleaned, so mention that you'd be glad to do it in order to free him or her to discuss the case with the horse's owner.

"You might suggest, too, that while the vet is actually treating the horse, you could write down data about the case, and even hold instruments."

Back at the office, says Carson, you could make yourself useful by replacing soiled instruments, laying out a new set of sterile instruments, and feeding any horses that might be on the premises.

"Remember," insists Carson. "You're not out necessarily to earn any money at this point. The vet probably got along just fine without your services and is not likely to part with hard-earned money for services that can be — and have been — performed alone. The idea is for you to see and hear and smell and feel what equine medicine is really about. To get such an opportunity you've got to offer something — like your time — in return.

"The vet will be doing you a big favor," she adds. "If you adopt that attitude, you're more likely to make a good impression and get what you need."

TWO

The Jockey

IT WAS TWENTY MINUTES till show time.

The grooms were leading their brushed and combed chargers into the paddock area, where the Thoroughbreds would be dressed for their matinee performance. The last of the grooms to enter was Georgia Sweet, leading Little Villain.

He was a giant of an athlete, Villain was — a big-framed, broad-backed, big-boned chaser, whose dappled gray rump and shoulders sloped perfectly toward long and strong and fast legs. He tossed his head carelessly, snorting and prancing behind his groom, who led him into the seventh stall. There she removed Villain's leg wraps, and then the silver-and-black blanket of vinyl that had protected him from the pelting rain during the walk from the stable. After she wiped him dry, she began to braid his tail.

Her boss, trainer Jordan Winters, had insisted on the tail-braiding, because the track would be extremely muddy. Winters theorized that the braiding would prevent Villain's tail from picking up mud, which would add extra ounces of weight to the horse's mile-and-a-half ordeal. Even *ounces*, Winters insisted, could mean the difference between cheers and jeers for Villain.

Photo by Henry Carfagna

Anything for an edge, he argued.

While Georgia braided, a man with a notebook walked into the stall. He gently grabbed Villain's muzzle and turned back his upper lip, comparing the tatooed number inside the lip with the number on the registration papers in his notebook. He made other comparisons, too — of Villain's color and markings — against other notations on the registration papers, checking on every last detail, including the five black hairs over Villain's right eyelid. Satisfied that Villain was indeed Villain, he made his way to stall number eight.

The track veterinarian visited Villain next. As soon as he determined that Villain was fit to run, he left quickly, bumping into Winky Barnes on his way out.

Barnes, dressed in a gray work shirt and gray pants like all the other *valets* at the track, was carrying a saddle. Behind him was Jordan Winters.

The groom held Villain's bridle and captured his attention with her raspy voice while Winters and Barnes performed the saddling ritual. As usual, the trainer stood to Villain's left, the valet to his right. First, they placed the saddlecloth on the racehorse's back. It had Villain's program number — 7 — sewn onto it.

Next, a pad with flat lead bars sewn into its cloth pockets was placed over the saddlecloth. Then came the foam rubber saddle pad and, finally, the tiny racing saddle, which they fitted high up on Villain's withers. Two girths were cinched tight, to make doubly sure the saddle wouldn't slip. One of them even went over the top of the saddle — anything for an edge.

Winters checked the bridle, making certain that the bit had been placed correctly. Satisfied, he then looped a long piece of gauze through Villain's mouth and tied it under the horse's chin, so Villain couldn't swallow his tongue — anything for an edge.

The paddock judge strolled by. He had a book that listed each item of equipment that the eight horses would race with

— even down to the gauze. The judge approved Villain's equipment, and, as he stepped out of the stall, he stopped to watch eight short, tough people in colorful shirts and tight white breeches strut one by one into the paddock. They were the costars of the upcoming two-minute performance — the jockeys.

Last in their single-file parade was Willie Silk, the rookie, the *bug boy*, the apprentice jock. Winky Barnes greeted him with a handshake and handed him his riding whip. Willie was all smiles, despite the fact that the upcoming race would be the first he'd ever ridden in that really mattered. Why was Winters willing to gamble on the heart and hands of a twenty-year-old kid who'd never raced professionally before today?

Because Willie Silk was an edge — anything for an edge.

The rules of racing grant the apprentice — or new — jockey like Willie Silk a slight advantage, in order to offset his inexperience and encourage owners and trainers to give him mounts to ride. An apprentice jockey's horse is required to carry less weight in his lead pad than horses with veteran — or *journeymen* — jockeys riding them.

Once in a while this weight reduction helps a horse win a race he might otherwise lose. In fact, Jordan Winters is one of those horse racing devotees who insists that every pound or two that a horse doesn't have to carry across the finish line can mean a fifth of a second faster performance for that horse — which is why he was so willing to give apprentice Willie Silk an opportunity to ride, despite his inexperience.

The weight reduction for Willie Silk would be substantial. Until he won five races, he'd be given a ten-pound advantage. After the fifth win, he would have a seven-pound advantage until he had visited the winner's circle thirty-five times. Then he'd continue riding with a five-pound advantage until one full year after the date of his fifth victory.

The weight allowances would be noted by asterisks (*) next to Willie's name in the racing program. Three asterisks would indicate the ten-pound advantage; two asterisks, seven pounds, and one asterisk, five pounds. In racetrack jargon, the asterisks are called "bugs," and apprentice jockeys are known as "bug boys."

Jordan Winters had known many apprentice jocks who had ridden for months as "triple bug boys," never winning even five races. They eventually left racing altogether, or gave up their jockeys' licenses, without ever having shed the three bugs that marked their continued failures.

It was a gamble, then, to use an apprentice — the weight advantage notwithstanding. Still, Winters liked the idea of using triple bug boy Willie Silk in the lucrative holiday race. Villain could use the ten-pound advantage over the other, lighter horses.

But Winters realized that what Villain needed, even more than the weight advantage, was a smart jockey. Villain, you see, had won only one race in thirteen tries. And even the one victory was an accident. The horse that came in ahead of Villain was subsequently disqualified because of his jockey's disdain for sportsmanlike conduct. Still, a victory is a victory, argued Winters — even if it was a gift.

Overall, Villain had finished second six times and third four times, finishing "out of the money" (fourth place or worse) only twice in his two-year-old racing career. Not bad, really. His record proved that he could run, and run well. Winters was aware of that. The problem was that Villain had almost no desire to fight his way to the finish line, which explained so many second- and third-place finishes.

"Some horses," Winters had explained to Willie when he told the boy he wanted him to ride Villain, "actually inherit a competitive spirit. You can see it in them the first few times they're turned out to pasture with the other weanlings. It's their nature to beat other horses. One tries to get in front of the other, just like a little bitty game.

"Then there are the horses who have to be taught how to be competitive," he added. "Villain's one of them. The problem with him, though, is that somewhere along the line he absorbed a message that he's supposed to catch all the horses on the track — and then stop, once he's in front.

"I suppose he thinks he's done his job as soon as he takes the lead. Trouble is, he always takes it before the finish line."

Winters knew that an apprentice like Willie, no matter how good a rider he was, would find it difficult, at best, to push stubborn Villain at the end of the race. So he and Willie had decided on another strategy: Willie would trick Villain into winning — if he could. It was a tall enough order for even a journeyman jockey — a skyscraping order for an apprentice.

"Remember," advised Winters. "He'll use any fool excuse to stop trying once he gets ahead. You'll have to hold off till the last second, then pull his trigger. Understand?"

"Yessir," said Willie, all five feet one inch of him standing soldier-erect and attentive. "I can handle it, Mr. Winters."

"Riders up!" yelled the paddock judge. It was ten minutes to post time.

Winters cupped his strong hands, took Willie's left boot in them, and hoisted the one-hundred-pound athlete onto Villain's long and broad back.

"I want a winner right off," thought Willie. "The only way I'll get more horses to ride is to make people notice me."

"Good luck," said Winters, slapping Villain's hindquarters.

*

"They're at the post!" boomed the track announcer.

From the grandstand, a couple of hundred yards away, it looked to the spectators as though the Thoroughbreds were milling around in confusion behind the starting gate. It was a complex operation, certainly, requiring one man per starting stall to guide the eight kicking, snorting, high-spirited runners smoothly into their narrow confines. All of the horses had been schooled to start from the electric machine. In fact, each horse had been approved by the official starter — the man who would open the gates — before it was allowed to enter its first race.

Still, many of the horses were fractious — including Villain.

The crew of assistant starters led, pushed, or otherwise

coerced the nervous animals into the numbered metal stalls in order of their post positions — beginning with number one, Decoy, at the infield rail. The assistants knew how each individual runner should be controlled. Some, like Decoy, had to be "headed" into the gate, so a man perched on the metal framework grabbed Decoy's bridle and pulled him in. Others, like Contact, had to be "tailed" in. And some, like Villain, had permission to be loaded last, because they couldn't endure standing in the narrow stall and waiting.

The starter stood on a raised platform a few yards down the track from the gate. He could see everything, despite the near-blinding rain in his face.

Willie watched the starter. In a second or two, he would ride a thousand-pound beast at forty miles an hour through wind and rain and mud, competing against seven other thousand-pound ground-gorgers who would go just as fast and want to win just as much. Wouldn't it be enough, he thought, just to be able to stay on the half-pound saddle all the way around the track? To summon up just enough strength and coordination, balance and timing, rhythm and sensitivity, to ride the two-minute storm?

No. It wouldn't be enough. He wanted to stay on, certainly. He wanted to cross the wire first, too. He would prove that he belonged. He had a good enough horse to win — if he could only outsmart him.

In the instant of time when the starter thought he saw all of the runners with their heads forward and four feet on the ground — wham! He pressed the button, the stall doors clanged open, a bell sounded, the jockeys whooped and hollered, and hooves thundered.

"They'rrrre off!" boomed the track announcer.

Two sprinters bolted in front of the pack and battled each other for the lead. The bettors' favorite, Decoy, eased into position just behind them.

Willie held Villain behind every horse but one. He planned to launch Villain's move a half-mile from the finish — if he could hold back his stubborn charger till then.

By the far turn, the plan was working. In fact, Willie had his horse so far behind the leaders that he could barely even feel the wet hunks of mud they were kicking back at him. Indeed, to everyone at the track except Willie — and perhaps Jordan Winters — it looked as though the race was slipping hopelessly out of reach for Villain.

Young Willie had remained nearly motionless atop the easy-striding gray, his solid little body packed forward and balanced harmoniously on top of Villain's withers. His mud-speckled hands were his communicators, sending messages through the reins, the bit, and into Villain's big heart. "Relax, plenty of time," the message was saying.

Villain understood. He ran with long, loping, effortless strides, and therefore wasted no energy by straining for more speed or fighting his jockey . . .

Villain and Willie were on the same wavelength.

*

At the half-mile pole, just as he had planned, Willie made his move.

One inch at a time, he lowered his little frame over Villain and asked his horse for more speed. The motion was so smooth, so in tune with the multiple movements of his mount, that no one but Villain would have noticed.

Then, reaching back — to ensure that Villain was giving him everything he was asking for — Willie spoke to his horse with several right-handed slashes of his whip.

"We were way off the lead by then," he would later explain to a reporter. "Maybe twelve, thirteen lengths behind. When I hit him, Villain *really* moved out. It was incredible. To ask him for speed and have him rev up his engines like that . . . it was like blasting off to the moon or something. Incredible."

*

With only a sixteenth of a mile left, Willie had his hands full.

His horse was pulling as hard as he could on the bit and charging into contention along the outside. The crowd cheered wildly. Long-shot Villain looked as if he had a chance.

But Jordan Winters crossed his fingers and talked to himself. His horse had looked like a winner thirteen times before. He expected the usual — that is, the worst. He was now uncertain whether a rookie jock could actually pull the whole thing off after all.

Later, he explained his last-minute concern.

"All the other jockeys had always rushed Villain to the lead too soon. Don't get me wrong. When your horse is bearin' down on that finish line it's just a natural reaction for a jockey to want to let him run all out. I wouldn't blame a jock."

But with Willie, things would be different. Although the finish line was fast approaching, he didn't move a muscle. He waited . . . and then he waited some more. At the last possible second, he got into Villain again. This time, the horse took the lead for the first time in the race — right at the wire.

Little Villain had been tricked into winning.

A few yards later — as if in demonstration of his resentment — Villain dug his toes into the mud, sending Willie sailing.

For only a moment Willie lay in the wet mud. He then picked himself up and strutted to the winner's circle with a smile so big it nearly hid the rest of his face.

Meanwhile, back in the jockeys' room, the other riders were grinning too, preparing for the initiation rite that greets every young jock on the occasion of his first racing victory.

Willie had naturally heard about the ritual, but it was the furthest thing from his mind as he strode through the cement corridor from the paddock and swaggered into the ambush. Instantly, a thousand pounds of jockeys pounced on the unsuspecting rookie. Most were armed with dirty rags covered with greasy black boot polish. A few others wielded dispensers full of shaving cream and containers of anything they thought would be sticky and uncomfortable. They laughed uncontrollably, remembering when they had been on the receiving end.

Willie struggled, but it was no use. Only when all the dispensers were empty and all the black grease transferred from the rags to Willie's face and hair could he work his way free and stumble away. The white-and-black reminders of his first victory were washed quickly away by the shower. Nothing would remain, save the memory.

*

Those who admire the art that is race riding insist that, pound for pound, the finest of all the athletes in the world is the jockey.

"He's got to have the strength to control something ten times his own size," says Jordan Winters, "as well as the guts to defy death and bone-breaking catastrophe every single time he breaks a horse from the starting gate.

"On top of all that," adds Winters, "a jockey needs an unusual sense of timing, split-second reflexes, and the ability to communicate with a horse through his hands. It's not easy."

Oftentimes a jockey's skills are overlooked by disappointed bettors at trackside, but they can't possibly be taken for granted by anyone who's ever ridden a headstrong Thoroughbred.

"The job demands are formidable," insists Winters, "and the jockey is a formidable little man or woman."

In the early days of racing, in Great Britain, only men — and full-sized ones, at that — rode racehorses. Then some of the horse owners, realizing the great importance of weight, began using small boys to ride their horses. One boy, for example, weighed only fifty-six pounds when he won the Chester Cup race in 1884. That's about half the weight of the modern-day jockey.

The problem was that horse owners had to employ younger and younger boys in order to be competitive. This ultimately proved disastrous, as several youngsters were actually killed and many more suffered debilitating injuries.

Finally, Britain's House of Lords and Jockey Club cosponsored a law which made it mandatory for a horse to carry at least seventy-seven pounds in a race. The thinking was that most boys of that weight would be at least twelve years old. That law, however, did not solve the problem. Only when the British Parliament ultimately passed the Education Act was there a law that prevented boys under twelve years of age from being employed in any job — including, of course, race riding.

Today in the United States, state racing associations will not license a jockey unless he or she is at least sixteen years old. Without the license, no legitimate racetrack will allow a person to ride in a race.

*

Like most other jockeys who have ridden before him, Willie Silk didn't just decide one day that he wanted to be a jockey, jump on a horse, and win the ninth race at Aqueduct. Actually, before he'd even considered being a jockey, he had begun preparing for it — in his own family's barn.

By the time he was ten years old he had learned how to groom a horse: how to bathe his father's stallion with a soft sponge and a mild detergent, how to work the currycomb and wipe away the dandruff that would dull the stallion's coat and, even worse, clog his pores.

Willie could even apply the standing leg bandages that would keep Rascal from kicking himself, or use the brush and rub rag with such skill and such energy that the stallion's coat would reflect Willie's image. In truth, the family's barn was like a classroom to him.

But the extracurricular activities — the rump-hurting trials and the bone-breaking errors at thirty miles an hour — were equally important to him. Without them, he'd never have graduated.

"He never refused an opportunity to ride a horse," remembers Willie's brother, Billy Ray. "I recall a time when he was about fourteen. He got on this one horse — I swear that son-of-a-gun bucked Willie at least ten feet straight up into the air. He came a-*slammin'* down on the ground.

"Next thing I knew, Willie had brushed himself off and was back on top of that horse again."

Lightweight young people who want to become jockeys — and who, like Willie Silk, have had previous experience around horses — usually either have to know someone connected with a racetrack, or have to go into the "backstretch" area and all but make pests of themselves by asking anyone and everyone for a job — that is, anyone and everyone who happens to train racehorses at the racetrack.

It's the racehorse trainer who generally hires a would-be jockey. Usually, the first rung on the career ladder is work as a stableboy. For Willie, the $60-per-week job included chores like carrying water buckets, cleaning tack, mucking out stalls, walking "hots" — that is, leading horses that had just raced or worked out, in an endless circle until they'd cooled off and could be rubbed and fed — and any other less-than-glamorous chores that popped up every day.

When Willie Silk got that first racetrack job — with Jordan Winters's twenty-horse stable — the seventeen-year-old was up before the sun every morning so he could be in the barn by daybreak.

"Hot-walking took up maybe fifty percent of my time as a stableboy," he recalls. "Being in New England, our track was usually frozen on really cold mornings in the winter. The wind would whip up and the temperature was always below freezing, and all I'd do for three, maybe four hours, every single day was walk horses. Sometimes I wondered if it was all worth it.

"It wasn't an easy job. The money was terrible. I couldn't afford an apartment, so I lived in the trailer that Mr. Winters provides the stableboys. It was like a medium-sized horse trailer with three stalls. We had heat and a mattress — that's it. Some people would tell us the horses lived better.

"No matter what I was being paid, though, hot-walking was still an important job because it was a way for me to prove myself to Mr. Winters. I had to keep an eye on my horse all the time. I had to know when he wanted a drink of water, when I should slip the cooler over his withers, when he wanted to relieve himself. Things like that.

"Besides the weather, what made the job really hard was that it was pretty boring sometimes. Say a horse was worked six furlongs — three quarters of a mile — in the morning. Mr. Winters might want me to cool him off for forty-five minutes. Just walk him for forty-five minutes. Most of the time I'd have to walk three or four horses every day like that.

"You learn fast how to daydream real good," insists Willie, "while you keep one eye cocked on your horse. The two-year-olds are toughest. They're just at that point where they're learning the business, so to speak. If I daydreamed too much when I was leading one of them, he'd take off on me.

"That's no way to make points with the boss, either."

The next step up the jockey ladder for Willie was when Winters made him a groom — at $100 per week. "The increase in money wasn't the big thing," Willie insists. "I mean, where was I going to spend it, anyway? I was working all day and too darned tired to do anything at night.

"The big deal about it, though, was that now I got to work pretty close with Mr. Winters and learn about horses from him."

Willie still had to be at the barn by sunrise every morning. First he'd check that all the horses had passed the night without harm. Then he'd supervise the stableboys as they mucked out the stalls.

Once Winters arrived with the training schedule for the day, Willie got the horses ready to either be walked around the shed row, galloped, or "breezed." Winters spent a lot of time now with his aspiring jockey. They'd been together for more than a year by that time, and the trainer knew Willie was serious about becoming a jockey. Winters went out of his

way to educate the boy, spelling out everything for him —
like the reasons for *blistering* this horse or *pinfiring* that one.
He and Willie were in constant communication regarding the
health of all the horses.

"It was like being in school," says Willie. "Only better. I'd
tell Mr. Winters that one of the horses had a warm ankle.
Then he'd tell me, 'Okay, this is what we'll do — do the ankle
in mud tonight, alcohol and bandages tomorrow.'

"It was a tremendous education, when I look back on it. By
being a groom I learned that there are a lot of different factors
responsible for a horse's being a winner at the racetrack."

*

Stableboy . . . hot-walker . . . groom. Willie was now ready
to assume even more responsibility. Jordan Winters promoted
him to the position of exercise rider — at $150 per week.

"My first day as an exercise rider was hilarious," Willie
recalls. "There's something about galloping a horse. There's
no way to really prepare for it.

"I went all the way around the mile-and-an-eighth track
that first day on this crazy horse named Crazy Horse. When
I finally got up to the back side where Mr. Winters pulled us
up, I couldn't even feel my legs anymore. I jumped off the
horse and there was nothing — I mean *nothing* — there to
hold me up. I went right down to the ground. Bam!

"Mr. Winters laughed like anything. 'It happens to everybody,' he said. 'Don't feel bad.' But he couldn't help me feel
any less silly."

Despite the inauspicious debut, Willie soon became a competent exercise rider. First, he learned to *gallop* horses. In a
gallop, the horse is eased along at a leisurely clip, while the
rider stands up in the stirrups and maintains a firm, restraining grip on the reins.

"Galloping a horse is very physically demanding," says
Willie. "You've got to remember that a Thoroughbred is born

and raised to do one thing: show his speed. Every single stage of his education is geared toward the day when he'll be asked to run as fast and as far as he can in competition.

"When you gallop a horse on the track and he sees other horses running past him, he'll lunge against the bit and want to burst full speed ahead. An exercise rider has to be tuned in to the first hint that his horse has that idea in mind. If not, he'll run off — with you on his back. Then it's like trying to stop a freight train with an elastic."

Controlling a horse at gallop, adds Willie, necessitates a firm and steady hand on the reins. "You don't meet too many exercise riders — men or women — with weak handshakes," he says.

But strength alone, although it is important, is not the only attribute of a good exercise rider. He also has to have — or develop — the ability to transmit "messages" to the horse through his hands and the reins. "There should always be a minimum of struggle between me and my horse," says Willie. "If I challenge him to a test of strength, I can bet on one thing — I'll lose. Every time."

The other half of an exercise rider's job involves "breezing" the racehorses. Strength here is less important than when galloping a horse, because restraining the horse is less of a problem in breezing. Instead, the rider must be concerned with how fast his horse is running.

"Breezing is really the advanced stage of learning to exercise a racehorse," says Jordan Winters, "because the jockey has to learn how to *pace* his horse."

Training a racehorse demands tremendous patience. Before the horse can be tested for speed, the trainer has to build up the horse's muscles and respiratory system in long gallops. Then, in a painstaking series of *breezes* — or sprints — the horse is asked to demonstrate small increases in all-out speed. "But," says Winters, "if the horse runs at a pace that his body just isn't in shape to handle, the entire training program can be set back to day one. The horse would have to be rebuilt all over again."

"There's a lot of pressure on an exercise rider," adds Willie. "If, say, Mr. Winters has a horse fit enough to do a half-mile in fifty seconds, and the exercise rider lets him run it in, say, forty-five, the training program can be ruined."

"And," says Winters, "that exercise rider would probably be out looking for another job."

*

All the while Willie was proving himself as an exercise rider, he was continuing his jockey's education by visiting the starting gate of as many races as he could.

"The start is the most important part of a race," he says. "There are a thousand ways your horse can get beat, but the most common way is if he messes up coming out of the starting gate."

"There's endless room for human error," adds Winters. "Some jockeys get in there and they're too nervous. Some are too relaxed. They actually get caught leaning back when the gate opens. But the good ones — like Willie — can sense what's going on and anticipate that moment of takeoff. That's a tremendous advantage."

"I had to watch a lot of starts to learn that," admits Willie. "But it got to the point where I could tell exactly when those gates were going to open."

*

Finally.

After three years with trainer Jordan Winters — three years of mucking out stalls, walking hots, and exercising horses — Willie Silk was officially apprenticed to Winters via a standard contract. It simply stipulated that Willie could ride horses for other trainers, but for at least the next three years Jordan Winters would have first option to use Willie in any race over any other competitor. In return, Winters would help Willie get his jockey's license.

Willie signed the contract — gladly. Only one more obstacle had to be overcome. Before he could actually ride in a race, he had to be licensed by the state's racing commission. He had to have a trainer — that is, Winters — vouch for his ability, and then he had to demonstrate, in front of track officials, that he could break a horse from a starting gate.

"That," says Willie, "was the least of my worries."

*

Several more rides like the one he rode on Little Villain were sufficient to show everyone at the track that Willie had a natural aptitude for his profession. Before long he was riding in as many as seven, eight, or nine races a day, six days a week. Every trainer at the track wanted to take advantage of his many skills — and his apprentice's weight allowance. "An unbeatable combo," attested a local sportswriter.

"Obviously," says Willie, "the name of this game is to get horses to ride if you're going to make money. But competing in so many races every day gets hectic once in a while. I usually get about ten or fifteen minutes between races to change silks, wash up, weigh in, and think about the next race."

Willie does get some help. He has to. First, he teamed up with a valet.

"I'm sort of like his slave," says Winky Barnes, grinning all the while. "I set out Willie's clothes for him in the locker room, help him get dressed for each different race, carry his tack to and from the weigh-in scales. I even saddle his horse for him."

Barnes takes care of four other jockeys at the track, too. He is paid a salary by the track itself and, in addition, receives ten percent of whatever his jockeys earn.

"My guess is that the average valet makes himself about fifteen thousand dollars a year. But if you get lucky and get hooked up with somebody like a Willie Silk who wins an awful lot of races, a valet can make some pretty decent change."

Willie also employs a second person — an agent named Christopher Cavalieri. "Chris is my right arm," says Willie. "He's at the track every day, making the rounds of all the trainers, trying to get me on the best horses to ride. A good agent like Chris means the difference between driving a Ford and a Rolls-Royce. That's why he gets twenty-five percent of everything I make. And he earns every penny of it, believe me."

"A jockey can make a lot of money," Cavalieri explains. "But he's got to win races to do it."

Here's why. In a race of $5,000 or more total purse money, for example, a jockey finishing fourth or worse earns $35 "jock mount." Third place gets $45, second place $55, and the first-place jock earns ten percent of the winning owner's share of the purse — which is usually sixty percent of the total purse. Thus, if the total racing purse is $5,000, the winning owner's share (at sixty percent) is $3,000. The jockey and the trainer would each receive $300 (ten percent) from the owner.

"So," says Willie, "let's say I've got three hundred dollars coming to me. But I still owe some bills. My agent gets twenty-five percent. That's seventy-five dollars. My valet gets ten percent. That's thirty dollars. That leaves me with a grand total of a hundred and ninety-five dollars for bringing my horse in first. And I've still got to take out taxes and expenses from that hundred and ninety-five.

"The point is, you have to win a lot of races to make any big money."

In 1977 there were 2,500 jockeys in this country. The top third were earning $100,000 or more annually; the middle third, about $30,000 to $50,000 annually; and the bottom third were just barely surviving.

"A jockey's expenses are high," Cavalieri continues. "But the big money is there if he wins. But don't forget, if he makes it to age thirty-five in this business, he's considered real lucky. By that time, he's either too heavy, or he's all done because of an injury. Some of them only last four, five, six years. In fact, the average racing lifetime is only six years. It's a case of making hay while the sun shines."

Winky Barnes agrees. "Even if they do make a bundle," he says, "they earn it. Being a jock is tough. Real tough. They get kicked, bumped, bitten, and bruised. They gallop horses at the crack of dawn when it's so cold the blood in their hands stands still, and they ride races on afternoons so hot they should melt right off their saddles."

"Don't forget their eating problems," says Cavalieri. "Most jockeys have to stick to a rigid diet because they can't afford to gain weight, and others' nerves won't let them eat anything."

"A lot of them," adds Barnes, "lead a gypsy sort of life, going from one racetrack to another, spending most of their time knocking on doors trying to get good mounts, until — if ever — their names are known."

"But above all," says Willie, "it's a very dangerous profession. I put my life on the line every single time I ride in a race. It's a fact of life in this business — you ride often enough, you get hurt. Period. The question is how bad — not what if.

"I was lucky until last year. My first accident came in March when I tore the cartilage in my knee in a spill. I wasn't even racing — just warming up my horse before the race. The horse did something wrong and I fell off him. He ran over my knee, tore the ligaments in my ankle, and broke my little finger. I had bruises all over my leg.

"Three months later I fell again. This time I got a concussion.

"The most common type of accident is when a horse 'clips' another horse's heels. If your horse trips on the other horse's heels in front of him, he'll automatically go down. What usually saves you is that you're moving so fast that when he does go down, you just sail about fifteen feet away.

"I don't even think about the danger. If I did, I'd never get on another horse again."

*

Must the would-be jockey always start at the bottom like Willie? Why can't a knowledgeable, experienced horseman begin his climb a substantial way up the career ladder — at the rung, say, of the exercise rider?

"You can," Willie insists. "But you've got to know what you're doing."

Unless you know a trainer who can help you find a job as an exercise rider — no racetrack will issue you a jockey's license unless you've worked there at least one continuous year as an exercise rider — the best bet is to go to the track's stable gate (for a list of racetracks, see Appendix II) and tell the person in charge that you're interested in galloping horses. If there's no immediate job available, leave your name and telephone number.

"If that approach fails," says Willie, "offer yourself as a hotwalker. Hot-walking jobs are plentiful. And once you're in the stable area, you'll be in a position to apply for an exercise rider's job as soon as one opens up."

There are two types of exercise riding jobs. A racing stable with at least ten horses in training usually has a salaried exercise rider. Other exercise riders are freelancers, who work for two or three stables each day and are paid a set fee — usually $5 — for each horse they exercise.

A beginning exercise rider working for a large stable can expect to earn $150 per week. The more experienced rider — either salaried or freelance — does nothing but ride: "Maybe ten or more horses each day," says Willie. "Seven days a week.

"When you contact a trainer about an exercise riding job, don't mislead him — for God's sake! — about the amount of experience you've had. A Thoroughbred is tough to handle. He's been taught one thing all his life — to run, and run *hard*. If you exaggerate your ability, you'll put yourself and everyone else on the track in danger."

*

If you are a high school graduate or have an equivalent certificate, you can choose from several vocational schools which prepare students for racetrack-related careers.

The Kentucky Equine Education Program (known as KEEP) was organized in 1975 to supply trained labor for Kentucky's Thoroughbred breeding, training, and racing industry. Each KEEP graduate is trained to enter a specific occupation: hotwalker, groom, or exercise rider.

Twenty-five students enroll in KEEP twice a year, in September and March. The course consists of six-hour-long sessions, five days per week. Students first learn the basics — stable care, grooming, nutrition, anatomy, health management, bandaging, and breaking horses — before they choose a specific job objective (i.e., groom, hot-walker, or exercise rider).

The course is open-ended — you graduate when you have reached an acceptable level of ability for employment in your chosen occupation. Six months is about average, although some students move along to paid positions after only four.

There is usually a six-month wait from the time of application to acceptance. Preference is given to Kentucky residents, although out-of-staters are encouraged to apply, too.

KEEP's administrators help place their students upon completion of their course work. Most of the job openings are in the Lexington, Kentucky, area, although if you wish to work out of state, KEEP officials will try to help place you wherever you wish.

Students must provide their own transportation and housing. The KEEP admissions office maintains apartment brochures that are made available upon request.

Applicants have to be at least sixteen years old and complete the "General Aptitude Test Battery" (GATB), which is given at most public employment offices nationwide. Your test score should then be sent to the Bureau of Manpower Services, 300 South Upper Street, Lexington, KY 40508, Attn: Testing Unit (KEEP). Lexington-area applicants can arrange to take the

GATB test by contacting the Director of Admissions at KEEP. After the GATB score is sent, the applicant should contact the Director of Admissions for an application and an interview.

For further information, contact the Director of Admissions, KEEP, P.O. Box 11188, Lexington, KY 40511.

Another racetrack-oriented school, Hawkeye Hill, offers instruction in exercise riding and/or stable management.

"Traditionally," says co-owner Lisa Mitchell, a licensed jockey, "anybody interested in a career at the track had to spend months or years at a track, working his way up from jobs like mucking out stalls and walking hots. We offer a shortcut. Our graduates step right into being full-fledged exercise riders, grooms, or even assistant trainers."

Lisa and her husband, Mitch — a licensed Thoroughbred trainer — are the instructors at Hawkeye Hill. Students — only six at a time — live with Lisa and Mitch in their home. The students work and ride together, but each follows an individual training program. Lisa and Mitch consider a student proficient enough to "graduate" when the student is capable of getting a job in his or her area of study. At that point, Lisa and Mitch certify the student, help him or her obtain a license if necessary, and help the student find a job.

Most Hawkeye Hill students require three weeks to graduate as grooms or assistant stable managers, four to five weeks as exercise riders. Room and board for the first three weeks is included in the tuition charge. Students staying more than three weeks pay an additional weekly charge for room and board. Before attending Hawkeye Hill, each student is sent a series of booklets prepared by Lisa and Mitch, which contain basic information and follow-up quizzes about horse anatomy, leg problems, tack, and other equine subjects.

Consisting of sixty-eight acres of land, Hawkeye Hill has a seven-eighths-mile regulation racetrack, a turf course, and starting gates. In addition to the training facilities, the school houses an extensive reference library.

For further information, write Hawkeye Hill, Route One, Box 189B, Commiskey, IN 47227.

Whiting's Neck Equestrian Center offers a three-month "Careers in Racing" program four times each year, starting in January, April, July, and October. The course enables graduates to enter the racing world as grooms and exercise riders.

Students ride in two one-hour-long sessions per day: one session on a young horse (a yearling or two-year-old) and one on an older horse. In that way, students learn to "break" (gentle) young horses as well as gallop and breeze racehorses in training. The main emphasis is on developing the skill of the rider in handling all situations that may arise in the exercising of a racehorse of any age or temperament.

In addition, every student is required to care for two horses under the supervision of a licensed trainer. The student is responsible for all aspects of the horses' care — including feeding, mucking out, grooming, and leg care. The routine is as highly disciplined as it is on the racetrack. The trainer-in-charge gives daily lectures and demonstrations on all phases of conditioning, basic veterinary care and medications, shoeing, feeding, bandaging, and psychology of the racehorse. There are frequent tests and discussions, as well as lectures by well-known guests.

Finally, all students are expected to keep training records on each of the horses they are responsible for. In that way, they learn the progression of a good conditioning program.

The cost of the program includes tuition and a room with cooking facilities. Food is not included, and all students cook for themselves.

For further information, write Whiting's Neck Equestrian Center Inc., Route 3, Box 105D, Martinsburg, WV 25401.

At the California Horse Racing Institute, the basic instruction lasts six weeks. Students are responsible for their own room and board. Students go to sessions four times per week — three evenings and one full day — where they learn to become grooms or hot-walkers.

The basic six-week instruction is followed by an advanced course in exercise riding. The Institute is equipped with a half-mile oval racetrack and starting gate for this purpose.

"Ninety percent of our students," says co-owner Rita Fresquez, "have never even touched a horse before. Two of our graduates — who are now jockeys — had never ridden a horse before they came here. They couldn't even lead a horse with a halter on. We work each student at his or her own pace. We have to, because everyone comes here with a different amount of experience. We don't put anyone up on a horse until they know exactly how to work around the animal."

For further information, write the California Horse Racing Institute, P.O. Box 417, Newhall, CA 91321.

THREE

The Breeding-Farm Manager

THE MARE WOULD HAVE HER FOAL anytime now, Morgan was almost certain.

Although Sassy's pasture bed was blanketed with knee-deep clover and warmed by the late-afternoon sunshine, Morgan knew the mare was not comfortable. Her tail swished ceaselessly at her chestnut-colored flanks, and she continuously turned her head to stare at her bulging belly.

"Let's get her inside," said Morgan, moving her teenaged figure between panels of bread-white fence. The birth of the foal would not be a new experience for her. She had spent nearly half her twenty-six years on breeding farms.

For the young woman following her, however — Alexis Sentry — the birth of a miniature-sized horse certainly would be a new experience, one she had begun to anticipate months earlier, when she had first written Morgan Singer for a part-time job.

"I want to learn *everything* about breeding horses," she had told Morgan — more than once — during their initial meeting. "I'm willing to start at the bottom . . . I know it will be difficult . . . I'll do *anything* that needs doing . . . I just want

Photo by David O. Aronson

a chance to *prove* myself. You'll see, Mrs. Singer. You won't regret hiring me. I *promise* you won't."

Morgan was intrigued by the young girl's enthusiasm — so much so that she was willing to overlook the fact that Alexis had had almost no practical experience with horses.

"How do you know you want to work with horses?" asked Morgan.

"I don't, actually," Alexis replied. "But I think I do. The only way I'll know for sure is if I give it a try. Right?"

Morgan admired the girl's sincerity. She hired the sixteen-year-old on a part-time basis — after school and on weekends — as a groom-in-training. "If we're both happy with each other by the time summer comes around," Morgan explained, "maybe you can join us full time, then — if you still want to. Meantime, you'll have to prove you're reliable."

Alexis was ready to do just that. But she had mistakenly thought she'd be more or less eased into her new situation. Instead, the first day on the job now appeared as though it would be one she'd not soon forget. "How can you tell," she asked, "that your mare's ready to foal?"

"See this?" asked Morgan, stooping down and pointing to Sassy's swollen udder. "You know what it is, don't you?"

"Sure. It's got milk-producing glands inside," said Alexis. As if on cue, a stream of white liquid squirted out of a teat. Alexis looked at Morgan as if something were wrong with the mare.

"Don't worry," said Morgan. "When the milk starts leaking like that, the foal is usually almost ready to be born. Let's get her to her stall. We can keep an eye on her there."

Morgan had emphasized the "usually" portion of her diagnosis because there is no definitive tip from a mare as to when she will actually deliver her foal. Mares like Sassy who drip milk do often foal during the night of the day they begin to drip profusely.

However, Morgan had seen some mares drip for a week or even two, before delivery — and others never dripped at all.

"Mares don't foal alike, any more than they look alike," she advised Alexis as the two of them observed Sassy in her stall. The mare was standing motionless, at the center. Then she peered back at one of her bulging sides, seeming to disbelieve she'd been able to carry another horse — albeit a small horse — inside herself for so long. She shook her head and then paced back and forth, back and forth, stopping at intervals to look back at her heavy sides.

"Delivery room looks great, Alexis. Good job!"

Alexis smiled. Her first official duty had been to prepare Sassy's foaling stall. As instructed, Alexis had removed all the previous straw and droppings with a pitchfork and wheelbarrow, and then she had swept the floor. Afterward, she disinfected the floor by washing its concrete surface with soap and water. Finally, she dusted the concrete with powdery white lime, to ensure its cleanliness, and prepared a clean, dry bed of straw over it.

"Be sure the straw's deep enough to be comfortable," Morgan had advised her, "but not so deep it'll be impossible for the foal to move around in."

Alexis had followed directions perfectly, even lying in the straw bed herself, to be absolutely certain it was comfortable enough. She had labored long and hard at her first responsibility, partly because of her inexperience, but partly, too, because of her strong desire to do well. Morgan was obviously pleased with her effort.

Sassy, however, hardly noticed the fancier-than-usual accommodations. Perspiration beads dotted her shoulders and chest. Her tail twitched again and again.

"Is she okay?" Alexis asked.

"Oh sure. She's just anxious to get it over with, that's all. She knows it's all about to end soon . . ." Morgan's voice tapered off. She stared at Sassy. "Did you see that?"

"What?"

"See her sides caving inward, just in front of her hips?" The foal was apparently moving around inside Sassy, changing its position, getting ready to be squeezed through the birth canal. "Time to wash her," said Morgan, stepping inside the stall.

Alexis watched her wrap Sassy's tail and cleanse the opening beneath it — called the *vulva* — with a mild soap and warm water.

"That's about all we can do for her now," said Morgan, patting Sassy's rump affectionately. "The rest is up to her. Let's give her some privacy."

*

The birth of Sassy's foal, like that of any foal, would be a series of little achievements. Each achievement would be accomplished by a series of straining efforts by Sassy, followed by a rest, followed by several more straining efforts, and so on, until the foal was literally pushed out into the world.

Sassy probably wouldn't need any help in delivering her foal — but if she did, Morgan would be ready. She and Alexis had removed themselves to the office at the other end of the foaling barn, where they were watching Sassy on a closed-circuit TV. The mare, seemingly mesmerized after an hour and a half of pacing, now stood quietly in her stall.

"Any idea how long it'll be, Mrs. Singer?" Alexis had glued her eyes to the TV since their arrival in the office. Morgan had advised her to relax, that Sassy might not deliver until the wee hours of the morning, if then. She had prepared a sleeping cot for Alexis, in anticipation of just such a situation, and was about to order some fish and chips from a diner in town. "Relax. You may be in for a long wait ——"

"Look!" shouted Alexis, pointing to the TV picture of Sassy. What looked like water — several gallons of it at that — was gushing out from beneath the mare's tail.

"*Fetal* fluid," Morgan announced, checking her wristwatch. She explained that the foal's foot had broken through the protective sac that had surrounded the foal for the last eleven months. It was the fluid inside the broken sac that was now spilling out of Sassy, signaling that birth would soon be following. "It'll also lubricate the birth canal," Morgan added, "and make it easier for the foal to squeeze through it."

"Why do you keep checking your watch?" Alexis asked.

"Remember how I told you that giving birth would involve a series of little achievements?"

Alexis nodded her head up and down, one eye on Morgan, the other on the TV.

"Well, no more than ten minutes should elapse between each of those achievements. If it takes longer than that, something could be wrong. And if I can't help, I'll have to call the vet."

"How long before the foal's completely out?"

"Oh, anywhere from fifteen to thirty minutes, usually," said Morgan. "If there are no complications."

"Do you think there will be?" Alexis got off her stool and stood directly beneath the TV, which was on a corner shelf about six feet off the floor. She looked up and stared into the screen, afraid of missing even the slightest happening.

"Chances are there won't be any problems at all," said Morgan. "Difficult births are the exception, not the rule. But once she starts pushing that foal out, if she does need help, she'll need it right away."

Even as Morgan spoke, the mare was working hard, lying now in the straw, squeezing powerfully — once, twice, four times. Rest for several seconds . . . then squeeze again. Finally, nearly ten minutes after the initial gush of fetal fluid, a grayish-white bulge poked its way out from beneath Sassy's tail. It looked like the remnants of a burst water balloon. One little foot was pressed against the saggy bulge. Soon, the other foot appeared, sliding itself out just slightly behind the first one.

"Is that the foal?" Alexis asked, standing on tiptoe, her face almost in the TV screen.

"Sure is. Delivery looks good, so far."

Seconds elapsed. The tip of a nose appeared, resting on the

skinny, protruding legs, at about the knees. More seconds elapsed. A head emerged, up to the brow.

"I can see its eyes!" Alexis shouted. Sassy continued to strain and rest, strain and rest. After several minutes, though, the foal's ears had still not appeared. Apparently, the little horse was stuck.

"Come on," said Morgan. "I think Sassy needs help."

*

One of the foal's feet was still slightly ahead of the other. Morgan gently grasped the lagging foot by the ankle and wiggled it back and forth. Then, she pulled on it just slightly. The leg came forward easily. The rest of the foal, though, was still stuck.

"The shoulders can't get by the pelvis," said Morgan. She waited until Sassy started to strain again, and this time pulled gently on both of the foal's legs. As soon as its chest slid free, Morgan stopped pulling, wiped the mucus from the foal's nostrils, and quickly held the palm of her hand close to them. "It's a boy," she announced. "And he's breathing!"

"I just don't believe it," said Alexis.

"What don't you believe?"

"I don't believe that something that *big* was inside that poor mare all these months. I just don't believe it."

Morgan laughed and moved away from Sassy and her newborn son. "Watch the umbilical cord," she said, pointing to the hoselike connection between mare and colt. It pulsated as it continued to send oxygen-rich blood from the mother to her offspring. After a minute the pulsing ceased, and the colt struggled its way free from the cord.

"Help me a minute, will you please?" Morgan asked. "We'll have to disinfect the navel stump."

Alexis looked puzzled.

"Where the umbilical cord was connected," said Morgan. "His belly button." She chuckled and instructed Alexis to hold the struggling colt in a standing position. Morgan knelt on the straw, removed the bottle of iodine from her vest pocket, and dabbed the orange liquid over the colt's navel. She was careful not to touch it with her hands. Nor did she tie a knot in what was left of the umbilical cord that protruded from the navel like a piece of thin garden hose.

"There'll be some drainage coming out of there," Morgan explained. "If I tied a knot, it'd block up that drainage and cause trouble for him later on."

Next, she gave the little horse an injection. "A vaccination. It'll build up his immunity to disease."

Finally, she took a sample of the colt's blood. She would examine it herself in the farm's laboratory. "I'll be looking for a high white count among the blood cells," she said, "to be certain the littly guy is healthy." While she was putting a stopper in the blood-sample vial, exhausted Sassy struggled to her feet. When she was stable, Morgan tied a doughnut-sized knot in the membrane that still hung from underneath the mother's tail. "The *afterbirth*," Morgan explained. "Never pull this from a mare. It'll drop off by itself in a little while."

"It looks like a soggy broken balloon hanging out of her," Alexis observed.

"Come on now," Morgan reprimanded with a smile. "You mustn't hurt our new mother's feelings, you know. She'll be self-conscious enough as it is till she loses some weight."

"Sorry, Sassy," said Alexis, stroking the mare's back. "What do we do now?"

"Watch," said Morgan. "Just watch them. Make sure the little guy gets fed." She and Alexis withdrew from the stall. While they had been talking, the colt had instinctively begun to search for his first real meal. Alexis and Morgan watched as Sassy, her teat swollen and sore, began halfheartedly kicking at her colt.

"Shouldn't we do something?" Alexis asked.

"Let's wait a minute. Sometimes a mare needs a little time off before she'll let her newborn nurse."

Sassy kept moving around and shifting her weight from one leg to another, making it all the more difficult for the colt to sustain a suck. Finally, though, she gave in to her persistent son. Dinner was served without further ado.

"Look at him go!" said Alexis. "He acts like he's starving to death!"

"That's okay. This first meal's really important. Sassy's milk will act as a laxative for him."

"Huh?"

"A *laxative* — you know, help him clean out his intestines, cause his bowels to move."

"Oh."

"You know something, Alexis?"

"No. What?"

"That little guy is making me hungry. What do you say we go get those fish and chips?"

*

Contrary to what Alexis admits she used to think, horses do not jump full-grown from the forehead of a Greek god, nor do they come from potato bags, as Morgan herself once told an inquisitive five-year-old. Instead, they are born, even as you and I, after a slightly longer period of gestation (pregnancy) — a little more than eleven months.

There are about two hundred and fifty different kinds, or *breeds,* of horses in the world, but only about thirty-two of them are commonly raised in the United States. A breed is a particular kind of horse — an Appaloosa, an Arabian, or a Thoroughbred, for example — with certain distinct physical characteristics.

For instance, the Appaloosa breed is always spotted. Usually the loins and hips of an Appaloosa are white, with dark round or oval spots that may be as large as four inches in diameter. Each eye is surrounded by a white circle, and the hooves are striped with black and white. Generally, an Appaloosa stands about fifteen hands (five feet) high and weighs about one thousand pounds.

Such distinct physical characteristics are transmitted to the offspring of two Appaloosas that mate and reproduce. *Breeding*, then, involves the *controlled* reproduction of horses in order to produce the kind of offspring desired.

The breeding industry in the United States is older than the country itself. George Washington not only traded and raced horses, he bred them, too. In 1787, for example, his mares numbered forty-nine (sixteen of which he bred regularly to his favorite stallion, Magnolia; the other thirty-three, to Jack Ass).

On a medium-sized breeding farm like Winterbrook, where Morgan and her husband, Lonnie, are managers, there are usually three or four top stallions and a couple of dozen mares to which those stallions are bred.

"We breed the stallions to our own mares," explains Morgan, "and sell the foals, usually. Also, there are horse owners from all over the country who transport their mares here to mate with our stallions." In addition, Winterbrook mares are shipped to other farms, occasionally, to be bred to "outside" stallions. When those mares return, of course, the Singers see to the birth and care of the foals, as well as the continued well-being of the mares.

The work at Winterbrook is cyclical. The tempo changes with the seasons. The early months of winter, for example, are comparatively slow ones, although there's plenty of routine work to keep everyone busy — things like mucking out stalls, feeding and grooming the horses, seeing that they get exercised, tending to their illnesses, and so on. "It's no different here in the winter," says Morgan, "than it is at any other horse farm. The usual things have to be done."

Morgan is in charge of the mares and foals, while Lonnie manages the stallions and the overall operation of the farm. "We oversee a full-time trainer, three other grooms besides

Alexis Sentry, and one full-time maintenance person," says Morgan. "In reality, all of our responsibilities overlap. I find myself helping Lonnie with the stallions, he helps me with the mares and foals, we both help the trainer, we both muck out stalls when necessary, and on and on. Everybody around here sort of does a little bit of everything. Just because we're managers — Lonnie and I — and have our particular specialties, doesn't mean we don't have to get our hands dirty.

"If a job's got to be done, it's a manager's responsibility to see that it gets done — regardless of whether or not he does it himself or has someone else do it. If you work on a breeding farm there's always physical labor involved. Always. No matter how much education you have."

According to Morgan, the pace at Winterbrook begins to quicken around the beginning of February. "By then," she says, "the breeding schedules have been arranged. We know which stallions will be covering which mares — not only Winterbrook's mares but those who'll be coming to the farm from the outside, too. We also know by then which of our mares we'll be shipping out to be bred to outside stallions at other farms."

In February, then, the visiting mares who will be bred to the Winterbrook stallions start arriving. In all, this usually involves some forty or fifty mares. "It's like a hotel around here then," says Morgan. "It seems like we're checking in a new guest every single day.

"Actually, it's important that they get here early so they can be checked to see that they're healthy, and that their heat cycles show they're ready to have a foal."

The breeding season — the time when the stallions and mares are mated to produce foals — actually lasts several months: from mid-February to mid-June. "By March," says Morgan, "the breeding season is in full swing around here. Our phone never stops ringing. We've got our own mares foaling — the ones that were bred last year — which seems to happen mostly at night, for some strange reason. In the daytime we're breeding the stallions to the other mares, accepting the arrival of outside mares, taking care of the usual chores. Sometimes I can't believe we accomplish all the things we do.

"If it weren't for the fact that we've got six very reliable people working for us, we'd be lost. But we help them too. Besides the fact that they're being paid well, they're also getting a heck of an education — like Alexis, for example — because Lonnie and I involve them in all aspects of what we do."

Even with the help, though, Morgan and Lonnie typically work fourteen or more hours a day during the breeding season. "With the stallions working a seven-day week covering as many mares as possible, we're busy taking care of the pregnant mares and the mares to be covered, supervising the foaling, and caring for the newborn. This place is like a beehive. And that," says Morgan, "doesn't even include breaking the yearlings and training our show horses."

The really hectic period generally stretches well into April. After that, the foals dropped in February and March are allowed to spend considerable time in the pastures, which makes life somewhat easier for the Singers.

"It's like being able to send your children off to school," Morgan says. "They're not underfoot anymore, so we've got extra time to spend on other work that's got to be done."

By May, things have slowed down to almost normal. The breeding season is all but over. Very few mares are left to be serviced by the stallions. "By that time," explains Morgan, "it's basically a situation where we're keeping close watch on the mares who are supposed to be pregnant. Plus tending to the foals already born — like fighting diarrhea, which is fairly common — as well as doing the normal chores that everyone else who owns horses must do."

In June, the pace picks up again. The five dozen or so outside mares that have been "visiting" the farm are now being shipped back to their home farms. "The paperwork is really heavy during that time," says Lonnie Singer. "Things like stud-fee bills have to be sent out. There are tax forms, health certificates, registry papers . . . It's endless, believe me."

Meanwhile, the Winterbrook foals are kept outside up to twelve hours or so a day by now. When July comes, their care, and the care of all the other horses on the farm, is still the major focus of attention, although Morgan and Lonnie must concern themselves primarily with the Winterbrook yearlings — the foals that were dropped last year — which are now ready to be sold.

"That involves a bit of traveling," says Lonnie. "Taking the yearlings to auctions and shows and whatnot. Plus advertising in horse magazines and so on. It's hectic, naturally."

With September and early fall, though, "the pace really slows down again," adds Morgan. "By the time the cold weather comes on in mid-October or November, the work around here is routine again — feeding, grooming, and whatever. Then, of course, February comes along again and the cycle begins once more."

*

Lonnie Singer is one of approximately 8,300 full-time breeding farm managers in the United States, but his $22,500 annual salary is some $5,000 more than the average manager earns, according to a 1977 study by the American Horse Council. Although he's involved with practically every aspect of Winterbrook's breeding operation, technically Lonnie Singer manages the stallions. His master's degree in equine reproduction qualifies him to assume such an important responsibility.

Lonnie makes full use of his formal education on a practical level, as well as in the farm's laboratory. Housed in the breeding barn, the lab has the capacity for routine blood analysis and culture work on stallions or mares when necessary. However, the lab's — and Lonnie's — primary responsibility is analysis of *semen,* the reproductive fluid produced by the stallions.

"I evaluate the stallions prior to the breeding season," says Lonnie. "I collect their semen, then look at the sperm count and motility, pH, and cell morphology, and check for any abnormalities that might be present." This is why Lonnie's job requires specialized training.

"If you want to manage a good-sized breeding farm today," he advises, "you've got to have the educational credentials as well as the practical experience of having worked around horses. It's a big-time business. If you want to manage on the top farms, you've got to know what you're doing. As far as I'm concerned, part of knowing what you're doing comes from getting specialized college training in *animal science* first, and then equine reproduction on the graduate level. I'm not saying you've got to have a degree in equine reproduction to get a job, but I am saying that I think that's the best route to follow if you intend to make a career out of it."

*

When a mare is delivered to the farm in February or March or April, the mare's owner, in effect, goes home and forgets her until she's ready to leave Winterbrook.

"What we have to be concerned about," says Lonnie, "is the safety of the horses — not just our own, but those that are sent to us too. In a way, we're like babysitters, among other things, of course. We accept a tremendous amount of responsibility. I mean, people send us mares worth fifty thousand dollars and up. Believe me — we have to treat each one like she's our very own. The owners expect that. They don't send their mares to Winterbrook only because they expect to get a top-notch foal out of it. They also come to us because they trust us. They know we have the safety and the hygiene of all the horses on our minds at all times. It takes a long time to build that kind of reputation. All it would take would be one careless accident to ruin it all for us."

"We keep the stallions away from the mares — except, of

course, when we breed them," adds Morgan. "Mostly for the protection of the stallions. Generally they'll try to breed any mare they can get to, whether she's in heat or not. That can be very dangerous for the stallions, since the mares are very capable of defending themselves when they don't wish to be bothered."

Aside from safety and hygiene, the Singers' other major problem is determining when the mares are in heat and can be safely bred to conceive. "Horses," Morgan explains, "are seasonal breeders. The spring and summer months are the peak periods of sexual activity. Longer days, green grass, and mild weather bring on the establishment of regular heat periods in the mare — those times when she is able and willing to conceive. But it's a tricky thing to be sure when, exactly, a particular mare is ready to accept a stallion."

The *estrus,* or *heat,* period of the typical mare averages about one week long, although it can vary from three to ten days. Usually, those week-long periods come along every three weeks. Thus, one week out of every month is the only time a mare can become pregnant (conceive). Determining when that heat period is can be difficult.

"In general," says Morgan, "mares in heat will demonstrate an obvious desire for the company of a stallion. They won't fight when a stallion comes near. Also, the muscles of the mare's vulva, just underneath her tail, begin to *wink* — they twitch — and you can usually see a mucous discharge coming from the vaginal tract." Some mares, however, will not exhibit any obvious indications of being in heat, and the Singers are left to determine the mare's heat period. Fortunately, there are means at their disposal.

"In extremely difficult cases, we call the vet," says Morgan. But the most common means by which the Singers determine the heat periods of the mares is by "teasing" them. Teasing a mare involves bringing her in close contact with a stallion without actually allowing the stallion to mount her. Then the mare will indicate her sexual cooperativeness if she is in heat, or she may actually be aroused enough by the presence of the teaser stallion to come into heat.

"A mare should be teased just prior to actually covering her," says Morgan. "Lonnie sets the stallion in the stall above the breeding area, and we bring in the mares that we intend to cover that day and place them in stalls just below and in front of the teaser stallion. Then we bring one mare at a time out of the stall to be cleaned — and restrained, if necessary."

Usually Lonnie and Morgan can tell whether or not a mare will be unruly to a stallion — whether she'll be apt to kick or otherwise be a "bad actress," says Morgan. If so, restraint is applied in the form of a twitch, a leg strap on one foreleg, or breeding hobbles.

"Then," explains Morgan, "we wrap the mare's tail. This keeps it out of the way and helps prevent infection from spreading. We make certain that all mud and dirt are cleaned from the whole posterior of the mare, and we wash her vulva and buttocks thoroughly with warm water and a mild disinfectant."

The breeding stallion is then brought into the breeding area and he is washed, too. "Washing the stallion is probably the single most important part of any breeding situation," says Lonnie. "Before and after each cover. First we wash his genital organs with a disinfectant, followed by a rinse of clear warm water. We never wash a mare and a stallion from the same bucket. We never use a sponge, either. Instead, we use a disposable sterile cotton pad. All of the equipment is disinfected and cleaned after use too. We don't want to spread any diseases through carelessness. That's the fastest way to ruin a breeding business."

Once the covering has taken place, the next concern is whether or not the mare has conceived. "One way for us to tell," Morgan says, "is that the mare doesn't come back into heat during her next usual cycle even when she's teased. But the absence of a regular heat cycle isn't enough of an indication that the mare is with foal. What we do is call in our vet about thirty to forty days after the mare was covered. The vet can definitely determine pregnancy."

*

During the time the Winterbrook mares are carrying foals, Morgan's main responsibility involves keeping them in good physical condition and feeding them properly. "Exercise for the mares is important during pregnancy," she insists. "A mare's muscles have to be kept in good condition. A pregnant mare should never get soft and flabby. If she does, she'll be likely to have trouble giving birth to her foal. I keep the mares in a pasture where they have lots of room to move around."

Feeding, adds Morgan, is especially important for pregnant mares. The amount of milk a mare produces after she foals is largely determined by the feed she consumes during her first four months of pregnancy. "A mare's feed has to be nutritious, plentiful enough to keep her in good shape, but not enough to make her fat." The proper development of the foals, then — even before they're born — is directly linked to the care the mares receive from Morgan. "If a mare is undernourished, run-down, or has a deficiency in vitamins or minerals," she says, "the foal will likely be underdeveloped and weak, or it may not even survive."

Morgan works closely with Winterbrook's veterinarian to be certain the mares receive enough vitamins. "The vet comes in regularly," she says, "and gives all the mothers shots of vitamins and a little calcium."

Like Lonnie, Morgan has received formal training in breeding-farm procedures — she holds a bachelor's degree in animal science — though she earns less money than he does. "But that's only fair," she insists. "He has more education, more specialized skills than I have. It's only fair that he earn more than I."

Morgan earns $18,000 per year — slightly above the national norm. "Basically," she says, "there are two ways you can qualify yourself to manage a breeding farm like Winterbrook. First, you can sort of apprentice yourself at the bottom of the ladder at a breeding farm and work your way up. Be forewarned, though, that you'll have to take on the most difficult — and least glamorous — of all the chores at the farm when you begin. And don't expect to be paid much. If you're real lucky, you might be able to squeeze out sixty dollars a week from the farm owner. Maybe less. Maybe more. The point is to get your feet planted firmly on the farm and be able to get a realistic perspective about the whole thing. If you're conscientious enough, eventually you'll be given more and more responsibility. And with additional responsibility comes more pay and more knowledge. Who knows how long it'll take you to get to the top that way, though?

"I advise a second route. Team up with a breeder on a volunteer basis at first, while you're still in high school, say. Explain to the breeder that you're interested in breeding as a career, and that you'd like to volunteer your time in return for some hands-on experience and education. If you do it that way, you're likely to avoid the real lowly work like mucking out stalls and carrying water buckets — because you're not being paid — *and* be able to work directly with the people in charge. Mind you, now. I'm not saying that you shouldn't get your hands dirty. You'll have to sooner or later. The point is, you're not out to make money — you're out to find out what managing a breeding farm is all about. You can only do that by slipping into the manager's shoes.

"Once I had a summer or two under my belt and I was certain it's what I wanted, then I'd seek a formal education — first a bachelor's degree in animal science, maybe. Then a master's degree in equine reproduction. Let me emphasize that that's only one route to follow. Formal education in breeding doesn't necessarily mean enrolling in a degree program. But I think the more education you have in this field, the further you can go in terms of managing the top-notch farms in the states like Kentucky, where breeding horses is certainly big business."

*

"I think," says E. L. Squires, associate professor of animal reproduction at Colorado State University, "that the most valuable thing for a young student in high school is to concentrate on obtaining good grades in general, so that he is readily accepted into a well-respected college or university. In addition, the high school student should try to obtain experience working around horses so that he becomes quite comfortable being around them.

"The breeding farm managers in today's world are much more sophisticated than in years gone by, in that a lot of these managers have a working knowledge of artificial insemination, preventive health, and so on. Thus, a college student should make an effort to take such courses as anatomy and physiology, artificial insemination, inorganic and organic chemistry, diseases of livestock, and so forth. In addition, it is imperative that the college student continue to obtain practical experience working with horses.

"I assist up to six students per year in obtaining jobs on breeding farms. Some of those students have a master's degree in equine reproduction and, naturally, they are more valuable to the farm owners than students with only a bachelor's degree — or no formal education at all.

"The master's degree students have the ability to take full control of an artificial insemination program, for example. In addition, these students know the techniques of rectal palpation, embryo transfer, culture diagnosis, and biopsy.

"Of course, not all breeding farm managers have master's degrees. But many of them still have some formal education. They've taken college courses in equine reproduction. In combination with practical experience around horses, my feeling is that they've got a definite advantage in searching for jobs over someone with no formal schooling.

"I think a lot of the major breeders are aware of the universities and colleges that have an equine reproduction program. Thus, many of the job opportunities come directly to the attention of the universities, either by word of mouth or inquiry by letter.

"In addition, the universities may have other advantages in placing graduates. For instance, at Colorado State University, we hold continuing education programs for equine breeders. Thus, in a single year's time we have approximately two hundred and fifty equine breeders visit us from all over the country. During this time our students have the opportunity of interviewing with those breeders for possible job openings on their farms.

"Our master's degree graduates have been able to go out into the industry and obtain a salary between twenty and twenty-five thousand dollars per year. Our bachelor's degree graduates — who, naturally, assume less responsibility because of their briefer training — have been starting out at a yearly salary of between ten and fifteen thousand dollars.

"Specialized training, then — in the form of a degree from an accredited college or university — combined with practical experience working around horses while you're in high school and college, is what I recommend."

Whether you have a degree and you're looking to manage a breeding farm, or you're just looking to gain some practical experience, probably the best way to find out where breeding farms are located is to consult horse magazines and state breeding associations.

First, select the particular breed of horse you'd most like to work with. Then, either subscribe to a magazine that specializes in that breed (see Appendix III for a list of equine breed magazines) and watch for ads of breeders that appear in the magazine or write to the appropriate breed association (see Appendix IV for a list) and request the names of breeders in your area.

Either way, once you've acquired the names and addresses

of, say, three or four breeders, write them each a letter explaining what it is you want to do, and ask if you can visit their farms.

"There's a heavy turnover of entry-level people," says Morgan. "People who do the maintenance chores, like mucking out stalls and the like. There's always a need for such individuals, so don't be discouraged if the first farm you contact has no need for you. There are plenty of farms around that are dying to have responsible, dependable young people who are willing to do anything to learn the business from the ground up.

"And remember one very important thing," she adds. "The people managing those farms you contact were in the very same position as you, perhaps not so long ago. So they're probably willing to lend a helping hand — *if* they feel you're sincere."

*

In most colleges and universities in the United States, the department of veterinary and/or animal sciences offers the courses of study that lead to a bachelor's or master's degree in the area of equine reproduction (see Appendix VII for a list of those colleges and universities). Animal science majors are usually required to take a group of basic science courses — zoology, chemistry, biochemistry, and statistics, for example — as well as courses in genetics, nutrition, physiology, management, pathology, and so forth, and then to focus further educational attention on specific, equine-oriented training. The equine courses taken will depend on the student's career goals, and the courses may focus on either equitation-oriented skills or horse-management-oriented skills.

On the next page is a sample four-year degree program at a major university in the United States. The degree earned at its completion is a bachelor of science, with a major in animal science, equine-oriented.

BACHELOR OF SCIENCE DEGREE
Animal Science Major
Equine Studies Option

Freshman Year

1st Semester

Rhetoric
Zoology
Chemistry
Math or Statistics
Animal Science Introduction
Equitation I

2nd Semester

Rhetoric
Humanities
Chemistry
Math or Statistics
Social Science
Equitation II

Sophomore Year

Humanities
Social Science
Animal Pathogens
Horse Management
Physiology of Reproduction
Equitation III

Systemic Animal Physiology
Biochemistry
Horse Breeds, Types, and Selection
Humanities
Equitation IV

Junior Year

Principles of Animal Nutrition
Principles of Animal Genetics
Physiology of Homeostasis
Accounting I

Applied Animal Genetics
Applied Animal Nutrition
Theories and Methods of Equitation
   Instruction
Reproduction Laboratory
Accounting II

Senior Year

Special Problems in Training the
   Horse
Research in Animal Management
Entomology
English
Kinesiology

Animal Pathology
Equine Stud Farm Management
Special Topics in Horse Farm
   Management
Journalistic Studies
General Business

Many major colleges and universities throughout the country offer similar degree programs that qualify you to manage most breeding farms in the United States. Employment, of course, will depend on the qualifications the breeding farm owner is looking for in his or her manager. Perhaps the owner will insist that the manager have more advanced training in the form of a master's degree. Even then, the bachelor's degree is still a necessary step in the right direction.

The following are brief explanations of some of the courses listed in the degree program outlined above:

Animal Science Introduction — An introduction to modern animal agriculture and the many scientific disciplines it encompasses. The roles of nutrition, genetics, economics, physiology, and pathology in animal research and production are examined. The dairy, poultry, meat, recreational, and laboratory-animal industries are evaluated in their roles in serving mankind.

Equitation I — An introductory course for those with no previous riding experience, or for those who have not had formal riding instruction. The overall aim of this course is to establish the correctly balanced seating position and the proper use of the aids. The course teaches grooming, bridling and saddling, the walk, trot (sitting and rising), diagonals, and the start of canter work.

Equitation II — A continuation of the work done in Equitation I. This course is aimed at strengthening the position and security of the rider and introducing basic riding theory. Work without stirrups is done at the walk and trot, and the canter is developed.

Animal Pathogens — An introduction to the major groups of organisms that cause diseases in animals — bacteria, viruses, nematodes, trematodes, and protozoa. This introduction to characteristics of pathogens relates practically to prevention and control of infectious diseases.

Horse Management — A general course that surveys the history, evolution, and development of the horse breeds and provides an introduction to the management of horses.

Physiology of Reproduction — A lecture course concerned with a major aspect of animal productivity. A comparative approach to the anatomical and physiological aspects of reproduction and lactation in the higher vertebrates, and the manipulation of these activities.

Equitation III — This course deals more extensively with developing the balanced-seat position at the walk, trot (sitting and rising), and canter — with and without stirrups. The jump position at the walk, trot, and canter is practiced over cavalletti. Circles, figure eights, transitions, and individual tests are utilized to develop control and position.

Systemic Animal Physiology — An in-depth study of the function and regulation of the different organ systems in the body. Emphasis is placed upon the physiological application to animals and man.

Horse Breeds, Types, and Selection — The history and development of the breeds and their present-day type, conformation, and use. Emphasis on the importance of anatomy and conformation and the relationship of form to function. An organized and systematic approach to selection.

Equitation IV — This course is an extension of Equitation III. With the riders secure in their positions, they walk, trot (sitting and rising), canter, and go over cavalletti — with and without stirrups. The horses used at this level are more difficult in that they are either younger, untrained horses or the more sensitive, schooled horses. Beginning dressage, cross-country, and stadium jumping are the areas of concentration.

Principles of Animal Nutrition — An in-depth study of the basic metabolic functions and interactions of nutrients in the body under normal and abnormal dietary intake levels, with emphasis on the comparative aspects of monogastric and ruminant animals — that is, animals with a single stomach, like a horse, and those with several stomachs, like a cow, that chew their food more than once.

Principles of Animal Genetics — A study of the identification, transmission, expression, and arrangement of hereditary material. Some of the specific areas covered include Mendelian genetics, the physical and chemical bases of heredity, genetic regulation of protein syntheses, mutations, gene interactions, sex determination, linkage, and chromosome variations. Whenever possible, horses will be used as the primary example.

Applied Animal Nutrition — This course emphasizes the application of basic nutritional principles to the establishment of nutritional requirements for maintenance, production, and reproduction through laboratory animal experimentation.

Theories and Methods of Equitation Instruction — A comprehensive course to help prepare students to be potential riding instructors. The topics include theory, equitation instruction, practical application under supervision, and riding school management.

Reproduction Laboratory — A laboratory course concerned largely with techniques used to regulate the reproductive performance of a horse.

Special Problems in Training the Horse — A course designed to teach the student the fundamentals of training a horse, via practical application.

Research Animal Management — The humane care, handling, and management of animals used in research. Emphasis is placed on the practical aspects of feeding, breeding, housing, restraining, identifying, injecting, withdrawing blood, and performing surgery. Euthanasia is also discussed.

Animal Pathology — An introduction to the study of animal diseases — their causes, development, transmission, and control — with special attention to diseases of the horse.

Equine Stud Farm Management — Modern horse breeding practices, including heat detection, breeding procedures, pregnancy detection, and foaling procedures. This course combines scientific principles with practical experience in handling stallions and mares.

Special Topics in Horse Farm Management — Selected topics concerned with specific aspects of horse farm management. Topics include equine diseases, reproduction, nutrition, etc.

FOUR

The Riding Instructor

"THE KEY TO LEARNING how to ride," said Hoover Ginn, "is confidence. Really. You've got to have confidence in your ability to *communicate* with your horse . . ."

Hoover was addressing four people whom she'd known only a few minutes, four new riding students who not only had never ridden before, but — except for the redheaded teenager — had never even had occasion to be near a horse. Even the redhead had never actually ridden one. The four of them had come to the college to attend the special five-week-long summer riding program for beginners.

The college's chief — and only — riding instructor, Hoover Ginn, stood in the middle of the indoor riding arena as she spoke to her new students, who had arranged themselves in a semicircle opposite her. The redhead and another teenage girl with blonde braids stood with their hands on their hips, their weight shifted to one leg, announcing to all the world that they were at ease. The older man and the young-looking mother chose, however, to stand almost at attention, their legs shoulder-width apart, arms folded, indicating that they were sincerely interested in eating up every single word their instructor spoke.

Photo by David O. Aronson

Hoover had already taken them on a brief tour of the facilities. She had also talked a little bit about herself. Now she was explaining her philosophy of teaching riding, saying that it was to approach the project in much the same way as the students had been sent on up through grades in school. In all, the students would — if they continued taking lessons with her — ultimately pass through six "grades," or levels, of riding proficiency. "First grade" was for students like themselves, who had little or no previous experience around horses.

"Safe horsemanship," she said, "is only achieved when both horse and rider are never asked to perform beyond their abilities. That's why I believe in starting off with a good, solid foundation of basic skills."

This morning's lesson, then, would be the first at the "first grade" level. In all, there would be ten hours of instruction — ten lessons — at this level. Considering there would be two of these hour-long lessons per week, Hoover expected that all four students would be ready to graduate to the more advanced second level at the conclusion of the five-week summer program.

"In your situation," she continued, "there's no need at this point for you to run right out and buy a lot of expensive riding clothes. But," she added, "certain things are essential — for both your safety and comfort." She led her students to the entrance of the indoor arena, next to which hung a dozen or more hard black hats. "These," said Hoover, "are called *riding hats* or *hunt caps*. You've seen them before, I'm sure."

"Yes," said the young-looking mother. "On television. The Olympics. But I thought you only wore them for show." The older gentleman nodded his silver-sideburned head in agreement.

"Definitely not," said Hoover. "I'm glad you mentioned that. There's no law that says you have to wear a riding hat like there is in some states where you have to wear a helmet if you ride a motorcycle, say. Nevertheless, you should always, always be sure to wear one whenever you're riding. In fact, most riding stables — including ours — won't allow you on a horse without one. You'd be an insurance risk." She asked the students to sort through the riding hats and select one that fit. Once that had been accomplished, they all reassembled in the middle of the arena.

At the time the students had registered for the lessons, they had received a letter from Hoover explaining what they were to wear to the first class. Consequently, all four of them were wearing close-fitting jeans or pants and some style of boots with enough heel to keep the foot from slipping into the stirrup. Hoover thanked them for having followed her advice. "I'd also advise," she said, "that you get yourselves a pair of what we call *string gloves.*"

"String gloves?" asked the blonde-braided girl.

"That's right. You can get them at any tack shop. They'll help prevent the reins from sliding out of your hands and protect the skin between your fingers. At this stage of the game, that's all the equipment you really need. Of course, if you should decide to really get into riding and want to compete at shows and the whole bit, there are things you'll need — like a jacket, breeches, and riding boots. But that's putting the cart before the horse. What I'd like to do this morning is first introduce you to the horses you'll be riding —"

"We're going to ride this morning?" asked the mother. "Isn't that kind of fast? Dangerous, I mean?"

Hoover smiled. "I appreciate your concern," she said. "But don't worry. You won't actually be riding — you'll be sitting on your horse and he'll be walking. I assure you. Besides, by the time we get that far you'll have made good friends with your horse."

"I hope so," replied the mother, and returned Hoover's smile.

"I have a question for you, Hoover," said the older man. He cleared his throat before he continued. "Will we actually be able to ride a horse pretty well after just ten lessons? That doesn't seem like much time."

Hoover folded her arms. "I know what you mean," she said. "Ten hours in the saddle doesn't seem like much time. But look at it this way. We just met a little while ago, right?"

"That's right."

"Would you say you know me well?"

"Not at all."

"Would you say you're at least a little bit more comfortable with me now than you were before you met me?" Hoover asked.

He thought for just a second. "I'd say so."

"Good," said Hoover. "We've only known each other now for . . ." She slid the sleeve of her green sweat shirt up her forearm. "Ten minutes. Now imagine how much better you'll know me after ten *hours*."

The man grinned. "I see what you mean."

"Ten hours is really a lot of time to spend on a horse," said Hoover. "You'll be pleasantly surprised at the progress you're going to make. Believe me."

"I hope so," added the redhead. "It took me a year just to learn how to ride a bike — a *tri*cycle, at that!" She grinned. Everyone else did, too. And for the first time, there was spontaneous laughter. Everyone looked at each other. The tension had been broken.

"Okay, everyone. Follow me, please," Hoover instructed, leading them to Sorcerer's stall. The strawberry roan gelding had anticipated the moment. He was always the first resident of the stable to whom Hoover brought new students — with good reason. Sorcerer had the gentlest disposition.

His head and neck were stretched as far as possible over the Dutch door of his stall as the group approached him. Hoover placed her gentle hands on Sorcerer's starred face, speaking softly to him all the while. The horse responded to the affection, poking his muzzle into Hoover's face. She opened the stall door and walked in. Placing a hand on the gelding's muscular shoulder, she rubbed him in small circles and gave him a pat. The she moved to his head, attached a lead line to his halter, and led him onto the stage — the middle of the arena. Sorcerer would be the focus of attention for a while, and he'd love it.

"Did you notice that I greeted him and spoke softly to him?" asked Hoover.

The students nodded in unison.

"There's a reason why I did all that. Horses are very sensitive creatures."

"What do you mean, *sensitive?*" asked the mother.

"They're basically timid animals," Hoover replied.

"Timid?" The mother's voice had risen an octave.

"Yes. Definitely," said Hoover. "Their first reaction to an unusual situation is to panic and run away."

"It's hard to believe," said the mother. "They're so *big!*"

Hoover grinned. "I know. I felt the same way once. Why don't you come on over here and make friends with him?"

The mother swallowed — hard. "Me?" she asked.

"Why not? He's the gentlest horse in the stable."

The mother took one step forward, then stopped. She dug deep into her jeans pocket. "I thought these might come in handy," she said, pulling out several small cubes of sugar.

"Wish I'd thought of that!" said the blonde-braided girl.

"I hope you brought enough for all the horses," said Hoover.

"All the horses?" the mother asked.

"We can't give Sorcerer here any special treatment, you know. If he gets a treat they all get a treat."

The mother looked puzzled for just a moment. "That won't be a problem," she said, realizing the wisdom in Hoover's philosophy. She smiled at Hoover and patted a rather large-looking lump in her pocket.

"Good," said Hoover. "Now, all you have to do is place a cube in the palm of your hand. Then just let him lip it away. Don't be afraid. He won't bite you." Her voice was firm, yet contained a tone of compassion — a voice that could be trusted. At least that's what the mother thought. She followed Hoover's directions. Sorcerer lowered his head and lipped the white morsel into his mouth. "Good boy!" said the mother, looking as though she'd just won a trip to some faraway, exotic paradise. The other students applauded her bravery.

"That wasn't too bad, eh?" asked Hoover.

"Not at all," replied the mother. "You were right."

"Good. You and Sorcerer are a team. Okay?"

"Okay."

"Don't forget. Before we leave, all the other horses have to get a treat too. No favorites around here."

"For sure," agreed the mother as she rejoined her comrades. Hoover continued with the lesson.

"Just as we all wash up before we begin our day's work," she said, "a horse has to be washed, or *groomed*, every day — before and after he's used." She led Sorcerer back to his stall and secured him to a ring on the wall just outside his stall. Then she proceeded to demonstrate how to groom Sorcerer.

One after another, she gently lifted all his feet, removing caked dirt and tiny pebbles with a piece of iron that looked like a hooked finger. Next, she rubbed Sorcerer's eyes and lips and nostrils with a soft, damp sponge. With a second sponge, she cleaned underneath his tail. Then she worked over the horse's head and neck, chest, and forelegs, with the soft, short bristles of the body brush. As she began working on the rear half of the strawberry roan's body, Sorcerer reacted to the soothing massage by stretching his long, sleek neck and moving his head up and down, up and down.

"Feels good, doesn't it?" Hoover asked.

Finally, she concluded her grooming demonstration by brushing Sorcerer's mane and tail so that every hair hung in its proper place.

"For your age," said Hoover, "you look really good. You know that?"

When she was certain that all four students understood the grooming procedures, she introduced each of them — except the mother, because she'd be working with Sorcerer — to the horses they'd be teamed up with for the duration of the summer program. Each horse was secured outside his stall. The older man would work with a bay gelding named Moses; the redhead, with a half-Arabian mare named Moon Spinner; and the blonde-braided girl, with a piebald gelding named Ajax.

Once again, Hoover reviewed the grooming procedures. This time, however, the students performed the tasks as Hoover explained and observed and corrected. Even the mother participated, despite the fact that Sorcerer had been groomed already, because the grooming process was a vital part of this first lesson. It would help the students establish initial contact with their horses, thereby helping them to gain some degree of confidence around the animals.

After the grooming, Hoover announced that the next step would be for the students to learn how to bridle and saddle their horses. That, too, went smoothly enough. Then Hoover demonstrated how they were to lead their horses around the arena, to limber their muscles. Although she had emphasized that the students were to walk at the horse's left (near) side, the mother had some difficulty with this at first. She was afraid that even if she walked at Sorcerer's side, he would still step on her. She was thus awkward with the procedure at first. But Hoover spent extra time with her and enabled her to overcome her anxiety.

The next step would be for the students to learn how to mount their horses. A big step, indeed. None had ever been on a horse before.

Hoover had them walk their horses into the middle of the arena, one at a time — thus making certain that there would be ample room between them. All four teams stood at attention, prepared for work. The grooming, bridling, saddling, and limbering-up procedures had been carried out by each student and observed, controlled, and corrected by Hoover — a most effective introduction to their first riding lesson. She had laid for them a foundation of confidence between them and their horses. The horses had become acquainted with their riders' voices and movements and would not be confronted by completely strange creatures when the actual riding began. The students, in turn, had learned that their horses were by no means wild beasts or stupid animals. It was an important bonding that Hoover had consciously sought to establish.

Having made her students familiar, then, with their horses, Hoover proceeded to the next fundamental step of the first lesson: to demonstrate the correct riding seat. To do that, though, she first had to show them how to mount their horses.

She explained very slowly that they were always to mount a horse from the left, or near, side. Before they did so, she showed each student how to check the girth for tightness.

"Who wants to be first?" she asked.

"Well," said the mother. "I might as well keep on being your guinea pig, if it's okay with everyone else."

It was.

Hoover brought over a *mounting block* and placed it beside Sorcerer. "This will make it easier for all of you the first time," she explained. She showed the mother how to gather the reins in her left hand, checking to be sure that she maintained just a light contact with Sorcerer's mouth. "Take care," said Hoover, "not to keep the left rein too short. Your horse might start to circle when you try to mount." She then placed the mother's left hand on the *pommel* of the English saddle and had her stand on the wooden mounting block and turn her body so that her back was to Sorcerer's head, her left shoulder next to the horse's left shoulder.

"How am I doing so far?" the mother asked, just a tinge of nervousness in her voice.

"Just fine and dandy," said Hoover. "Now, take the stirrup iron in your right hand . . . turn it clockwise, toward you . . . that's it . . . and place the ball of your left foot into the iron . . . that's right."

Hoover then instructed her to place her right hand over the waist of the saddle and shift the weight of her body to her left foot. Then with a boost from Hoover, the young mother sprang upward. Her right leg swung over the saddle and she delicately lowered herself into it with an ear-to-ear smile.

"Put your right foot in the *offside* iron," said Hoover. She tightened the girth to be sure the saddle was secure and then adjusted the stirrup leathers to the correct length. To do that, she had the student take her feet out of the irons and let them hang down naturally. Hoover adjusted the leather of each stirrup so that the bottom of the iron touched the inside point of the anklebone. Finally, she showed the mother how to hold the reins slightly apart — about four inches from each other — between the ring and little fingers of each hand, with the slack held by the thumbs.

When all the other students were also sitting smartly atop their mounts, Hoover continued their primary education. "Riding," she explained, "is really the art of controlling a horse while mounted on its back. Many *styles* of riding exist to do that, depending upon the task you're going to ask your horse to perform."

"What do you mean, *style* of riding?" asked the redhead.

"I mean," said Hoover, "the way you ride. For example, a person might ride with his back straight, rising right up out of his saddle. 'Like a cowboy, say. Another might ride bent over his horse's neck."

"Like a jockey," said the blonde-braided girl.

"Exactly," said Hoover. "Those are examples of riding styles. And those styles are dictated by the task each rider is to perform with his horse. The jockey's job, for instance, is to get his horse to run as fast as he can. Consequently he adopts a certain riding style — leaning forward — in order to help his horse accomplish its task — to go as fast as possible."

Hoover emphasized that perhaps the most important aspect of any rider's style is his *seat* — his position in the saddle, be it an English saddle or a *stock*, or *Western*, saddle. A rider's seat, Hoover explained, is based on balance, whereby the rider maintains his position atop his horse without resorting to gripping with his knees or thighs or holding on to the saddle with his hands.

"Since we're using English saddles," said Hoover, "we'll have to adopt a style of riding that fits our equipment. So we'll be learning the *balanced seat* style of riding, which is the style of the majority of riders in the world."

"The balanced seat?" asked the man.

"The balanced seat," said Hoover. "Also referred to as the *hunt seat.*"

"How many kinds of seats are there?"

"Three, mainly. Hunt seat is the style, or position, that best enables a rider to ride a horse over fences and across country. Then you've got what's called the *saddle seat.* And then there's the *stock* or *Western seat.*"

"What's the difference between them?" the man asked.

"Well," said Hoover, taking in a deep breath and exhaling slowly. "That would take me the length of a book to explain fully. But I can give you a quick example of some of the major differences between Western seat and hunt seat, say, just to help clarify the whole thing a little for you. For one thing, in the Western seat, or style, the rider sits farther back in the saddle than we'll be sitting, and his reins are usually held in one hand. That style was developed so that one hand could be left free for using a lariat. Remember I told you that riding styles developed to fit the task that the horse and rider had to perform? Well, the Western seat was developed by the cowboy, whose primary responsibility was working cattle.

"Another difference between Western and hunt seat is in the length of the stirrups. Western seat riders use a lot longer stirrup than you're using." Hoover paused. "I suppose the biggest single difference between hunt seat and Western seat is that the Western rider's goal is not to remain in the center of his horse, because the task he'll be asking his horse to perform — let's say it's cutting cattle — is quite different from what the English rider will ask his horse to do — let's say it's to jump over a fallen tree."

Hoover checked her watch. It was getting late. There was still much to cover in the last fifteen minutes.

"Your seat," she continued, "is probably the most important part of riding. If you don't learn first to position yourselves correctly in the saddle, you'll never progress very far." A correct hunt seat, she said, meant that they would be balanced on top of their horses — secure, yet responsive to their horses' every movement. She asked them to all imagine that they were sitting on a triangle, two of its points being the seat bones and the third point the crotch of the body.

"You all should be sitting in the middle — the lowest — part of your saddle," advised Hoover. "Keep your backs straight and your shoulders square." As she spoke, she went to each student and placed her hand behind him or her, flat on the saddle. "There should be just enough room for my hand between you and the *cantle*," she said, repositioning the older man.

"The next thing I'd like you all to do," Hoover continued, "is to open your legs away from your horse's flanks . . . good. Now draw your thighs into position from behind." This, she explained, would bring the large inside thigh muscle under and to the back of the thigh, thus flattening that area and allowing it to rest close to the saddle and the horse. Then, by pushing their weight down in the heels, they would feel their seats lower all the way into their saddles.

"So far, so good," said Hoover. "You all look like you were born to be in those saddles. Now, your lower legs should be hanging down to rest . . ."

Ten minutes later, the morning's lesson was finished, a little more than an hour after it had begun. Hoover helped the students unsaddle their horses — grooming them a second time, she said, would be unnecessary, since the horses had only walked around the arena three times — and then quarter them all comfortably.

She made certain, also, that the mother kept her promise and treated all of Sorcerer's stable friends to sugar cubes too.

The students were all smiling and extremely pleased with themselves as they filed out of the stable. After all, they had actually "ridden" a horse — albeit a slowly *walking* horse — for the very first time in their lives — and under their own control! Quite an accomplishment, they told each other.

Hoover too was pleased. She had started her new students along a logical road that she had studied step by step, one that after this morning's good start would lead to happy riders and happy horses, even at an elementary level, by summer's end. She disappeared into the stable manager's office to get ready to work on her own next steps on her own horse. Beebo would not be used today or tomorrow by any students, so Hoover would have to exercise him.

She did so in the field next to the outdoor riding ring, nearly disappearing into Beebo's big black back. It was hard work riding him. But Hoover was doing one of the things she enjoyed doing most in life. The late-morning sun, however, was uncomfortably hot, and she perspired freely. Still, her legs remained cemented to the saddle as she gave Beebo a tour of the jumping facilities. One hundred and fifteen pounds of determination was in total control of twelve hundred pounds of brute strength.

Hoover stopped Beebo in front of the first jump and let him examine it. She flicked some sweat from her brow with a quick forefinger and walked Beebo to all the other obstacles, letting him examine those, too. Then it was down to business.

Teacher and mount practiced their crafts for forty-five hot minutes. It was work. It was fun. When it was over, they headed back to the stable.

In the meantime, the vet had arrived to attend to Snark, who had had indigestion the night before. The vet and the stable manager conferred in Snark's stall while Snora, the St. Bernard, waited outside, keeping one eye ever so slightly open as she lay stretched out on the cool dirt of the riding ring.

Hoover arrived with Beebo and cooled him down by walking him leisurely around the indoor ring. His coat was crayon-black where he had sweated underneath the saddle pad. Soon Hoover moved him to the stable entrance, sponging his warm body with cold water to bring his temperature down. Several more leisurely strolls around the ring and Beebo was finally ready for his lunch. The groom would take care of that, though, so Hoover could now enjoy her own noontime meal — an egg salad sandwich and a Coke — in the stable manager's office.

There were days, like yesterday, when she simply didn't have the time to sit down and enjoy lunch. On those occasions, an apple, eaten while on the back of a horse, had to suffice.

Lunch was concluded in twenty minutes. The vet, having joined Hoover and the stable manager for a bite to eat, said goodbye. Now it was time for Hoover to be a barber and shave the whiskers off all the horses.

Normally, the grooming of the horses was not her responsibility. From September through early June, when the college was in session, Hoover's primary responsibility — her only responsibility — was teaching riding. However, during the summer, when all the college students had gone home for summer vacation, the riding classes were made up of people from the surrounding communities. Since there simply weren't enough people to fill up classes all day long, Hoover occupied her time by helping with various stable chores, in addition to exercising the horses.

"Any instructor worth her salt," says Hoover, "is much more than just an instructor, anyway. I'm really several things all rolled into one: an equestrienne, a teacher, a trainer, and a bit of a stable manager, too. I have to be, and so does anyone else who expects to get anywhere as an instructor."

The groom patrolled outside the stalls, walking back and forth, looking for volunteers to be shaved. "Who wants to be first?" he kept repeating. When it became obvious that none of the horses was going to step forward, the groom chose Sorcerer. Hoover brought out a long electric cord and shaving shears from the office. She showed Sorcerer the apparatus before turning it on, even rubbing the silent machine softly

over his nose. Then she switched it on, clipping first the whiskers around the muzzle, next the backs of all four ankles, and
finally tidying up Sorcerer's rather unkempt mane. In four
minutes it was all over. There were eleven more horses to do,
and each "customer" would react differently. For instance, the
electric rhythm tickled Tego's extra-sensitive nose, and he
quivered with pleasure while Hoover sheared him. Ajax, on
the other hand, was not nearly so cooperative. The groom had
to bend one of the horse's legs at the knee and hold it up so
that Ajax would keep the other three legs down for Hoover
to trim. "There, you *rav*ishing beauty, you!"

Bunty was next. Then Moon Spinner . . . Beebo . . . Moses.
They were all shorn by one-thirty.

"Can you make a trip to the tack shop?" asked the stable
manager. Hoover was "off " now until her next lesson, at six
o'clock. She would travel to another riding stable and exercise
some horses there.

"No problem," said Hoover.

"Pick me up two dozen cottons, please, and charge them to
the college. Thanks, Hoov."

*

How did Hoover Ginn become a riding instructor?

"My father and mother," she says, "are the ones who got
me interested in horses in general. We'd go on family trail
rides when I was very little — six or seven years old. When
I expressed an interest in getting better at riding, my father
observed which of the riding instructors were winning at local
shows and hooked me up with the instructor I still go to today
— Ruly Blue. I was about ten at the time. I took one private
lesson and one group lesson a week with Ruly, for years."

Of course, Hoover was fortunate in that she owned her own
horse and was thus able to practice between lessons. "I rode
constantly," she recalls. "Took lessons faithfully. Went to
shows and competed almost every weekend."

Over the years she was able to establish herself as one of

the premier English-style riders in her area. Then, at age seventeen, she got her first job teaching riding at a summer camp sponsored by the college at which she is now employed full time.

"Ruly Blue, my private riding instructor, had been the head instructor at the college for years before going off on her own. When she learned that the college needed a summer camp instructor, she recommended me," explains Hoover. The job was eight till four, five days a week throughout the summer. It paid $100 per week.

"That was pretty good money for a kid in high school," Hoover insists. "Plus I got to ride and be outdoors all day. That's what hooked me into this whole instructor thing in the first place. I'd never really given it any thought before that summer job.

"When summer was over, a few of the students wanted to keep on taking lessons from me on a private basis, so they would come to my parents' place after school or on weekends. It wasn't a steady thing. If it rained, for example, the lessons were off because we didn't have an indoor arena. Still, it kept me sharp."

In the meantime, Hoover returned to her summer camp job for two more summers. After her third stint there, a full-time instructor's job opened up at the college. "I had my foot in the door already," she says. "They knew what I could do. When the job opened up, I was kind of the natural choice."

She earns $150 per week ($7,800 annually) from the college, working there Monday through Friday. But because she gets time off during the slow summer months when school is out, she has the opportunity to earn extra money elsewhere. For example, she earns $5 for every horse she exercises at Ruly Blue's place. Generally, Hoover exercises three horses there per day, four days per week, during the summer — an average of $60 extra per week over and above her college salary.

In addition, she gives lessons at her parents' place after work — usually one night a week. "I have three regular students," she says. "I charge them twelve dollars apiece for the lesson, so that's another thirty-six dollars a week during the months from May through October.

"My parents are a really big help. My students board their horses at my parents' place. In return for them letting me use their facilities, I take care of my parents' horses for them. So I have no expensive overhead — yet I have a place at which to give lessons. With my base salary from the college, I have it made."

In effect, what Hoover's doing is building up her reputation in the area, looking forward to the day when she can leave her college teaching position and work full time for herself, so her weekends are filled with "work," too. "I'm at a show every single weekend during the spring and summer," she says. "The more ribbons I win, the more I establish myself as an accomplished rider, and the more I'm noticed by prospective students. The idea is to prove that you're a top rider first — attract people who want to learn your secrets. Then you try to establish your reputation as a good teacher, too. That happens if your riding students do well regularly when they compete. After that, it's all word-of-mouth advertising.

"My goal is to ultimately attract enough students so that — like Ruly Blue — I can offer riding instruction full time at my own place."

*

Is formal training necessary in order to become a riding instructor?

Technically, no. Unlike Great Britain, there is no national standard, no licensing of riding instructors. "But," says Hoover, "if you can possibly afford it, I think it's an excellent idea — to get a sound instructor's training at a reputable riding school. I'm not saying it's absolutely necessary — after all, I never went to a Morven Park or a Meredith Manor. But, then again, I had a rather fortunate situation. Everything — including instruction and horses and facilities — has always been at my disposal. I'd say I'm somewhat unusual in that respect, which is why I'd advise — for most people — that a formal course in riding *and* riding *instruction* is a good idea."

Of course, it seems obvious that a riding instructor should be a good rider first and foremost. But that is not always the way it is. The good riding instructor is the one who, at any given moment, can demonstrate an exercise on horseback as correctly as he demands it from his pupils. "A student has the right," says Hoover, "to expect the same qualities in a riding teacher as he would in any other kind of teacher — a thorough knowledge of the subject he's teaching."

She's certainly not alone in her opinion.

Prince Philip, president of the International Equestrian Federation, in the foreword to his book *Great Riding Schools of the World* writes: "People can teach themselves to do almost anything, and many people who have achieved success are proud to say that they are self-taught. That system works, but only when there is exceptional talent and, then, exceptional application. . . . Far better results will always be achieved by a combination of natural talent and good basic instruction. Good instruction in its turn comes from the accumulation and refinement of experience and the rational application of consistently successful techniques."

In short, most riding schools, Prince Philip argues, maintain proper standards of teaching by using well-proven principles of instruction. William Steinkraus, equestrian extraordinaire, agrees with Prince Philip. In his preface to the prince's book, Mr. Steinkraus writes: "The best way to learn any difficult and complex subject is to study it systematically, drawing from past knowledge. . . . Man's progress in the equestrian art depends upon the systematic transmission of accrued knowledge about it . . . through oral instruction and practical demonstration, as customarily offered in serious riding academies."

Be advised, though, that riding schools vary as to the riding *styles* taught. Morven Park International Equestrian Institute in Leesburg, Virginia, offers an "Equitation Instructor's Course" that is based "on the understanding and adoption of a balanced seat which will enable the rider to perform on the flat and over fences, in the hunting field and in competition." In other words, a student learns the *hunter seat* style of riding there. At another school — like Meredith Manor in Waverly, West Virginia, for example — a student could learn the hunter seat or the *Western seat* style of riding. If your goal is to ride an American Saddle Horse, a Tennessee Walker, or a Morgan, particularly on the show circuit, then you look for a school teaching the *saddle seat* style.

A reputable riding school will ensure that its students' basic riding techniques are correct, that their theoretical knowledge is also based on correct principles and understanding, and that the qualities of a good riding instructor are instilled in its students — sympathy, patience, humility, firmness, and an ability to transmit confidence and enthusiasm to pupils.

In addition to learning the "rational application of consistently successful techniques" in riding and instructing, a student graduating from a "serious" riding academy may receive other benefits. "We offer a placement service," says Morven Park's director, Lt. Col. Mark Daley. "A small portion of our students have their employment already arranged before they come here. In some cases their jobs have been dependent on their completing our course. Another small portion go home and seek employment locally, intending to live at home and instruct on a full- or part-time basis. The great majority of our graduates have an open mind and have no personal restrictions on where they will operate. It's with those individuals that our placement service is most effective."

At the same time, the horse industry is unlikely to welcome graduates of riding schools — notwithstanding their knowledge and ability — if they can't take a horse's temperature and muck out a stall. Any good school, then, in addition to an average of fifteen riding hours a week, will include instruction in stable management in theory and practice and a veterinary program, as well as teaching techniques.

But training in itself — however formal and however thorough — will still not necessarily make you a good riding instructor. Unfortunately, having considerable knowledge of any subject does not automatically mean that one is able to impart knowledge in an attractive and attention-getting way.

"Other than not knowing what you're talking about," explains Hoover, "dullness is probably the most damaging criticism anyone can level against the ability of any riding instructor."

Why? Because so much more is required of an instructor — from any teacher, for that matter — than the mere transfer of factual information. "A good riding instructor," adds Hoover, "has a duty to influence students to extend themselves, to exercise their minds, to be enthusiastic. In other words, he has an obligation to get the most out of his students by any way he can, and that often requires extra effort and imagination.

"I've heard some instructors say, 'My students are just a dull lot. They have no enthusiasm to learn. They're lazy!' That might be true once in a while," says Hoover. "But not most of the time. If the attitude of the majority of this group of students remains unchanged after being with the instructor for some weeks, then I think it's an indication that the instructor has failed to make an impact on them. And *that's* the instructor's fault."

A riding instructor who attains a reputation as a good teacher as well as a good rider, says Hoover, "talks in an interesting manner and gives demonstrations in an interesting way. All the hard work, the acquisition of knowledge, and a high standard of riding will not by themselves be responsible for an instructor's achieving a national reputation — or even a substantial local or regional following. The ability to communicate effectively and to motivate, and willingness to help pupils develop themselves — all of these are essential factors that are quite noticeable in the top instructors.

"Being able to ride a horse well, being able to tell people

what to do, knowing how different horses should be ridden under different conditions, and being capable of looking after horses won't by themselves make anyone a good riding instructor. An instructor, maybe — but not necessarily a good one.

"The good one realizes that unless he obtains the cooperative interest of his pupils, much of the knowledge he imparts will be wasted. The good instructor — like the good classroom teacher — knows how to obtain that interest and really cares about obtaining it.

"It's simple: no instructor who's dull can shine professionally. And to not be dull takes imagination, creativity, extra effort — which is *very* demanding. I assure you."

*

After a quick stop at the tack shop, Hoover arrived at Ruly Blue's by two-fifteen. She would exercise Chopin and Mummer today.

Manx, the barn cat, greeted her in the stable by bowing his head in anticipation of being rubbed. Hoover obliged him only a minute, and then she was into the tack room, putting on her paddock shoes and wrapping her ankles and calves in the blue bandages she'd later wrap Mummer's legs in. By the time she'd finished, Ruly had arrived with two of her students.

Ruly's pupils take two lessons from her per week, at $20 each per lesson. In addition, Ruly boards some of the students' horses. All told, her six boarders bring in $1,200 per month — enough to pay for their own upkeep and the upkeep of Ruly's own horses and to pay two part-time grooms. The lessons earn her about $300 per week. In addition, she buys horses, trains them herself, and resells them at a profit. Last year, her take-home income was $27,000 — well above the average of $11,200 the nation's five thousand full-time instructors earn annually.

Ruly is able to attract students because she has earned a

reputation as an outstanding teacher. Her students place high at horse shows. But to get to where she is today, she had to "pay dues," just as Hoover is doing — lots of hours in the saddle, continuous improvement and training, weekend horse shows, and all the rest.

"I'll get there," Hoover insists. This week, for example, she would earn $246 — $150 of it from the college, $60 from Ruly for exercising horses, and $36 for giving one group lesson at her parents' place. Her yearly income last year was just under $12,000. "I'll probably never be rich," she says. "But riding and teaching is exactly what I love to do. It's healthy. It's fun. The money is definitely secondary to me."

By four o'clock, she had left Ruly's and stopped for potato chips and a soda at the town drugstore. Then it was off to her parents' place to feed their horses before going back to the college for the final lesson of the day.

The day hadn't been a hectic one, but it had never stopped demanding something from her. As she moseyed into the college's stable at five-forty-five, her legs were moving decidedly slower than they had been when she left the stable four hours earlier.

And she still had an hour-and-a-half lesson to get up for. It would be eight o'clock in the evening before she could put her tired feet up and call it a day.

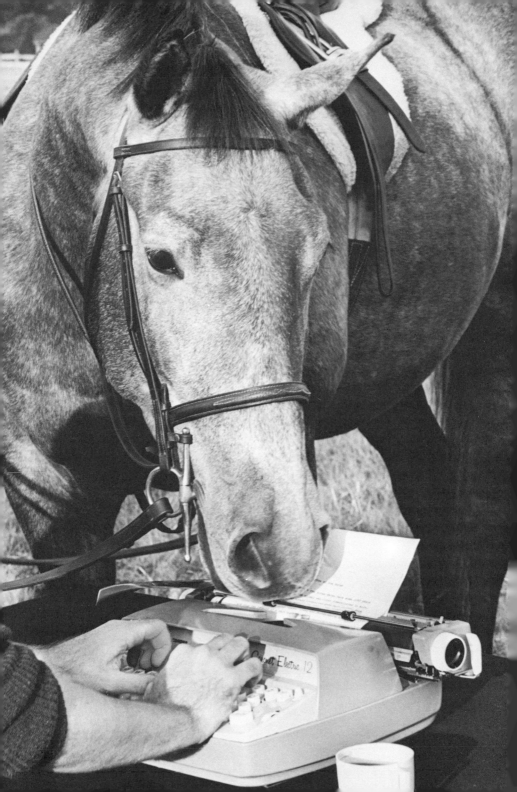

FIVE

The Equine Writer

"Last stall on the left," the old man mumbled, pointing an arthritic finger toward the end of a dimly lit barn. "Better watch out, too — he's a real striker, that one is."

Carlos Gria grinned at the old man. A tall man standing next to Gria nudged him with an elbow. "What's he mean, Carlos — a real *striker?*"

"He means the horse likes to rear up," Gria explained, "and hammer anyone he doesn't like." Picking up his pail of tools, he marched bowleggedly to the last stall on the left. As he approached the field of battle, his blue-black opponent snorted a stay-away warning, bared his brown-stained teeth, and fixed a wild-looking eyeball Gria's way.

The tall man — Dakin McAdoo — had not moved. Why, he wondered, would any *sane* person do what Gria was going to do?

"He's crazy," mumbled the old man with the arthritic finger, as if he could hear what Dakin had been thinking.

"Easy now, big fella," they heard Gria say as he stepped inside his opponent's stall, slowly sliding his boxer's hand into a protective glove of rubber.

Dakin hurried over to the stall. He watched every move

Photo by David O. Aronson

Gria made and scribbled observations onto his fingerprinted note pad. He was particularly intrigued by a cruelly carved skin scar above Gria's right forearm. It was as if something had bitten into it in the same manner Dakin might bite into a piece of chicken to strip away some meat. Guessing that it was the work of some dissatisfied patient, Dakin made a note to ask Gria about it later. As he did, a sudden movement in the stall caught his eye. In one quick spurt, Gria had wedged his rubberized hand between the stallion's mighty jaws and was pulling on its powerful tongue, forcing a mouthful of teeth wide open.

"Yup," said Gria, peering into the green-dark orifice. "One of 'em will have to come out." As if on cue, his wide-eyed patient heaved himself forward and pinned Gria's ribs to the wall. Gria groaned. Dakin dropped his note pad and rushed to the stall door.

"I'm okay," grunted Gria, forcing the stallion backwards as he would push a stalled car. He steered the frightened animal into a corner and hid its eyes behind his linebacker's forearm, then slipped a forceps into the horse's mouth. A twist, a turn . . .

"Okay, big fella," said Gria. "Party's over."

Indeed, the "party" was over for Gria and his patient. But it had only just begun for would-be writer Dakin McAdoo.

*

"You don't have to sport saddle sores," Dakin explained, peering over half-moon spectacles, "in order to write for horse magazines."

The fledgling equine writers were at the very edges of their steel seats, and they were all armed with brand-new notebooks, full of unused paper, and extra pens or pencils, in case their favorite writing instruments failed them. Dakin, they all thought, would be able to give them the magic secrets that would turn them into successful writers like himself. Everyone in the audience was familiar with his background, which was why most of them were in attendance. Dakin McAdoo, you see, is the quintessential writing success — the suffering malcontent who had long dreamed of being able to make his living by writing about subjects he enjoyed. If Dakin had been able to pull it off, perhaps a little bit of his magic might rub off on some of them.

Dakin understood why they were there. He, too, had once known their kind of frustration. Formerly an English teacher, he had been bothered by the fact that he had never written anything for publication. "What good is it calling yourself a writer," he once asked a friend with similar aspirations, "if no one ever reads what you write?"

The friend was in total agreement with Dakin's rhetorical muse. "It's like dancing," said the friend. "You need a partner, an audience."

Four years later, Dakin had his audience — a big audience, at that. Even though most of them had never met him personally, they knew his byline. Some, for instance, were avid readers of his monthly column in the *Practical Equestrian*. Others looked forward to his monthly personality profile in *Horse World* magazine, or his regular feature articles in *Equine* magazine. But his largest audience, by far, were those who — having read his first two books — were eagerly awaiting his third. Whoever they were, Dakin's audience associated his name with lively, entertaining writing about horses and the people who rode and maintained them.

"The handwriting," Dakin continued, "is on the stall — if you'll pardon my paraphrase. The horse population in this country is the largest it's ever been. It seems like half our nation speaks a foreign language, punctuated with words like *hackamore* and *skid boots* and *gaskin*. The magazine and book markets are loaded with literature on all sorts of equine topics.

"And," he added, "I'll let you all in on a little secret. Not one of those thousands of books and articles writes itself!" He paused for a moment to sip some water from the glass on his podium. "I can hear many of you now," he said. "'But I don't know a *surcingle* from a *snaffle bit*. And besides, I live in East Oshkosh, Caledonia, where horses and horse people have been extinct for hundreds of years.'" His audience chuckled and smiled. Dakin had read them correctly.

"Well," he said. "Let me tell you all something. I had that very same problem when I started out. I knew little about horses. But I did know that I wanted to know *more* about them."

A hand rocketed above the audience. A voice asked, "Could you tell us how you came to write and sell your first article?"

"I suppose that would be helpful," Dakin replied. He recalled how, while he was a teacher, he would drive by a farm on his way to work every day. "And every day," he said, "there would be people out there, riding horses.

"I'd been wondering about what I could write an article on. I figured, what the heck? I've been interested in horses most all my life. I'll drop by the farm one day after work and poke my nose around. If there's something or someone there that interests me, I thought, then maybe it'll also interest someone else — like the editor of a newspaper or magazine." He paused once again for a sip of water. Then he touched his dark mustache to whisk away any droplets that might have clung to it. It was a habit, the preoccupation with his mustache. Some people chew on pencils or drum their fingers; Dakin twirls and toys with his mustache. Constantly.

"By the way," he added. "That's still the way I decide whether a subject will make a good article — or book. If it interests me, it'll interest someone else too. It's also a heck of a lot easier to light a fire under me when my curiosity's piqued."

He went on to explain that, while "poking around" at the horse farm he passed by on his way to work every day, he met Carlos Gria, the horse dentist. "I introduced myself to him," said Dakin. "I explained to him that I was a freelance writer who was interested in horses and was looking to do a story about someone with a *different* kind of an equine occupation. I remember being scared that he would think I was just being nosy or I wasn't *really* a writer and that he'd tell me to go get lost. I couldn't believe his reaction to me. He was completely overwhelmed that I would want to write about him. Overwhelmed, mind you."

Another hand rocketed out of the audience. "Did you tell this horse dentist that you'd never written a magazine article before?"

"Good question. The subject never came up," said Dakin, "so why would I volunteer the information? He did ask me, though, for what magazine I was writing the piece. I told him I was writing the article for *Horse People*. He recognized the name of the magazine immediately, and he became even more flattered."

"Excuse me, but — wasn't that sort of lying to the man?" asked someone in the front row.

"Nope," Dakin replied, matter-of-factly. "I was going to write the article *for Horse People* magazine. Whether or not *Horse People* would *accept* what I was going to send them would be another matter."

"Did this Mr. Gria ask you anything else?"

"Nope," Dakin replied. "They never do."

One disbeliever in the third row spoke up. "You mean," she said, "that horse dentist actually believed you were a writer — just like that?"

Dakin couldn't help himself. His laughter exploded into the microphone. "Forgive me," he said, trying very hard to restrain himself. "That's such a natural question for you to ask. I assure you I'm not laughing at you. I was just remembering what I thought, before I approached him for the interview: What if he asked me about some of the articles I'd had published? What could I tell him?

"Well, now I know that a writer doesn't wear a special costume that says W-R-I-T-E-R on the back, isn't necessarily six feet two inches tall with a gorgeous tan, and doesn't have to speak as though he'd just memorized the dictionary. In short, ladies and gentlemen — what does a writer look like? I'll tell you. A writer looks exactly like you and me." Dakin paused to watch members of the audience look at one another in disbelief.

"Think about it," Dakin continued. "Who am I to question whether or not you are a writer — if that's what you say you are? People will believe you, if you sound sure of yourself. That's really rule number one if you want to succeed as a writer — you've got to assume the *identity* of a writer. You've got to be able to look somebody in the eye and tell him you're a writer, pure and simple. If you believe you are, so will everyone else."

A person in the next-to-last row had a question. "Don't you ever feel like you're imposing on the people you're interviewing?" she asked.

Dakin shook his head. "No way," he said. "Most people — in fact, nearly every single one I've ever interviewed — were not only happy to give me their time, they were absolutely flattered that someone else, especially a writer, would be even the least bit interested in them. Believe me. People love to talk about themselves, even if they don't like to admit it."

Dakin went on to the outcome of his experience with Carlos Gria. "About four weeks after I had sent the piece to *Horse People* magazine," he recalled, "I got a letter back from its editor-in-chief. He told me he loved the article, enclosed a check for sixty-five dollars, and asked me if I had any more articles I'd like to submit. There's still a hole in my living room ceiling," said Dakin with an ear-to-ear smile, "where I hit when I jumped for joy."

He detailed how he wrote several more personality profiles for *Horse People*. "By the fourth piece, the editor was impressed enough with what I could offer him that he started sending me assignments. Imagine my state of mind *then*. One thing led to another. I started branching out, sending other articles to other magazines. Eventually everything started to snowball."

*

The reason that everything began to "snowball" for Dakin is because he is an extremely organized person. "A writer has to be," he insists. "It's not an easy thing to be, that's for sure. There's no boss hanging over me every morning, giving me the incentive to write. It's all got to come from within *me*.

"Writing is a job — make no mistake about it. Some of the tasks associated with it are fun, certainly — like meeting a movie star like Charles Bronson to do a piece about him and his equine hobby. But the actual writing of an article or book is work, plain and simple. It's work because it's got to be done on a regular basis. There is no such thing as *waiting for inspiration* if you're making your living as a writer. Your stomach can't eat inspiration."

Does Dakin believe it's possible to make a living by writing about horses and horse people?

"Definitely," he insists. "If — and only if — you're systematic about it. The nice thing about this kind of work is that you can keep a full- or part-time job in the horse world while you're establishing yourself with editors and publishers."

He suggests you begin selling to horse publications by first finding out who will buy what from you. The initial step, then, is to obtain copies of all the horse magazines in which you'd like to see your work appear. The problem with this approach is that most equine publications cannot be found on news-stands. Most go to subscribers only — via the U.S. mail.

"That problem's easily solved," says Dakin. Locate the names and addresses of at least six of your favorite horse magazines (see Appendix XII for a list of publications published in the U.S.). Then write to each of those and request a sample copy of the magazine."

Dakin sends a postcard like this one:

Dear _____:

    I wish to become a regular contributor to your magazine. Please, therefore, forward me a copy of your publication, plus a guideline for writers if available.

    Thank you.

His Name
_____

His Address
_____

"About four to six weeks later," says Dakin, "your six magazines will have arrived. Then what? Simple. Take heed of rule number two in how to be a successful writer for the equine magazines — the only reason a magazine will buy your article is because it meets the magazine's requirements. You certainly wouldn't buy something that you don't need. Neither will a magazine editor. The only way you can find out what a magazine needs is by studying that magazine, from cover to cover. That's exactly what I did to get started. That's what I still do, whenever I want to break into a new publication."

Ninety percent of all rejections of equine articles, says Dakin, stem from the fact that the would-be contributor doesn't sit down first, study the magazine, and then gear the article he's writing to precisely what the magazine obviously wants.

"They'll only accept certain kinds of articles," he explains, "written in certain ways, that interest their specific audiences. In a nutshell, that's the *secret* to getting your articles published — analyze your intended market and then give it what it wants. It's sort of like matching a birthday gift to a person. You wouldn't send your eighty-year-old grandmother — the one who happens to be confined to a wheelchair — a pair of riding breeches. Same goes for a magazine editor. Give him what he needs. That's what making a living as a writer is all about."

*

"So. You studied the horse magazines, right?" asked a young man with several questions written on his face. "You knew what each one's requirements were. But where do you get your ideas about what to write? You even admitted that your horse dentist article happened almost by accident."

"Good question," said Dakin. "Where do my article ideas — or book ideas, for that matter — come from?" He was silent for several moments. "I had one horseman tell me once that he marveled at the variety of subjects we professional writers can find to write about, as if we have some special kind of gift. That's a lot of bunk. Every one of us here can sit at our desks and think up enough article ideas in an hour to last us the next three months!"

He explained that after he's studied a magazine thoroughly so that he's fairly certain as to the type of article it needs, he starts to see article possibilities everywhere. He says, "It becomes a habit after a while. You train yourself to look at every person, every experience, and every event with the idea that here is a possible article idea some horse enthusiast will be interested in."

Dakin first begins with some broad topic. "Some subject," he explained, "like equine dentistry. Once I've decided on the broad topic, then I try to narrow it down, find an *angle* on that topic that the magazine's readers will likely be interested in. I find such an angle — such a narrow focus — by asking myself questions like, How does one prepare for a job as an equine dentist? How dangerous is the job? How is a horse's tooth actually pulled? Why do horses' teeth have to be pulled at all? Is there any preventive maintenance recommended? What's the day-to-day routine of a horse dentist? And so on.

"Each one of those questions is about a particular aspect of the broader topic of equine dentistry. Since *Horse People* articles tend to focus on the day-to-day realities of those horse people with unusual ways of earning their living, I knew how I had to focus my piece on Carlos Gria. It didn't have to be technical, but it did have to paint a picture for the readers of what a typical day is like for one equine dentist.

"The point is this. I look at every situation I either run into, read about, or hear about, by asking myself questions. Then I match the topic and the angle with the magazine's interest."

He further explained that newspapers — and the horse magazines themselves — are excellent sources for article ideas. "They're gold mines," he insisted. "Every single day — whether I'm on the road, on vacation, or wherever — I scan several newspapers and magazines for possible ideas. If something interests me, I cut it out and file it. My file contains about two hundred different manila folders, each one containing information about a different subject.

"Example: I have a file on how to purchase a stallion. About three dozen articles I've clipped on the subject from various sources over the last three years. I guarantee you that when one of my editors calls me and asks me to come up with a piece on how to buy a stallion, I'll have all my background information, my research, at my fingertips. And I'll be sure to give him something that's never been done before — a new slant on the subject."

Another person in the audience had a question. "I thought that being a writer was sort of a glamorous kind of job," she said, pulling absentmindedly on a light brown braid. "Sounds like all you ever do is cut out things." The audience laughed.

Dakin smiled. "Glamorous, huh? Where in the world did you ever get that idea, young lady?"

He explained to her that he works seven days a week, although on two of those seven days the "work" involves merely an hour's worth of scanning publications for possible article ideas. The other days' mornings — Monday through Friday — always begin at eight o'clock sharp.

"I begin every workday by answering my mail," he said. "Maybe a thank-you letter to someone I interviewed for an article. Maybe a letter requesting certain information from an organization or an expert on some subject. Whatever the reason, it gets me going, gets me writing.

"By nine I'm at my desk working. I write for three solid hours every single workday that I'm not on the road. Yesterday morning, for example, I wrote the fifth chapter of my new book during the first two hours, and then I worked the last hour on a piece I'm doing for a regional newspaper on where to find trail rides in my area. I assure you it's all very unglamorous. It's work — daily, regular, unremitting work. If you really enjoy writing and want to achieve something with it, you can't sit around idle and wait for inspiration to strike you. None of the professional writers I know spend one day writing and the next three riding the plains for pleasure. They work, as I do, every day, with regular hours day in and day out. Writing is a solitary and secluded business, once you get back from the interview or the show or the barn."

By noontime, then, Dakin, has usually worked for four hours and is ready for a break. He takes an hour and a half for lunch — "Not that I need that much time to eat," he explained, "but I do need that much time to recharge my mental batteries. Usually I'll jog a few miles, then come back to the house and have a bite to eat. That's when I really appreciate the job I have, being my own boss and not having to leave home to go to work. It's nice . . . real nice."

By one-thirty he's back at his desk again, revising what he wrote during the morning. "Revising is really a different task altogether from writing," Dakin explained. "When I write, I pretty much have to squeeze my imagination so that the words will squirt onto the paper. That's hard and tiring. When I rewrite, however, all the *hard* work's already been done. Everything is ready and waiting for me. It's still work, mind you. I go over and over and over what I wrote, cutting and changing words to bring out meaning more clearly. Sometimes

I rewrite a single sentence a dozen, maybe two dozen times. Almost never is one of my paragraphs perfect the first time. That's why rewriting is necessary. But it's fun — tremendous fun — to start off in the morning with a blank page of paper and, by late afternoon, have that same piece of paper alive and singing. It's a real turn-on for me, to be able to create something out of nothing."

At three o'clock — "after my fifth cup of coffee," he notes — Dakin spends an hour going through his files looking for possible article ideas to suggest to editors. If he finds something he thinks a particular editor might like, he composes a "query letter" to that editor.

"Basically," said Dakin, "a query letter simply explains what my article idea is and why the editor should be interested in it. It's like bait. I've been dealing with the same editors regularly enough so that when they get a query letter from me, they know I'll come up with something appropriate for their magazines, so they usually end up writing or calling me with a go-ahead on the idea."

By four o'clock on the typical workday, Dakin told the audience, he performs one of two tasks. He's either in his darkroom producing photographs he's taken in conjunction with an article he's writing, or he's preparing for tomorrow. "Preparation might entail getting my camera equipment ready for a shoot the next morning. Or preparing a list of questions for someone I'll be interviewing the next day. Or it might even involve running to the camera store for some film."

By five, he starts winding up his day by reading newspapers and magazines he subscribes to. "I'm always looking for new article ideas," he said. "Also, the only way I can keep contributing is by spending time studying what the magazines are doing, so that I'll have a good idea of what they might be doing in the future."

Eight in the morning till five-thirty in the evening with one and a half hours off for lunch. An eight-hour workday for Dakin McAdoo. The only time he ever varies his routine is when he has to travel in conjunction with an article. He tries to schedule such travel for Wednesdays. "No special reason," he admitted, "other than it breaks up the week for me."

Not all his travel, though, can be reserved for Wednesday. "If I get an assignment to cover, say, the All-American Quarter Horse Congress or the International Jumping Derby, then I've got to work weekends. It doesn't happen often. When it does I really don't mind. That's when the job finally gets a little glamorous. A press pass gets me into places that the ordinary spectator could never go."

Other than special assignments, Dakin confines his time away from his "office" to one day a week, then. "My telephone and the U.S. mail help me out a heck of a lot. It's tempting to jump into my car on a beautiful summer day, say, and drive to the United States Equestrian Team Headquarters, on the North Shore of Massachusetts, to get an interview with the team's coach or one of its stars. But I don't get into that habit. I interview over the phone or through the mail whenever possible. Of course, if photographs are absolutely essential for the article — and they usually are, by the way, so you'd better become handy with a camera — then I schedule that trip for the midweek. Otherwise I use the phone or the mail. Time not wasted traveling is time I can spend writing — and earning money."

*

According to Dakin, making money as a writer for the equine market means turning out writing in volume. "Not one article a month," he insists, "because, in general, the horse publications just aren't the top-paying markets."

On the average, a 1,500-word article ("That's about five double-spaced pages," says Dakin) with three photographs earns him $225. "You don't have to be a mathematical genius to realize that to earn ten thousand dollars at that rate, you need to produce forty articles for the year," says Dakin. "Can it be done? Can you produce — and sell — one article every week and a half? Certainly. But," he adds, "only if you're organized about it.

"In my particular case I don't have to live on the ten thousand dollars from the magazines alone, because I have royalty checks coming in from my previous two books — every June and December they arrive. This year I expect my royalties to amount to about fifteen thousand dollars. Plus I got an additional advance of five thousand dollars for starting my third book. The nice thing about writing books is that once they're finished, they're finished — but they still can keep earning you money for several years to come."

In fact, Dakin emphasizes that the reason he is able to write full time is simply because of the income from the books. "There's a big, big difference," he says, "between ten thousand dollars and thirty thousand dollars. I wouldn't be happy making only ten thousand dollars a year. I'd have to get some sort of part-time job to supplement my magazine income if I didn't have the book royalties. That's the only side of this writing business that really displeases me. Pay rates among most equine magazines are oftentimes ridiculous."

For example, he says, *Equine World* — a magazine with a circulation of some 150,000 copies every month — only pays its freelance contributors 2 cents per word for an article and $2 per photograph used with the piece. In other words, the typical article in that magazine yields the writer a whopping $30 — plus another $2 to $6 for photos. And they have the added drawback that they pay that paltry sum of money "on publication."

"That means," says Dakin, "that they can hold your articles and photos as long as they want with no pay to you. Why? Simple. Suppose this pay-on-publication magazine accepts your article. Then comes an editorial decision to hold it for six months before printing it, because a competing magazine just came out with a similar piece. So your article is put in the freezer — through no fault of yours. It could be the greatest piece ever written. But you still won't see your ridiculous thirty-two- or thirty-six-dollar check until your article actually appears in the magazine."

According to Dakin, most freelancers working the equine market, were you to divide the number of hours they work into the number of dollars they earn, probably don't make the minimum wage. So why do they continue to write for the equine publications?

"Lots of reasons," Dakin explains. "One is definitely ego. It's quite a trip to see your name on an article that's being read and enjoyed by maybe a quarter-million people. You're recognized at horse shows and other horse-related affairs and get lots of attention. It's a profession to be proud of. Most of the feedback is very positive. I think the public views a writer as someone special, and it shows in the way they react to you at a party or an interview or whatever.

"By far, though, I think most of us don't mind hustling the horse magazines because we realize it's a necessary step before getting an opportunity to do a book. Writers can spend most of their lives pulling down modest bucks a year from their writing efforts for the horse mags, but there's always that chance, that hope, that dream, that they're going to sell enough articles to get a chance at a book, which in turn will become two books, and three books, and so on, and allow the writer to do what he wants most to do in his life — write, full time. In the beginning you've really got to hustle. But it does seem to get easier after a while."

Dakin also earns extra money by speaking to groups and by teaching writing workshops. "But without a couple of good-selling books under my belt," he insists, "I literally couldn't afford to write full time."

*

"As you become a recognized name in the various horse magazines," says Dakin, "whether you're writing on a full-time or a part-time basis, books should eventually furnish at least a part of your regular writing income. Someday soon, I expect to be able to make my living entirely from writing books."

His first book, unlike his first magazine article, did not come about by accident. He had been searching for a good book idea for some time. When he finally decided on one — a how-to on grooming the backyard horse for competition — he had already published approximately one hundred magazine articles, some of which were directly related to his book's subject. He consulted the *Subject Guide to Books in Print* at his local library and looked up all the books ever written on his subject. To his amazement, there were only four — and not one of them was anywhere near as thorough as the book he had planned.

Encouraged, he consulted another library book, *The Writer's Market*, and made a list of all the book publishers he thought might be interested in his idea. "Book publishers are like magazines," Dakin says. "They have individual preferences for the type of work they publish. Therefore, you should study the book publishers, too, and try to learn what kinds of books they publish and how they like their subjects handled. For example, some book publishers won't have anything to do with children's books. You've got to home in on their individual preferences."

His next step was then to compose and send a query letter to several publishers. "It was basically a magazine-type query letter," he recalls. "One page, single-spaced. It presented my idea, gave reasons why it was a good subject to publish now, and talked briefly about how I was qualified to write about the subject." Dakin doesn't think his publisher would have given him the go-ahead on his first book idea if he hadn't had some impressive credentials to prove to the publisher that he was, in fact, capable of writing the book he said he was.

"By that time," he says, "the articles I had had published in horse magazines proved I was a professional. Obviously, if I had a column in one major equine mag, was a contributing editor to another, and so on, they were certain I could pull off my idea."

Why was he so certain that a busy book editor at a major

publishing company would read his one-in-a-thousand query letter? "There are ways to get your mail read," he insists. "The simplest way is to address the letter to the editor in chief of the publishing house. In fact, address your letter to him by name, not just by title. Your library should have a large, paperbound book called *LMP: Literary Market Place/Directory of American Book Publishers*. It's published and updated every year and lists every book publisher in the U.S., along with their addresses, and it also lists the names of responsible editors in those publishing houses. Believe me, editors are only human. A letter addressed personally to one of them — by *name* — will be read."

The trick, he says, is to write the query letter so that it will make the editor have the desire to read your novel or book. "You've got to pique his interest. If your letter reflects sincerity and intelligence, and your idea is a good one, you will probably be asked to submit either your entire manuscript or a couple of chapters of it. Just remember that editors are every bit as hungry to buy good manuscripts as you are hungry to sell yours."

*

Dakin sells his books not by writing the entire book first, and then looking for a publisher, but by writing only a couple of chapters of the proposed book. For example, with his second book, a novel, he created a story idea, some characters, a theme, and a plot outline. Then he wrote the first two chapters and the last chapter — three chapters in all. He also wrote a chapter-by-chapter outline for the rest of the book.

"At that point," he says, "I had a marketable piece of writing that had taken me only about a month to produce." An experienced editor could look at what he had written and know right away whether or not it was a book that would sell.

"The beauty of working that way is that when you sell the book, you get half the advance right up front." In other words, he explains, he signed a contract with the book publisher, stating that he would finish the book by a certain date. In return, the publisher agreed to pay him an advance of $6,000 — half of which he received immediately, the other half when he finished the book six months later. In addition, the publisher agreed to pay Dakin a royalty of one dollar for every book of his that sold. That money would be paid each June and December.

"I call it the pay-as-you-write plan," says Dakin. "It's one of the best reasons writers try to get a book idea contracted before it's written. That way they don't waste time by writing a book that won't sell. And, more importantly, they get half the advance to help pay the grocery bills while they're writing the book.

"Again, though, I emphasize the importance of earning publishing credits before you try to tackle a book. You've got to be able to assure an editor that you are a writer who can *produce,* that you are a *good* writer, and that you have a *special knowledge* about horses or the people who ride them. That's why it certainly helps to have been published at least a few dozen times or more in some respectable horse magazines.

"If you've never published anything before and your idea happens to be a really good one, the editor may write and tell you that he likes your book idea and that he wants you to be sure to send the completed book to him for a look-see. But you receive no money and certainly no guarantee that the editor will even like your finished book. If it takes you a year to finish it, and it doesn't sell, then what? The best way is to get your money up front if you can. The only way to do that is to convince an editor not only that you've got a great idea, but that you can definitely put the idea together. And the only way to be so convincing is to show what you've already had published — so we're back to the horse mags again."

*

"Nothing but the common mechanics of writing," says Dakin whenever he's asked what it takes to become a writer. "Like spelling, grammar, syntax — everything you should have learned in school. It's not absolutely essential that you go to college and major in English to become a writer. A good friend of mine, for example, is only a high school graduate. Yet not only is he a full-time writer and doing well at it, but he's just published his first book — on how to write!

"In other words, the accepted mechanics of writing — spelling, grammar, and so forth — represent one of two preparations every writer must have. If you've paid attention in grade school, junior high, and high school, you should possess the mechanics of a writer already. Writing *skills,* then, can be taught — and it's more efficient to learn them from experienced and skillful elders than to teach yourself. After all, that's why teams have coaches. Writing is a craft, not some mystical activity. In that sense, a degree or courses in writing or English at the college level (see Appendix VIII for a list of U.S. institutions which offer courses and degree programs in writing) is certainly good preparation, too — a good place to *polish,* let's say, the writing skills, the mechanics, that you've been acquiring all along."

The other attribute of every writer, Dakin says, is possessed by every one of us. "But only by actually writing will you learn if your tools are sharp enough, unique enough, and appreciated enough so that you can shape a successful career as a writer. What I'm talking about is everything that has shaped and molded you into the person you are — the things that make you the inquiring, persistent person you must be in order to be a writer.

"It would be helpful, I think, if your background involved communicating information via the written or spoken word. In my particular case, of course, having been a teacher, communication was the nature of my job. But even the ability to write letters of great human interest or to exhibit skill and persuasion in talking or writing are all encouraging evidence of your potential writing talent."

Dakin also notes that another background qualification that

may lead you to a successful writing career is *expertise* — a specialized knowledge about horses. "The reading public," he says, "has demonstrated a great interest in acquiring knowledge on subjects about which they themselves are not so knowledgeable. And they appreciate learning it from experts. For instance, let's say you're a riding instructor. There's a writing market wide open for you if you can translate the complex and the obscure elements of riding into easily understood everyday language.

"I was once asked how to become a writer. I remember telling the young man that there are three rules for becoming a writer — unfortunately, nobody knows what they are!

"My point, of course, is that no one can *teach* you how to *be* a writer. People can teach you the difference between a noun and a verb — mechanical skills. But your writing is a personal creation uniquely your own, planted and fertilized not by pedagogy, but by your experiences, observations, sensory perceptions, and imagination.

"Maybe I should warn you that writing is hard work, and that anyone not willing to approach it as a job requiring complete dedication should not aspire to the profession. If any accomplishment by humans deserves to be called *self-acquired,* it's writing.

"A little help along the way, though, sure won't hurt you."

SIX

The Horse Photographer

"IT'S A PRETTY SPOT all right," said Tory Keeps, testing the pond's temperature with a finger. "But there's not enough light here this early — not with those tall trees all around."

A young exhibitor studied the towering oaks from atop her impatient horse. She nodded her approval of Tory's observation. "Any suggestions?" she asked.

Tory mentally catalogued her other favorite photogenic sites on the sprawling ranch. In the time it takes to load a roll of film, she had an answer for the little girl in the big cowboy hat. "Why don't you bring him over to the weanlings' pasture. There'll be no distracting background there, and the light'll be better. See you in five minutes. Okay?"

Ailie agreed and rode immediately for the rendezvous point. Tory hurried through the swaying trees and over a sleeping meadow, heading for the small pickup truck she had parked outside the show arena. Her pigtails bounced up and down on her yellow-shirted shoulders as she arrived at the lot and jogged through a mini-city of campers and tent trailers and tied horses. The horse show had attracted several hundred participants. It was obvious that most of them had chosen to camp in the parking lot, as opposed to renting a hotel room

Photo by William Haggis

many miles away. Despite the congestion, Tory found her way to her truck.

She lifted a strongbox out of the back and pulled out the equipment she'd use for the morning's shoot — two 35mm cameras and a portable electronic flash unit. Then she removed several boxes of color film from a picnic cooler. Finally, she stuck her hand inside a leather pouch and pulled out four long, skinny batteries. "Oh, good!" she announced, to no one in particular. "I remembered to bring the flash batteries this time!" A group of campers next door overheard her self-congratulatory remarks and applauded her. Slightly embarrassed, Tory continued her preparations, stamping her name on a receipt she'd already prepared for Ailie's parents and tucking the folded piece of paper into her jeans. She was now prepared to meet her first customer of the day.

Ailie Calhoun was already in the weanlings' pasture, standing with Trumpeter by a white-railed fence that separated the less-than-a-year-old weanlings from their grateful mothers. Ailie's parents were also standing with her. Tory exchanged pleasantries with the Calhouns and then got down to business. It had to be that way, since this portrait would be just the first of many Tory would shoot today.

"Could you get a mane comb for your horse, please?" she asked Ailie. Tory studied the gelding's conformation — his body build. She was looking for any physical *faults* that Trumpeter might have, faults that she would have to take into consideration when she composed the photograph. She watched carefully as Ailie combed the minutest snarls from her horse's brown mane. Tory insisted that the good looks of Ailie's horse would be of the utmost importance for the portrait. "It's the same as when you primp before your school picture is taken. The idea is to get Trumpeter to look as good as possible," she explained.

Tory always insisted that the horses she photographed be immaculately groomed. She was quite stubborn about that point, never clicking her camera's shutter until she thought the horse was groomed as well as it could be. After all, she argued with many a lazy customer, if the horse didn't look good, it was bad for the owner — and certainly not healthy for her reputation as a photographer. So Tory was always insistent. And it paid off. One trainer was once overheard telling another: "Tory Keeps is the only photographer I know of in these parts who can make a two-thousand-dollar horse look like a twenty-thousand-dollar horse."

That's why she is so successful. She's aware that perfection is impossible to achieve, but that never keeps her from striving to attain it anyway.

As Ailie combed through Trumpeter's tail, Tory settled herself in the shade of a nearby elm tree and attached her flash to one of her cameras. Then she delicately wiped both cameras' lenses with an especially soft tissue. She would only use one of the cameras during this morning's shooting. The other was there as a backup, in case the first one malfunctioned in any way. "How's he going to be with his ears?"

"Dad'll take care of that," said Ailie.

Mr. Calhoun proudly exhibited a New Year's Eve noisemaker, a small boxlike creation which could be spun around its stick-handle to produce a strange, loud noise. "If this doesn't get his attention," said Mr. Calhoun, "nothing will."

The sun was already hot, although it was only eight-thirty in the morning. Its yellow beams were rocketing past the near (left) side of Trumpeter from the rear, at a forty-five-degree angle. It was pretty.

"Will you be wanting riding shots too? Or just portraits this time?" Tory asked.

"Just portraits, thank you," said Mrs. Calhoun.

"Fine," Tory replied. She adjusted the camera's *f-stop* — the size of its lens opening — and set the shutter speed so that it could be synchronized with the flash. The flash would be necessary to fill in the dark areas of Trumpeter's body and the parts of Ailie's face that were shadowed by her wide-brimmed hat, as the sun was shining from behind them. Tory then had Ailie position the gelding. "We'll be wanting his mane to show for these shots," she explained, "so let's get him turned around the other way . . . Hold it! A little to the left . . . Turn his head a little, please, toward me . . . Nope — too much . . . Never mind. I don't like that background anyway."

She could see that the background was too distracting. She knew that if she took the picture there, the result would be that the center of attention in the photograph would be the well-lighted white fence and trees behind the horse, instead of the horse and its handler. Since she'd want the picture-viewer's eyes to be drawn to Ailie and Trumpeter, she moved the pair to a less distracting background.

They stood now in a shaft of light that came from behind and over a group of trees. The dark trees behind them would provide a perfect background for the well-lighted horse and its handler, Ailie. But Tory still had to look for ground that was flat and level. She didn't want Trumpeter to appear as though he were going either uphill or downhill in the picture. Worse yet, uneven ground could make each half of his magnificent body seem to go off in different directions. She was also careful to choose an area with short grass. She wanted nothing in the final pictures to detract from her main subjects.

"Back to your left a little, please," Tory instructed Ailie. "Keep turning him . . . turning him . . . Nope! That won't work either. We need a more level spot."

"God! She's a perfectionist," Mrs. Calhoun mumbled.

"Nothing wrong with that," said Mr. Calhoun.

Ailie moved herself and Trumpeter back about twenty feet. "Nope," said Tory. "That telephone pole in the background is no good." Five more sun-hot minutes boiled away before Tory stamped her approval on the perfect spot for the pictures. "Okay. Just square him up now . . . Widen the two front legs just a smidgeon. Mr. Calhoun, you're the official ear-getter-upper, right?"

"Yes, ma'am."

"Great. Why don't you go over by the gate," Tory suggested. She then turned back to Ailie. "Toe your feet out, please . . . I want your left shoulder like this," she said, pointing herself so that Ailie's tiny body would be at a diagonal to the horse's big shoulder. "That's good . . . Now turn your head and raise his just a smidgeon."

Everything seemed ready. Tory turned to Mr. Calhoun, who was standing about forty yards away, sitting on the gate. "Okay, Mr. Calhoun! We're ready! Start making noise, please!"

Mr. Calhoun spun the small boxlike creation on its stick-handle, churning out a noise that sounded like metal scraping against metal. Trumpeter's ears shot forward instantly.

"Smile," said Tory. *Click.* "Bring his muzzle a little toward you, Ailie," said Tory, never looking away from her viewfinder. She had them in her sights, as if she were looking through a submarine's periscope at the designated target. There was no need for her to look up. "Keep making noise, please!" she instructed Mr. Calhoun. The noisemaker churned again and spat out its staccato metallic clatter. Trumpeter's ears again responded, like metal to a magnet. "Great!" *Click.* "Oh! that looks *sooo* good!" *Click.* "Bring his muzzle a little bit more toward you . . . Smile . . . Now!" *Click.* "Great! Let's get a couple of profile shots next."

Ailie moved her horse so that he was facing the camera sideways. Tory examined the new pose with eyes like microscopes, capable of noticing even the minutest details. "His back end's slightly uphill. Move him just a bit forward, please . . . just a smidgeon . . . That's fine. Mrs. Calhoun, could you bring me that rake, please?"

Mrs. Calhoun grabbed the wooden rake that had been leaning on the lawn side of the fence and delivered it faster than she could throw a saddle on a horse. Tory then proceeded to claw at some dead grass in front of where Trumpeter was standing.

"They told us you were a perfectionist," shouted Mr. Calhoun from his gate-perch. "But we had no idea . . ."

Tory smiled. "Everything's got to be just right, you know," she insisted, raking vigorously. "Okay, Mr. Calhoun. Get ready to start the noisemaker, please."

As soon as she was in position, Tory gave Mr. Calhoun the signal to begin. Once more Trumpeter's ears cocked forward instantly. "That looks good," said Tory, looking through the camera's viewfinder. "Smile!" *Click.* She looked up and then approached the target. Trumpeter had moved one of his hind legs.

Tory lifted the nearside hind leg, positioning it so that it was perpendicular to the ground. Trumpeter moved it. Tory placed it back again — ever so carefully, as though laying down an expensive vase. Then she moved the offside hind leg slightly forward, so that it showed behind the other hind leg at the hock. "Beautiful," appraised Tory, backing up to her former camera position. "Lift his muzzle just a smidgeon." She ducked her eyes into the viewfinder and sighted her targets. "Don't lean back, Ailie . . . Turn his head just a smidgeon . . . Okay, Mr. Calhoun!" *Click.* "That does it, folks."

It had taken nearly an hour, but Tory finally had all the pictures that she wanted in her camera. Mr. and Mrs. Calhoun thanked her and handed her a check for fifty dollars.

"I should have them in the mail to you within ten days," said Tory, handing the Calhouns the receipt she dug out of her jeans.

"Can't wait," said Ailie. "Think they'll be good?"

"Are you kidding?" asked her father. "They'll be master-pieces." Everyone laughed.

In the meantime, two other horse-show exhibitors had mean-dered into the pasture. "Can you do our horses?" asked the taller boy.

"Absolutely," said Tory. "What kind of pictures do you want?"

"Halter shots, if you don't mind," said the shorter boy. He was putting a tie on his Western shirt.

"No problem," replied Tory, flicking beads of perspiration

from her forehead with a quick swipe of a forefinger. The late July sun was glowing even more mercilessly by now, beating on her head. Tory knew it was going to be a very long day. It usually was, whenever she took portraits like this at a weekend show. She had no idea, as usual, how many customers would make their way to the pasture to take advantage of her photographic expertise. She never made appointments in advance of the day she would shoot. She just showed up. The horse people knew her well, knew her fine talent. They would see her and seek her out. Tory would stay around for as long as the customers would keep coming — even if that meant all day long . . .

And it would. There would be no time for breaks of any kind. The portrait-seekers would arrive in a never-ending procession.

"Close his mouth, please," Tory instructed the taller boy. "And let the shank hang down under his chin . . . That's it. Now smile." *Click.* "Good. Keep smiling." *Click.* "Step a little closer to him, please . . . Whoa, right there. Now smile." *Click.* "Good." *Click.* "Let him turn his head just a smidgeon . . . That's it." *Click.*

Suddenly, the stallion reared up. A horsefly had bitten him on the rump. Fortunately, the boy was able to get him back under control in a hurry, but the horse would have to be set up again.

The perspiration was now surfacing on Tory's forehead even more profusely as she placed her camera on the grass and approached the stallion. First, she turned his huge head toward her camera, just enough so that only the brow of his offside eye would be seen. She then noticed that his rear legs were in their proper position, but that the front legs weren't. She gingerly placed the nearside front leg perpendicular to the ground so that it ran straight up to the body like a leg underneath a table. Then she moved the offside front leg slightly back, so that it broke from the other at the knee.

"No way I could do your job for a living," said the taller boy. "I'd get so aggravated with the horses."

Tory hardly heard him. She was concentrating on the stallion, examining him. "That's perfect," she observed, backing away. As she turned around to pick up her camera, the pesky fly returned to resume his torture — this time on the horse's ear. The stallion reared once again.

"Darn!" cried Tory. She reached into her equipment bag and grabbed the fly spray, underhanding a throw to the taller boy. He sprayed his horse as two more customers made their way to Tory's "studio."

"We've been looking all over for you," said the young man leading the chestnut filly. "When can you do us?"

" 'Bout thirty minutes or so," said Tory.

"We'll wait," said the second young man, looking around for a shady spot.

Tory nodded and then continued to reposition. For twenty sweltering minutes, she tried to get the obstinate stallion to resume his former pose. When he reared up a third time, Tory admitted defeat — temporarily. "Let's put him away for a while," she suggested. "Maybe later on he'll be in a better mood."

By now, another two customers had joined the previous two young men, so that four people were standing in the elm shade waiting to be photographed. Tory saw them all applying fly spray as though it were spray paint. She tied a red-and-white bandana around her forehead to keep the salty perspiration from dripping into her valuable eyes. Meanwhile, customer number three got into position.

"Problem I'll have with her," Tory advised the young man, "is her neck. It's a little short and thick. I'll really have to get her to extend herself."

And so it continued, on through the lunch hour and into the late afternoon. By the end of the day, Tory Keeps had photographed fourteen horses — at fifty dollars each. She had labored seven sweaty hours, with not even a break for a cold drink. But her customers were all satisfied, and Tory's pockets contained seven hundred dollars' worth of paper. She would return to the show tomorrow and shoot eight more horses. All told, the weekend would see her earn eleven hundred dollars. After the film was processed, the prints made, the pictures mailed, and taxes set aside, she would realize a profit of eight hundred and forty dollars for her eleven-hour-long effort.

*

According to Tory, in order to capture such magnificent creatures on film — be it a portrait or a candid shot — the horse photographer must first be intimately familiar with them.

"The key to success in any kind of photography," Tory insists, "is a thorough knowledge of the subject you're photographing. And nowhere is that truer than in the photography of horses.

"You've got to know their behavior well enough," she explains, "to be able to anticipate — or even control — what they're going to do next. And have a keen sense of timing — of when to release the shutter to get that perfect moment on film. Some of the horse photographer's skills can be learned. Other skills must be instinctual, like timing, knowing when to *anticipate* what's coming up next.

"If you're involved with horses already, you're one giant step ahead of other would-be horse photographers, because you already know your subject well."

Tory herself was an equine enthusiast before she ever picked up a camera. Admittedly, though, she started both enthusiasms — photography and horses — a little bit later in life than most people. She was twenty-one years old when she purchased her first horse, although she had ridden pleasure horses with her family for five years prior to that time. The interest in photography began when she desired "some nice pictures" of the horse she bought. "So," she says, "I got myself a very inexpensive little camera and took some snapshots. They were awful."

She had no technical expertise in photography at that point, although she had always been keenly interested in beautiful photographs. In her early teens she had acquired every horse book and picture and poster she could lay her hands on.

At twenty-one, then — with a horse of her own and a deep-rooted need to create lasting beauty — she apprenticed herself to a freelance photographer she was introduced to at a friend's wedding. "I agreed to do all his darkroom chores for free," says Tory, "in exchange for his teaching me about the basics of photography. At first all I did was really simple darkroom work that anyone could do — mix chemicals, clean up, things like that. But that freed him so that he could be out taking pictures and making money. In return, he'd take me on a shooting with him a couple of times a week and give me a photography lesson."

Tory was an avid student. Within six months, having studied several beginners' guides to photography and then having her photographer friend clarify and demonstrate difficult concepts for her, she became comfortable enough with a camera to purchase some good equipment and carry it with her at the horse shows in which she was competing with her own horse.

"Whenever I wasn't competing in a class," she says, "I'd go around to the winner's circle after an event and take a picture of the awards ceremony. By that time I had set up a makeshift darkroom in my apartment. I'd process the film myself that night, print up the pictures, and then take them back with me to the show the next day. I'd be sure to show them to the winners and ask if they wanted to buy a photograph for five dollars.

"Obviously, that's not a lot of money. But that wasn't my purpose, to make a lot of money. All I wanted to do was to get known — and get better at photography. Practice, with a camera, really does make perfect."

Her scheme worked well. After a half-dozen successful

shows, a ring secretary asked Tory if she'd be interested in being the show's official photographer and taking all the winner's-circle shots. "That's very unglamorous, straightforward photography," she says. "But it pays — and it gets you established with the horse people."

Before too long, she was known not only as an exhibitor at the various shows, but as an excellent, courteous, and dependable photographer as well. Ultimately, people started approaching her and asking if she'd take portraits of them and their horses to be used as advertisements in magazines, or even just to hang in a recreation room.

Today, there are horse owners who fly her to their ranches to take portraits of their horses. These portraits are used in equine magazines to help sell the horses — which is why the owners want a photographer like Tory Keeps, who can "make a two-thousand-dollar horse look like a twenty-thousand-dollar horse."

*

"There are thousands of photography studios in this country," says Tory, "where *people* can go to get their portraits taken for weddings, engagements, graduation, whatever. But, if you want a professional portrait done of your horse, no such studio exists, as far as I know. That's why I'm able to make a living at it — by going to my customers."

She specializes in portraits of one particular kind of horse — the quarter horse. "The reason for specializing is simple," she says. "Each breed exhibits something special about its conformation, its build. A horse photographer has to know what those special physical attributes are, and then be able to accentuate them in the photograph. I happen to stick with quarter horses because I know a lot about them — I own one. It's tough enough to be knowledgeable about one breed, never mind several."

Accentuating a horse's good points isn't as difficult a task as it might sound. "It's really a question of being a good observer," Tory insists. "When you glue your eye to the camera, you've got to get into the habit of examining everything about the picture in general. Then find the horse's good points and stay away from his bad ones. For example, if a quarter horse is narrow-chested as I look at him straight on, my job is to make him look barrel-chested, because that's how a quarter horse is supposed to look."

How does she accomplish such magic?

"Very simply. I just don't photograph the horse head-on. I photograph him with his body parallel to my camera, so you can't see that narrow chest. Just remember that what you see in the viewfinder of a 35mm camera is exactly what you'll get in the photograph. It's just a question of moving your camera position until the problem goes away."

But what if — to carry the example of the narrow-chested horse further — that same horse had a great big "Roman" nose? If Tory shot the horse in profile, the unsightly nose would be accentuated. What could she do then? "I'd have to be certain I turned the horse's head directly toward me so that you wouldn't be apt to notice the size of his nose," she says.

Tory is as much an artist as a canvas painter. "But we photographers have it more difficult than canvas painters," she says. "We have to work with what we get. If a horse has an ugly nose, the canvas painter can repaint it, ignore it. The photographer has to be more inventive."

She insists that in order to be a good horse portrait photographer, you must first learn the prominent characteristics of the particular breed of horse in which you're interested. "Quarter horse people are neck-conscious," she says. "If I can't bring that characteristic out in my pictures, I won't get any customers."

To become familiar with how a particular breed of horse should look in a photograph, Tory suggests that you subscribe to a magazine which features the breed in which you're interested (for a list of such magazines, see Appendix III). Then, she says, it becomes a case of carefully studying the photographs appearing in the magazine to get ideas.

"You can go to school to learn the basics of photography," Tory says. "But there are no schools I know of which specialize in teaching how to take a good horse portrait. The only way to learn, outside of working as an apprentice for an established equine photographer, is by looking at what other successful photographers are doing. Study their pictures. How did they pose the horse? Why? What characteristics of the horse are accentuated by the pose? Why did the photographer use the background that he did? And so on.

"I still study the quarter horse magazines," she admits. "As soon as I look at a photograph, I'm automatically analyzing the picture, trying to figure out how I would have handled the same situation. It's great practice. I'm convinced it's one of the best ways to learn — that is, to imitate the masters first, and then develop your own personal style.

"And don't be afraid of asking horse people — and other photographers — their opinions about photographs, whether they're your photographs or someone else's. Get feedback, especially about your own work."

*

In her horse portrait business, Tory shoots ten pictures for $50. She has a custom lab process the film and make prints for her, which she then mails to her customers. Because she is able to do so well at one show, she only visits them once every three weeks, from May through October. Nine shows in all — approximately $9,000 in income.

"I wouldn't want to work any more shows than that," she says. "They're extremely demanding and tend to get monotonous. I prefer diversity in my working life." And diversity is precisely what she gets. She spends her "typical" Monday-through-Friday workweek shooting *stock* photographs of horses. A stock photo is any picture that belongs to the photographer, but whose sale is handled by a picture *agency*. The basic function of any stock-photo agency is to bridge the gap between those who produce pictures — like Tory — and those who buy them — like horse magazines, book publishers, and calendar companies.

Although Tory's agency charges a seemingly steep fifty percent commission on every one of her photographs it sells, the agency exposes her work — she has almost five thousand slides and black-and-white prints on file with them, by the way — to far more potential picture buyers than she herself could ever hope to reach. Moreover, her stock-photo agency takes care of all the business details like getting her work circulated, billing buyers, and collecting money.

"It's gravy income," says Tory. "All I do is concentrate on taking pictures. My agency takes care of all the other details, and it doesn't cost me a penny up front. They only take their commission when a photo sells."

Fortunately for Tory's agency, her pictures sell — well. Her stock photos of horses have been published in scores of magazines and books, and even appear on calendars and greeting cards. One shot of a mare giving birth to a foal, just as the sun was rising in the background through an early-morning mist, has sold twelve different times in the last two years, earning Tory nearly $5,000. In fact, last year alone, sales from her stock photos earned her $11,000.

"Once the picture's been taken and the agency is distributing it to possible buyers," she says, "I can just sit back and wait for the money to roll in." But that money "rolls in" not only because Tory is an outstanding photographer, but also because she has an excellent idea of the kinds of pictures that are salable. And, too, her success is due in large part to the fact that she shoots pictures constantly.

"I have definite territories I roam," she explains. "Each week I'll choose a particular horse farm or riding stable or whatever, and just take pictures there all week long. I'll shoot several rolls from maybe seven to ten in the morning, scout out the area for other possible shots during the afternoon when the lighting is uninteresting, and then shoot several more rolls from maybe three till sunset." On the average, she shoots ten rolls of film — both color and black-and-white — per day, fifty rolls per week. That adds up to some eighteen hundred pictures every week.

"My main expenses are film and gas. I try to keep my traveling to within a fifty-mile radius of my home. You don't have to go to Kentucky, say, to get a good racehorse action picture. There's a racetrack thirty miles from me."

Her expenses are minimal in comparison to what her work sells for. For example, some of her color photos appearing on the covers of various books have earned as much as $500 each. A calendar shot brought in $1,000. One-time use of a color photo of a colt for an encyclopedia earned $350. In each instance, Tory split the fee right down the middle with her New York–based agency. But in each case, too, she'd never have sold the pictures to those markets on her own.

*

When the agency agreed to market Tory Keeps's photographs, it was with certain "understandings" which were written into a contract, which Tory signed — details like the fifty percent commission and how often she would be paid.

The way in which she established her relationship with the agency was simple. She wrote to several (see Appendix X for a list of stock-photo agencies) and asked about what subjects they specialized in and their procedures for handling a photographer's work. Once Tory decided which agency would be most interested in her equine subjects, she submitted her "credentials" in the form of twenty-four of her very finest slides. In a brief note, she explained how many photos she planned to send immediately thereafter if they accepted her work, and how many and how frequently she expected to add to her account in the future.

"It's really important," Tory insists, "to let the agency know that you'll be contributing new photos on a regular basis, because it's costly — in terms of paperwork and people's time — for them to open a new account." Tory sends her agency three dozen new photos every month. "Your income from stock photos," she says, "assuming, of course, that they're good photos and show a reasonable variety, will hinge upon how many you have working for you. Obviously, your chances of making money in any given month are much higher if you have, say, one thousand photos in stock as opposed to one hundred. Ten times better, as a matter of fact."

*

Should you go to school in order to become a photographer? Is formal training absolutely necessary?

"Definitely not," says Tory. "You don't need a college degree to make a living as a photographer. Some people learn to be photographers by reading books and magazines and trying things out for themselves. Others go to a few workshops, seminars, or two-year photography schools, or even earn themselves a four-year degree in photography. The point is, there are as many paths to becoming a photographer as there are people who would be photographers."

What would Tory do if she were entertaining the idea of a career as a photographer today?

"First," she says, "I'd visit the local library for some basic instruction in photography. There are lots of excellent beginner's books. Then I'd go out and start taking as many pictures as I could. You learn by doing, especially in photography. Once I understood the fundamentals and felt comfortable with a camera, then I'd seek out more formal training."

*

Formal courses and degree programs in photography are being added all the time to the curricula of American colleges and universities. (See Appendix IX for a list of institutions in the U.S. which offer courses and degree programs in photography.)

In educational level they range from the most basic courses to extremely advanced study. "The nice thing," says Tory, "is that you don't have to be enrolled in a degree program to take a photography course or two at most colleges or universities."

Once you've selected a college or university, Tory suggests sending for its course catalogue and reading the descriptions of the photography courses being taught. "The course catalogue will also tell you the names of the instructors. That's vital information to you. You can write to the instructor of the course that interests you and find out if the course is really for you. For instance, is your level of ability what the instructor intends most of the other students' will be? Is there a darkroom you can use? How often? What's it equipped with? Will you be able to process color as well as black-and-white film? In other words, you can find out directly from the instructor what you can expect from the course. If it sounds like it'll meet your needs, fine. If not, there are others."

In addition to colleges and universities, there are schools and institutes that specialize in the teaching of photography (see Appendix IX). Courses usually take from six months to two years to complete. Tory suggests writing one of those schools for a catalogue, too. "I know you can't judge a book by its cover," she says, "but the quality of a photography school's printed catalogue is a clue to the quality of the instruction offered. The photographs in the catalogue of a school that *specializes* in photography should be top-notch. After all, if the school can't present modern and appealing photos in its own catalogue, how can it teach you to produce them?"

Be sure, too, she says, to check the school's credentials in its catalogue. Ideally, it should be licensed by its state's department of education to assure that it meets minimal educational standards.

"Above all," says Tory, "try to visit the college or institute or school you want to enroll in. Take a good look at its facilities, including any equipment you'll be able to use, and find out whether or not each student will have access to personal space in a darkroom. And be sure to talk with the students already enrolled. Get their reactions to the place. Talk to as many of them as you can before making a decision."

Probably the most convenient and, overall, least expensive formal training in photography can be had by studying at home, provided that you have the desire to do the work required. At one time, the limitation of home study was the lack of personal contact with an instructor. If something confused you, there was no one you could turn to. Today, this limitation is overcome in a number of ways.

After you study a few lessons, most correspondence schools have you mail in a photographic assignment in which you demonstrate what you've learned. Years ago, the student would then have received back a typewritten letter from an instructor who offered criticism and advice regarding the work. If the student had questions, he had to write to the school. Because of the necessary briefness and coldness of typed letters, this method was — at best — barely adequate.

Today, one of the leading correspondence schools has overcome that limitation by using a cassette tape recorder supplied with the course materials. When the student studies each lesson, a prerecorded "teacher on tape" leads him or her through the lesson like a tutor. Then, after the student sends in the photo assignment, he or she receives back the pictures from the assignment with a personally recorded cassette tape on which an instructor talks to the student by name about the pictures.

In this type of one-to-one critique, the student receives the personal attention that he or she might have gotten in a private workshop situation. In addition, at any time during the course the student can call the private phone number of his or her assigned instructor to discuss any questions or problems.

Home-study courses usually cost between $200 and $400, and the length of the course varies depending upon the amount of time the student can devote to it.

"I would have no qualms about recommending home-study courses to anyone," says Tory, "under certain conditions." First, she advises, be sure that the school offers the cassette-communication method of teaching, rather than the out-of-the-textbook-only approach. "And enroll only on a money-back inspection basis. Also, I'd call the school before I enrolled and ask to speak with the dean or the director. Since all schools promise personal service, I'd listen very carefully for the vibes I got during our conversation. If the person I was talking to sounded truly interested in me, then there's a chance I might actually get the personalized service they promise. On the other hand, if the dean or director sounds as though it's just a job to him, I'd choose another school — in a hurry."

Most photography magazines such as *Popular Photography* or *Modern Photography* always have school advertisements. "That would probably be the best way," says Tory, "to locate a home-study school."

Another way to learn photography is by enrolling in short courses. For example, your local camera dealer can arrange for a Kodak Photographic Seminar in your community. The dealer takes care of selling tickets for the seminar and arranging for a place at which it can be held. Kodak then provides the experts. Those courses are usually held on weekends for one day, from nine until five. You can find out more about them by asking your local camera dealer. The Kodak seminar covers subjects such as camera handling, composition, exposure control, films, lenses and lens attachments, and depth of field. In addition, various types of lighting — including outdoor, flash, and available light — are covered.

One of the longest-running short courses ever offered in the U.S. is sponsored by the Nikon School of Photography. They are regularly scheduled on various dates in various parts of the country throughout the year and run for two days. You can attend Friday evening and all day Saturday, or all day Sunday and Monday evening. They cover subjects such as composition, creative exposure metering, knowing your camera, films, filters, multiple exposures, motor drives, choosing a lens system, and more. In all, it's eleven hours of schooling. The price includes a meal for the all-day session and free reference books. To find out when the Nikon School will be held in your area, write the Nikon School of Photography, P.O. Box 14, Bellmore, NY 11710.

*

"Photography," says Tory, "whether it's of horses or butterflies or computers, is really two things. First, a working knowledge of the basics — how to use a camera, what the various lenses will do for you, the kind of film to use in any given situation. That's the technical side. Anyone — and I mean anyone — can master that technical side if he or she wants to badly enough. It just takes practice.

"But the second side to photography is really a side that can't be taught. You either have the 'eye' or you don't. You either have the ability to see a picture, or create a picture, or you don't. That ability can be groomed, for sure. But I don't think it can be taught.

"My advice is to learn the basics. Where you learn them is your choice. But shoot as many pictures as you can stand. Have people comment on them. And study other people's work. The difference between a good photographer and a great photographer is a dash of imagination. After you've shot several hundred rolls of film, you'll know if you've got it or not.

"I think what I enjoy most about being a horse photographer — beyond the money or the thrill of seeing my name under a picture — is the fact that the only criterion for acceptance of my work is that the work itself meet someone's needs. No one cares whether I'm a man or a woman. No one asks me what my education might have been. No one cares if I'm young or I'm old, what my religious beliefs are, the type of car I drive, or the camera I can afford to own. All that matters is the photographs I produce. If they meet the needs of someone, they'll be bought. It's the work I create that determines acceptance, not some arbitrary value unrelated to my pictures, like a degree from Harvard or something.

"In other words, what I like most about being a horse photographer is that if I make it, I make it for no other reason than that I *deserve* to."

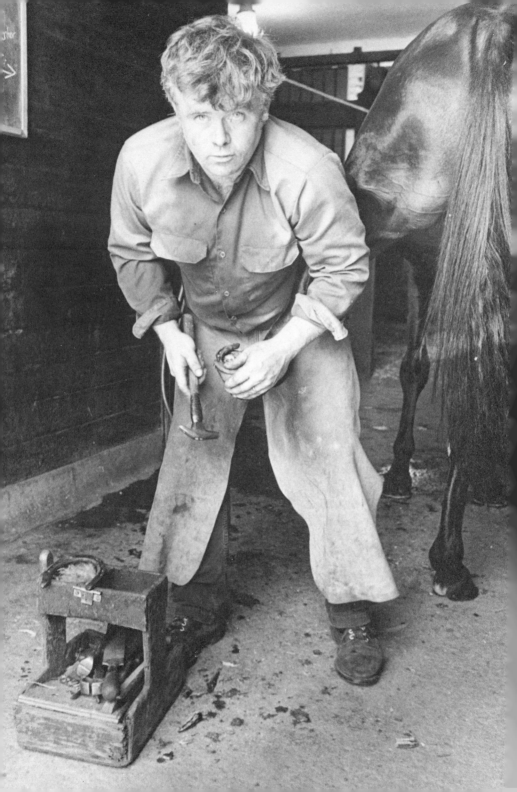

SEVEN

The Farrier

THE RED FIRE WAS HUNGRY. Its glowing, gaseous tongues licked and lapped at the empty belly of the black forge, set on the tailgate of the pickup truck.

Rory Sparrow fed four horseshoes into the little inferno and then placed his hands above the flames, the way he would over a campfire. The flames thawed the chill of January out of Rory's frozen fingers, and soon he was warm enough to make his way back to the cold barn.

Wild Thing was crosstied inside. Against the early morning sunlight shooting through the rear of the barn, the horse looked like some horned, silhouetted specter. When he saw Rory approaching, he backed up as far as he could, but the metal chains halted him after two steps. Rory set his toolbox on the cement floor in front of Thing. "You gonna act up on me again?"

"Naw," said a voice squeaking up from behind him. "You know Thing," said Nicky Cusker. "All snort and no bite." The little red-nosed man let out the kind of laugh that forces a chubby belly to bounce.

"Right," Rory replied. "I know. But at seventeen hands, that snort of his is more like a hurricane — and you know what

Photo by David O. Aronson

kind of bite one of those has." Facing Thing's rump and standing shoulder to shoulder with the four-legged giant, Rory gently placed his hand on the horse's shoulder and ran it slowly down Thing's leg, raising the hoof ever so delicately. He held the hoof between his knees and crouched over, his back as level as a tabletop.

"I don't know what's wrong with 'im," said Cusker. "All I can tell you is he's not right. Favors that darn leg all the time, like it hurts or something."

As Cusker spoke, Rory cleaned the sole of Thing's hoof — the bottom of his foot — with a *hoof pick*. He carved out dirt and pebbles with the metal hook, scooping out anything that didn't belong there. "Well," he replied, "let's get his shoe off first. Then maybe I can find out what's bothering him." Still holding the hoof, Rory turned around so that he now faced in the same direction as Thing. He walked Thing's foot forward until the leg was fully extended, and squatting slightly, his back arched this time like a mad cat's, Rory rested Thing's foot just above his own knee, on his apron.

He reached into his toolbox an arm's length away and felt for the *clinch cutter* — a tool a little like a small axe — and a hammer. Placing the cutter underneath one of the eight nails that had been bent over and filed on the outside of the hoof, Rory struck upward on the cutter's head with the hammer. He had to be careful not to gouge the surface of the hoof wall. He repeated the process on the seven other nails. Once they were all sticking out of the hoof, he smoothed their ends with a *rasp* so that they could be easily pulled through the wall when the shoe was removed.

"Thing's bein' real good, Rory. Don't you think?"

Rory grunted his affirmation. He had the *shoe puller* — a large pair of pliers — in both his hands. He closed its jaws on the left branch of the shoe and wiggled the puller from side to side until the shoe loosened. He did the same thing to the other branch of the shoe. Alternating the puller on either branch, Rory gradually loosened the entire shoe so that he could pull it from the hoof cleanly. The nails retreated through the wall of the hoof like little plastic swords from a sandwich.

"Pretty good touch there," said Cusker, stooping over Rory's shoulder to get a better view of what the farrier was doing. Cusker hadn't owned horses for very long. He had ridden them most of his life, but he knew little about how to take care of them. To his credit, he wanted to learn. Unfortunately, his desire to assimilate new knowledge oftentimes made him a pest. Rory didn't mind, though. He was used to someone watching over his shoulder. "Part of the job," he would always say, matter-of-factly.

He tossed the rusty iron shoe well away from Thing — a good idea, since the nails sticking out of it were ready to bite anything in retaliation for stepping on them. In five minutes, Rory had cleaned the other three hooves and removed their shoes, too. The real work, though, was yet to come.

*

Every six weeks or so, Nicky Cusker greets Rory. Then he watches as the farrier cleans his horses' feet, pulls their shoes, trims their hooves, and resets or fits new shoes. Then he pays Rory twenty-five dollars.

Although Cusker and a couple hundred more horse owners like him pay Rory for shoeing their horses, it is in the balancing of each foot that Rory really earns his money — rasping and trimming excess hoof growth until the bottom surface lands absolutely flat on the ground whenever the horse is in motion. "Anybody can nail a shoe to a horse's hoof," he insists. "But a farrier has to be an artist at it."

Rory is not exaggerating. A farrier's "art" is entirely a question of balancing all four of a horse's feet. Anything less than pure artwork will bring catastrophic results for the horse and for the farrier's reputation.

The importance of a knowledgeable farrier is driven home when you consider how the horse moves. "At a fast gallop," Rory explains, "each foreleg absorbs as much as five thousand pounds of concussion whenever its hoof strikes the ground. That kind of impact sends shock waves all through the horse's body, like an earthquake sending tremors through the earth. Such tremendous force can literally cripple a horse for life, if those shock waves aren't properly absorbed and distributed by the hooves."

Thus "balance" — and, therefore, the services of a good farrier — are vital to every horse's well-being. "Four balanced feet," says Rory, "four *level* feet, allow for the proper distribution of those powerful shock waves, so that all parts of the foot and the legs and the body get their fair share of the wear and tear."

In the wild, horses have no problems with foot balance. The rough surfaces of the plains, for example, wear their bare feet to a perfect shape, allowing each foot to make flat contact with the ground at every stride. When man began subjecting horses to hay-floored stalls, soft-dirt paddocks, and iron shoes, the hoof walls no longer were filed down naturally. They continued to grow, like toenails, and thus needed regular trimming, as is the case with us humans. Cutting off the excess hoof that nature used to scrape away gave birth to modern farriery.

But the farrier's constant challenge entails more than just the ability to slice off excess growth from a hoof. The challenge — and the difficulty — lies in his being able to make an accurate diagnosis — to see exactly where the hoof is out of balance — and then to cure the imbalance by properly trimming and/or shoeing the horse.

"Watching a horse as he trots barefooted," says Rory, "will tell me if each foot is striking flat on the ground, if each foot is in balance. Then a closer look at his lower legs when he's standing still should confirm the diagnosis I reached when I saw the horse in motion."

*

As soon as Rory had finished removing the last shoe from Thing, he walked to the far end of the barn and got down onto the concrete floor as though he were going to do pushups. With his eyes a foot away from the floor, he instructed Cusker to trot Thing directly at him. As they approached, Rory gave his concentration to the bottom surface of Thing's left forehoof — the one he suspected was out of balance, because it was that leg on which Thing was limping. He wanted to see how the hoof was striking the ground.

"Whoa, boy!" shouted Cusker, pulling on the lead shank when Thing was a stride away from the prone farrier's body. Rory never moved all the while the horse was barreling toward him. "How's it look?" asked Cusker.

"Tell you as soon as I know, Nicky. Could you trot him away from me now, please?" Again, Rory focused his attention on the same hoof. He muttered something indistinguishable as he observed that the hoof was not striking the cement in balance — the inside half of the bottom of the hoof was not hitting the cement at the same time as the outside half.

Rory moved to the side of the barn. "Okay, Nicky. Now trot him past me from right to left, please." Rory zeroed in once again on the same hoof from his pushup position on the cold cement. He shook his head. The front of the hoof — the toe — and the rear of the hoof — the heel — were not striking the ground in unison, either. The toe was hitting first, thus causing the ankle to bend backward.

"That's a mess," said Rory. "All out of whack. I told you to use the guy I recommended while I was on vacation . . ." He knew that the bones and ligaments below and above the fetlock joint were not being stressed properly, causing the huge horse to limp severely. He would have to find out why the hoof was out of balance and fix it.

First, though, he wanted to be certain of his diagnosis, that indeed it was the toe and the inside wall of the hoof that were out of balance. Moving to Thing's head, Rory stood directly in front of him, face to face. Thing nipped playfully at Rory's suspenders. Rory stepped back three paces and observed how Thing's front feet were placed.

"A foot will automatically turn toward the longer, out-of-balance side of the hoof," Rory explained. He pointed to the problem hoof. It was turned slightly inward, almost as if Thing were pigeon-toed. "That inside wall is definitely longer toward the toe area. But there's another way to prove it."

He would next check for displacement of the *coronary band* at the very top of the hoof, where it meets the leg. "Imagine," said Rory, "a horizontal line — parallel to the ground — going straight through that coronary band." Cusker replied that he could see that the left part of Thing's coronary band was higher than the imaginary line.

"That's because that inside wall, which is longer, has taken most of the impact," said Rory, "since it naturally has to hit the ground first. The greater shock has actually jammed the inside of the hoof wall higher than it should be. That's why the coronary band is higher on the left."

"Very interesting," said Cusker. "They were right about you, Rory. You really do know your stuff."

"Thanks, but I'm not done yet."

More checks would be necessary before Rory could be sure of his diagnosis. Facing Thing's rump one more time, he picked up the sorry hoof and stood as though he were going to clean it again, holding the leg behind the fetlock joint, the hoof dangling perpendicular to the ground. So that his head and eyes could be directly over the center of the hoof as he looked down at it, Rory tucked his head against Thing's belly. Thing stood stone-still.

"Yessir," said Rory. "That inside wall is what's causing the whole limping business." He ran his finger along the *frog* — the rubbery, V-shaped ridge at the center of the sole. Uneven contact with the ground had squashed the "V" toward the lower side of the wall, evidence which further proved Rory's diagnosis correct.

"So you were right after all?" Cusker asked.

"Unfortunately for Thing."

Fortunately, the imbalance could be corrected. Rory would

have to judiciously trim the inside wall of the hoof to bring
it into balance with the rest of the hoof wall.

*

"You're a real gentleman this morning, Thing, ol' boy," said
Rory. The stallion's ears cocked forward as if the word "gentleman" were an insult. He shook his head up and down once,
quickly. The chain crossties sounded as though they would be
torn from the spongy partitions to which they were attached.

Ignoring the frisky stallion, Rory stood by Thing's shoulder
and faced the horse's rump. He crouched into a flat-back position, raised the bad hoof, and propped it once again between
his legs. This time, he began clipping off the too-long inside
wall with his hoof nippers. It looked as if he had a gigantic
pair of toenail clippers and was working on a bigger-than-
usual toenail. In half a minute, a semicircle of clippings lay
on the floor.

Still supporting the hoof between his legs, and still crouched
over so that you could place a glass of water on his arrow-
straight back without spilling a drop, Rory reached to the floor
for his hoof knife. With it he skillfully trimmed the ragged
edges off the sole of Thing's foot.

Finally, he grabbed a rasp — a long strip of steel with raised
teeth — and smoothed the edges and leveled the wearing
surfaces of the foot, the way he would file a fingernail.

"A regular manicurist you are," complimented Cusker.

Kicking hoof clippings out of his way, Rory limped back to
his pickup and his hell-hot forge. He removed one of the shoes
with some metal tongs that looked like unusually big tweezers.
He examined the shoe, watching its raspberry-red colors blink
light and dark like part of a neon sign. He then laid the shoe
over the horn of his *anvil* — a heavy block of steel with a
smooth, flat top, on which the shoe would be hammered into
a different width to accommodate Thing's big foot.

Wang! Rory struck a blow to the molten shoe. *Wang!*
. . . another . . . *Wang!* . . . still another. Since the anvil

was on the tailgate of the pickup, the noise sounded as if he were banging the hammer on the tailgate itself. It was deafening. Ninety percent of Rory's shoeing involves this forge-and-hammer process, known as "hot shoeing," in which he heats the shoes in the forge to a temperature at which they can be bent, or shaped, with a hammer.

When the shoe had been widened at the toe — the curved end — Rory pounded out the branches. When the entire shoe had been widened to his satisfaction, he placed a *pritchel* — a tool originally used for punching nail holes — into one of the precut holes in the shoe. Using the pritchel for a handle, Rory carried the still-hot shoe to the barn.

Meanwhile, a mare in the pasture next door was racing back and forth, whinnying a love song Thing's way. Thing had quickly become excited, trying to peer back over his shoulder, rattling the crossties again in the process.

"Easy, big guy," Rory implored, standing directly in front of the brown-black behemoth. "She's only a tease anyway. She's not really interested in you, ol' boy." Cusker chuckled. Thing relaxed, figuring he had nothing to gain by fighting the chains that secured him. Rory picked up the trimmed hoof and set the hot shoe on it to check the fit. For an instant or two there was nothing . . . then a delayed-reaction sizzling and a smell as though Rory had just set someone's hair afire.

Thing didn't even swish his tail — until the mare whinnied once more. Then he neighed back, a deep, resonant exhortation that vibrated the pritchel in Rory's hand like a tuning fork. At that very moment, one of Cusker's dogs dashed into the barn, grapped a hoof clipping, and dashed away. Thing's eyeballs grew huge, but he remained still. Rory shook his head and calmly doused the hot shoe in a bucket of cold water. More sizzling. Clouds of steam rising into the light-and-dark barn. The mare outside whinnied a third time. "Hail Mary, full of grace . . . hope he keeps his feet in place," Rory mumbled.

"What was that?" asked Cusker.

"Oh, nothing important." From his pocket Rory drew eight nails and put them all between his lips. Again, he positioned the shoe on Thing's hoof, this time not needing the pritchel to hold it. The shoe was now cold.

"Ever swallow one of them nails?" Cusker asked. "On second thought, don't answer that right now."

One-*two,* one-*two,* one-*two* . . . half a dozen quick light strokes and a horseshoe nail angled through the shoe and into the lower part of Thing's hoof. The first one was always the most important. If Rory hadn't hit it right, he'd have to remove it and start all over again. He examined the nail. It had entered the bottom of the hoof at the white line that divides the outside wall of the hoof from the sole on the inside. The nail now protruded from the hoof wall approximately an inch above the shoe itself — a perfect strike.

After he added seven more nails, he clinched the tips of the nails by bending them downward with a *caliper* until they were flush against the hoof. He needed two hands then to hold the rasp, so he balanced Thing's hoof — now studded with shiny, jewel-like spikes — on his aproned knee.

By that time, Cusker had removed the bothersome mare to a far pasture, and Thing had calmed to the point where he was actually lethargic. His eyelids drooped and his head sank lower and lower. He even heaved a gusty, contented sigh.

"Now *that's* a good sign," said Cusker as he returned to the barn. "Never seen him like that before. Not when he's bein' worked on."

"It's okay by me," replied Rory. "I still have three more of his feet to shoe."

*

The outer wall of a horse's hoof — like a human's fingernail or toenail — grows constantly, at the rate of one-sixth to one-half an inch each month. The hind hooves grow faster than the front, and a mare's grow faster than a stallion's.

Many first-time horse owners aren't aware of these facts.

It comes as a total surprise to the city slicker turned country gentleman that there's still such a person as a farrier in twentieth-century, automobilized America. It comes as even more of a surprise to learn that, after the person who feeds the horse, his best friend is a good horseshoer — that is, a good farrier. Farriery is just as much a profession as doctoring or teaching. Consider, for example, that an incompetent farrier can lame a horse — that is, cripple him — for life. A really incompetent farrier can kill him.

The word *farrier* is actually derived from a Latin word, *ferrum,* which means "iron." That derivation is particularly appropriate, in that most people mistake a farrier for a blacksmith — one who works with iron. The association, however, is far from accurate. A farrier does shoe horses — as a blacksmith *might.* But the farrier's most vital duty is to care for and protect a horse's feet. Unlike a blacksmith, the farrier is a specialist who is concerned with every aspect of a horse's health that pertains to the bones of the leg and the hoof.

"In other words," Rory Sparrow explains, "a farrier does a whole lot more than just nail a shoe to a hoof."

An experienced farrier, for example, can discover lameness or problems in the legs and feet and will then work along with a veterinarian in a combined effort to solve a problem. Oftentimes the farrier is able to produce his own decisions regarding the nature of treatment required and then create a special shoe to remedy the problem, if necessary. In some instances, he may actually save a horse that might once have been destroyed.

Rory's customers, then, not only believe in his horseshoeing ability, but they trust and respect his judgment, too — which is why he is so successful. Very often he must handle a horse and enlighten a customer simultaneously. He must be able to express himself well and convince his customer of his knowledge and wisdom in handling horses, and in these areas Rory excels. His customers refer their friends and neighbors to him — not only because he's good with horses, but because he's good with people, too. Says one of his regulars: "Rory is very honest. He doesn't pretend he knows more than he really does. I trust him."

"I do a service for people," explains Rory. "The work I do is very important to the horse. Word about your ability — or lack of it — spreads pretty fast in the horse world."

There are some farriers who are incapable of rescuing the really critical cases, in which a horse might ultimately be destroyed because of severe leg and hoof difficulties. In those instances, an exhaustive awareness of the anatomy of a horse's leg and hoof — and of the mechanical function of the hoof — is essential to the proper resolution of the horse's problem. If the farrier can master this aspect of the profession, and not simply trim off excess hoof horn and slap a piece of cold iron on a hoof, it won't take long for his expertise to become known. "Well known," adds Rory.

*

Farriery is not as easy as Rory had once assumed it was.

"It's much more physical than I first thought," he says. "It's strenuous work, shoving thousand-pound animals around every day. There's a dangerous side to it, too. Anybody who works long enough around horses will eventually get hurt. The question is, how severely?"

Rory speaks from painful experience. His worst accident occurred during his second year in the profession. He was nailing the last shoe onto the rear foot of a pony when the pony suddenly lurched forward and kicked back at Rory's locked left knee. The blow tore the knee's ligaments — thin, ropelike tissues — which subsequently required surgery and a week's hospitalization. A cast was applied for six weeks, and crutches were necessary for three months. During the entire twelve weeks of recuperation, Rory was unable to work. For a self-employed person who pays his own salary, being out of work that long hurt as much as the pony's hard kick.

He still walks with a limp, three years later. He always will. "I was leery when I first started back," he admits. "But it's something I learned to live with."

A fidgety horse creates a potentially dangerous situation. When its handler is not present to hold and steady it, or when it is being trimmed or shod for the first time, a horse can become dangerously nervous. In those situations, sometimes the only way to calm a horse is by striking him hard with an open fist on the underbelly.

"You've got to be careful, though," Rory advises. "Some horses can be slapped and forced to behave. But there are those horses that resent it and just become more unruly, even unmanageable. With experience you can pretty much tell which ones you're dealing with. You've got to. If I make a mistake, I'm the one who suffers."

*

Despite the fact that there are some nine or ten million horses living in the United States and that they all need a farrier's attention periodically, the number of persons learning the farrier's profession has actually declined in recent years, according to the American Farriers' Association — which means that competition within the profession is by no means strenuous.

Nonetheless, as is the case with any other self-employment, the farrier may experience some difficulty, initially, in establishing a good practice and developing a firm clientele. "Loyalties and prejudices run deep in horse owners," says Rory, "and they're reflected in a reluctance to change or to accept a new farrier." A slow start, however, can be overcome with top-notch work.

Because advertising is almost exclusively by word of mouth, it doesn't take long for a farrier's ability to become well established. During the establishment period, earnings may be low and hours long or irregular. But once the farrier becomes known, he may find he just doesn't have the time to do all the horses he's asked to do.

A dedicated, competent farrier is in demand almost everywhere in the United States. Since most of those nine or ten million horses should be shod or trimmed every six to eight weeks and there are only some twenty-five hundred full-time farriers in the country, according to the American Horse Council's 1977 survey, there is tremendous demand and potential for high earnings. For example, Rory shoes and otherwise services anywhere from three hundred and fifty to four hundred horses every two months — ten per day, on the average, fifty per week — which translates into a yearly income of nearly $40,000, before taxes and expenses.

Initial overhead is minimal. A farrier can start off with an investment of $500 to $1,000 in equipment and materials, exclusive of the cost of his transportation. After that, the primary expenses are shoes and gasoline.

Farriers generally work out of doors, in or near stables or corrals where horses are kept. Some farriers have shops where horses are brought. But most often, a pickup truck or van is fitted as a mobile shop, which the farrier takes to the location of the horse or horses to be shod or trimmed. That may be a boarding stable, breeding farm, training stable, racetrack, farm, ranch, or someone's backyard. And because farriers are self-employed, they are free to choose where they want to work.

*

Rory's entry into the profession was somewhat unusual. The West Virginian is a former business administration major in college. When he graduated from the University of Texas, he went immediately to work for a credit bureau, of all places.

"I didn't particularly enjoy the nine-to-five routine and the jacket-and-tie bit," he says. "I first got the idea of becoming a farrier while watching one shoe my own horse. I thought I could learn the trade and moonlight with it on the side, for extra income." His career goal at that time was to become a state trooper. Having met all the requirements and passed all the entrance exams, he was waiting for his class of new recruits to convene. Because there was no way of knowing how long a wait there would be, he decided he would fill the interim by learning the farrier's art.

"It really wasn't too unusual a thing for me to pursue," he insists. "I had been around horses all my life. In high school I worked with hand tools such as files, hammers, chisels, and punches. I even took a course once in working with hot metals. When you consider that I had also studied biology and business management in college, I actually was pretty well prepared to undertake this sort of thing."

Upon the recommendation of his own farrier, Rory enrolled at an Oklahoma farriers' college. His schooling was eight weeks long, with each week seven days full. During his final week in Oklahoma, his wife, Tai, advertised his newly acquired professional services in local newspapers and church bulletins back home. As a result, Rory had several appointments waiting for him immediately after returning from school.

"After that," he recalls, "it was all word-of-mouth advertising, and my business mushroomed from there. Business got so good so fast that I decided to forget about becoming a state trooper.

"But," he adds, jabbing with a finger to emphasize his point, "this business can mushroom *against* you as well as for you. I take my time on a horse. It'll generally take me forty-five to seventy-five minutes to completely trim and shoe one horse. I could do it much quicker, but I want the job done right. There are a few farriers who are what we call *money shoers.* They'll shoe a horse in thirty minutes, or less. They'll do as many as they can in a day." Since earnings are dependent on the number of horses serviced, the profit incentive can be enough to foster less-than-impeccable work by the shoer if he's greedy.

"But," says Rory, "it'll come back to haunt you in the long

run. It's quality that makes you successful in this business, not quantity. Besides, I feel very proud of my work. Most farriers, I'm sure, feel the same way. I don't think I've ever shod a horse that I'd be ashamed to show to a vet or a show judge." Perhaps that's why Rory's yearly earnings are considerably higher than the $16,200 the American Horse Council estimates the typical farrier earns in a year.

*

Besides his basic blacksmithing skills in the use of the forge and its tools, a good farrier must have a thorough knowledge and understanding of the anatomy and physiology of the horse, especially the feet and lower legs. He must be able to recognize and differentiate between cause and effect of any imbalance in the way a horse is moving, or the probable results of any shoeing either contemplated or already completed. In addition, a good farrier knows horses and how to handle them — and their owners. He may work under the direction of a veterinarian in treating a particular problem, or he may consult the vet while pursuing his own course of diagnosis and treatment. He must be able to read and understand *radiographs* — X rays — and be familiar with medical terminology in order to communicate effectively with the vet.

"Also," says Rory, "a farrier uses a wide assortment of tools. Most of them are relatively simple instruments, but skill is required to use them properly. It's like a simple paintbrush. In the artistic hands of Picasso, it could do what it was supposed to do."

Of necessity, a farrier may occasionally have to fabricate a replacement part for his tools, or even design and make a specific tool for a specific job.

The knowledge and skill so vital to a farrier's profession may be self-taught or acquired over long periods of time by practice, observation, or serving as a trainee to an experienced farrier. "Working with an experienced farrier," Rory says, "usually offers training in the manual skills — like how to forge a shoe — and in handling and restraining techniques for the horses.

"However," he adds, "the more complicated *theories* of horseshoeing, like the concepts about a horse's anatomy and physiology, are usually neglected. The experienced farrier probably doesn't have time to explain why he's doing everything that he's doing. You've got to figure that any education you get from working with a farrier might be limited, then. A lot of them tend to specialize in one particular kind of horse, too, like racehorses or jumpers or gaited horses. That limits your education to a very narrow segment of what is really a broad field of care."

To overcome this problem, there are several score of farrier schools and colleges that have been formed in recent years. They purport to teach an overview of both the theory and practice of the art of farriery. But, depending upon the orientation of the particular school, a different balance between the two may actually be struck. So, too, may the emphasis of the school vary, depending upon the breeds of animals or the predominant use of the animals in the school's area.

During formal schooling, a student learns the basic skills of the trade from lectures, demonstrations, and actual performances. The proper use of the various tools is taught, as is handling of horses, animal psychology, public relations, professional image, business management principles, and anatomy and physiology of the horse.

"Completion of a farrier school's curriculum," says Rory, "doesn't necessarily produce a competent farrier, a person who is able to perform all that's expected of him. Much more practice is desirable and usually necessary — which you might acquire by working as a trainee for a while with an experienced farrier." Rory does recommend schooling first, though. He thinks, too, that the prospective student should be "very picky" about the farrier school in which he or she enrolls.

"One extremely important consideration," he says, "is the

ratio of students to instructors. In my opinion, if one instructor is responsible for more than a dozen or so students, I don't think those students are going to get the kind of individualized attention they really need."

Find out, too, says Rory, the number of horses that you'll actually trim and shoe during the course. "Obviously," he says, "the more horses you work on, the more experienced you'll be when you graduate. Nothing beats hands-on training."

Another consideration should be the length of the course. "Again, in my opinion — and I could be wrong, so get a few more on this one — if the farrier course is less than six or eight weeks long, you've got to wonder whether they'll be able to squeeze in everything in that short a time. Don't get me wrong," says Rory. "I'm not saying that, say, a two-week school is no good. What I am saying is that a shorter program than six or eight weeks must be looked into very carefully. That's all."

He also advises the prospective student to find out the ratio of time spent at forge work to time spent shoeing and trimming. "It should be about even," he says. You might ask, too, he adds, about the "depth" of the horseshoeing theory taught at the school. That is, does the school cover subjects such as anatomy? Physiology? Foot diseases and injuries? Nutritional deficiencies that affect a horse's feet? "You might also check to see if there is instruction in restraining techniques," says Rory, "and public relations and business management principles.

"Don't even consider a correspondence course or a three- or four-day *short course* or clinic as your basic education. They're just not thorough enough. How could they be, in that amount of time?

"And above all, don't assume that merely going to a farrier school for eight or twelve or fourteen weeks or whatever will make you an experienced, competent farrier. Schooling will give you a foundation upon which experience will build your professional skills. And the best way, in my opinion, to get that after-graduation experience is to work for a while as a trainee with an established farrier. You'll save yourself a lot of mistakes that way."

*

The following is a sample of a typical farrier school's curriculum.

Length of Course — *eight weeks* (seven days per week). All breeds of horses are brought to the school for foot care from the surrounding communities. Every student will have the opportunity to work on these horses under the supervision of qualified instructors. This provides the chance to gain experience with the tools, horses, and customers. One designated day each week, the public brings their horses to the school. There have been times when vehicles trailering the horses have waited in a line a quarter of a mile long. Because of this extensive demand, students will get to trim and shoe approximately one hundred head of horses during the course.

Blacksmithing — One of the primary skills needed to be a farrier is blacksmithing. This aspect of the course teaches you the production and handling of blacksmithing and horseshoeing tools. In your assigned forge area you will be instructed in the proper firing of coal and gas forges, the correct forge and metal temperatures, and the art of forge welding. You will also learn the identification and use of the appropriate metal for each job. (For instance, old railroad iron is very important in the production of steel racing shoes.) Smithing techniques such as proper bending, shaping, hammering, metal forging, level of fire to heat, slope of the side of the shoe, and toe-in or toe-out will all be covered.

Classroom Lectures — Knowledge of the anatomy and conformation of the horse is imperative to the correct fitting of shoes and braces. Through the use of specimens and diagrams of the hoof and leg structure, the student will learn the parts of the hoof, how the hoof is designed to support a horse's weight, blood vessel configuration, growth lines, etc. Many typical problems are revealed through demonstrations of special braces and corrective shoes. In addition, overhead projectors, films, and X-ray viewers are used with the lectures in order to illustrate, in depth, all facets of the farrier's trade.

Demonstrations — Through daily demonstrations, you will be taught techniques such as how to approach a horse, how to hold the foot while trimming and shoeing, and how to properly use ropes to tie and throw a horse without injury to you or the animal.

Training in the Field — You will visit large breeding farms and training farms in the local area. Your training will include working with horses from suckling foals to mature, powerful stallions. This training offers you experience with horses of varying age, breed, sex, and conformation. In addition, you will be able to gain a working knowledge of the dispositions and attributes peculiar to a horse's age and sex.

Corrective Shoeing and Surgery — In this part of the curriculum you will study corrective shoeing, braces, and surgery. Many good horses have failed in their show or race performance because of a correctable flaw in their feet. Therefore, knowledge of proper correction is a must in your training. Correction can mean anything from trimming to braces to artificial extensions of the legs. You will learn how to make artificial frogs, how to use plastic, heal thrush, and how to build up the foot on saddlebred and show horses. Since accidents and defects often require surgery, a veterinarian will teach you how braces are used to force the leg, ankle, cannon bone, etc., to heal properly.

Additional Instruction — You will be taught the basics of how to manage a stable — including correct saddling, bridling, bedding, exercising, and grooming techniques — in order to give you an all-around understanding of the raising and management of horses.

EIGHT

The Stable Manager

THE SUN HAD BARELY BEEN AWAKE an hour when Savannah Rainwater steered her jeep into Stonehenge Farm's parking lot. She bounced out of the vehicle and headed straight for the main barn.

Willis was waiting for her. He sprang out from under a hedge, looking like a miniature version of his dangerous cousin, the black panther.

"Mornin', Willis," said Savannah, stooping down to scratch her friend's plush head. "You rascal, you. Catch anything last night?" As Willis enjoyed the impromptu massage, a bicycle made its way into the parking lot transporting one of Savannah's new working students, a gangly, fair-haired young man. "Right on time, Coy. Good for you!" said Savannah.

"I haven't been up this early," said Coy, "since the Christmas I was five years old." He leaned his bike against the split rail fence that hugged the lot.

"It's good for you," said Savannah. "Morning's the best time of the whole day." She gave Willis a final pat and then led Coy into the main barn.

It was Friday, and the third week in June. School was officially finished for the summer. In return for a hands-on education in the basics of stable management, Coy would volunteer his services four days a week until school reopened in September. He would report directly to Stonehenge Farm's stable manager, Savannah Rainwater. Today would be Coy's first day on the job.

As soon as Savannah and Coy entered the barn, Big Bear, a half-asleep Newfoundland, and Scooter, a hyperactive Scottish terrier, made their ways to the door for the official morning greeting. Once salutations were exchanged, Savannah began introducing Coy to the stable's morning routine.

"Horses," she explained, leading Coy to R.D.'s stall, "are tough creatures. But, like any other animal, they can get sick or injured. The first thing I do, then — every morning — is go into each horse's stall and check him all over. Make sure nothing happened during the night." She stopped at her office for a moment to switch on the music over the stable's intercom. As soon as the first few bars of soft rock pulsed through the barn, several curious horses stuck their heads out of their hay-floored boudoirs. "Hope music doesn't bother you."

"Not at all," said Coy. He followed Savannah down the operating-room-clean corridor to the first stall on the right, R.D.'s. The Thoroughbred was wide awake and most happy to greet his caretaker, nuzzling Savannah's shoulder. "The minute I see my horses," she said, sliding her hand along R.D.'s sleek neck, "I can tell just by the way they're acting whether or not something's wrong. Each one of them has a different kind of personality, and it's pretty constant. When their personalities vary, chances are it's because something's wrong with them." R.D. shook his blazed head up and down and whinnied.

Coy chuckled. "I guess he agrees with you."

"He's a good boy — aren't you, R.D.?" Savannah opened the Dutch door and entered R.D.'s stall. Coy remained in the doorway.

"I look for certain things," said Savannah. "For instance." She rubbed a hand along R.D.'s ribs and hipbone. "These shouldn't be prominent. His hindquarters should be well rounded." She then positioned herself so that she was head-to-head with the horse. "He should stand just the way he is now. See how he's square on all four legs?"

Coy — hands in his pockets, a cowlick standing at attention at the back of his head — nodded.

"Give me your hand please, Coy." Savannah placed it at the base of R.D.'s ear. "Is it warm?" she asked the surprised young man.

"Yup."

"Good. That's the way it should be. Signs of illness vary. But there are some general symptoms which can warn you that trouble's brewing. If R.D. here were to stop eating, for example, or all of a sudden get extremely lazy — those are signs that would tell me something's not right with him.

"There are other things I check too. Discharge from the eyes or nostrils can be a sign of sickness. Just like us when we get runny noses." She love-slapped R.D. on his sturdy shoulder. "You're a good boy," she said as she left his stall. Coy closed the door and followed her down the corridor.

"The key to my job," said Savannah, unlatching the door to Macomber's quarters, "is for me to know every horse's usual physical and emotional health. Then be aware of the slightest change in either," she added as she entered the white-socked gelding's stall. "None of the horses in this stable can talk." Coy grinned at her. "They can't tell me when they don't feel well — if they've pulled a muscle or have a toothache or indigestion. It's up to me, then, to find out those things."

"I thought that's what a vet was for."

"It is," Savannah insisted. She picked up one of Macomber's feet for examination. "But our vet only visits us every couple of weeks, unless there's an emergency. If a horse goes that long without being checked, and he develops a serious problem in the meantime, he could die before the vet ever saw him." By now she had examined all four of Macomber's feet. "Two horses down, eight more to greet," she said, smiling at Coy.

"Many times," she added while leading the way to the third stall, "there's no emergency at all. But, if there is, I'm the one who has to take care of it."

"Is that what the first aid kit in your office is for?"

"Very observant of you, Coy. I like that." Savannah unlatched Spock's stall door. "Lots of times there's neither an emergency nor any real need to call the vet for advice. But the horse might still need some medical attention."

"What do you mean?"

"Oh," she said, touching a hand to the base of Spock's ears and thinking for two seconds. "Maybe a puncture wound. Like from a thorn, while the horse was being exercised. If it was deep and it looked like stitches would be necessary, of course I'd call the vet. Otherwise I'd take care of it myself. But," she added, picking up one of Spock's feet, "even if the vet had to come over, I'd still have to bring the bleeding under control."

Such a situation had occurred at the beginning of the week, she went on. Robert Frost, one of the newer horses at the stable, had punctured the skin just above his right hoof. Savannah went right to work. First, she applied a pressure bandage to stop the bleeding. "I used a folded handkerchief," she said. "I keep one with me all the time, just for that purpose." She pulled one from her jeans pocket and waved it in front of her.

She explained that she pressed the folded handkerchief directly over the wound. As soon as the bleeding stopped, she removed the cloth pad and carefully clipped the hair from the skin surrounding the wound. "After that," she said, leaving Spock's abode and walking toward Sneezy's, "I had to clean and disinfect the wound."

"How did you do that?"

Savannah stopped walking, turned, and looked at Coy. "I guess you really haven't had any experience around horses, have you?"

"That's what I told Mr. McNicholas. He said it didn't matter, as long as I was a good worker and was real serious about learning."

"I'm sure you are," said Savannah, entering Sneezy's stall. "Anyway, back to your question. I cleaned out the wound by trickling cold water from a hose over it. Then I rinsed it out with a solution of salt and water, dabbed on some antibiotic powder to kill any bacteria, and applied a bandage. Presto! The horse was on his way to recovery."

"Sounds like what my mother did to me once when I was a kid," Coy recalled, "when I cut my foot badly."

"It doesn't surprise me. A lot of what I do for the horses is just good ol' common sense."

*

When Savannah had checked all ten horses, she led Coy back to R.D.'s stall to initiate him in the morning's usual chores — the first of which would be grooming.

"The whole point of grooming a horse," Savannah explained, "is to keep him clean, massage his skin, and tone up his muscles. Actually, there are three phases to grooming. The first we call *quartering*, which is what we're going to do right now." She led R.D. into the corridor outside his stall and cross-tied him. She showed Coy her hoof pick and demonstrated for him how to remove dirt and pebbles and other foreign substances from R.D.'s foot. "It's sort of like digging an oyster out of its shell," she explained while moving the hoof pick along the edge of the first hoof.

"May I try it?"

"Sure," said Savannah without hesitation. She believed strongly that the best way for anyone to learn anything was by doing it. In the meantime, she fetched R.D.'s grooming tools from the trunk outside his stall. When Coy had finished cleaning R.D.'s feet, Savannah demonstrated how to clean the horse's eyes and muzzle, dabbing at them with a damp, soft sponge. She used a second sponge to cleanse the dock of the tail. Next she unbuckled the blue-and-white *rug* —the blanket that had kept R.D. warm during the night — and folded it back from his shoulders. Grabbing the soft, short-bristled *body brush,* Savannah showed Coy how to stroke R.D.'s head, neck, chest, and forelegs with it. "Look at him," she said, ceasing her massage routine for a moment. "He loves to be rubbed with this brush."

When Savannah had finished working over the front half of R.D.'s body, Coy returned the rug to its original position, while Savannah folded the rear half away from R.D.'s rump and repeated the body-brush process on the hind end of the hardwood-brown body. Finally, she brushed out the animal's mane and tail. When the first grooming of the day was complete, Savannah stepped back. She whistled. "I'll tell you something, R.D. ol' boy. You look good enough to lead the Rose Bowl parade." She was leaning against a corridor wall with her hands behind her body, as though she had a gift in one of her hands and R.D. would have to choose which hand it was in. She looked at Coy. "What do you suppose we should do with him now?"

"Water, maybe." Coy's brow furrowed. "Feed him, too?"

"Right-o!" said Savannah. "Go to the head of the class, Coy." She instructed him to move R.D. back into his stall and then fill his water bucket.

"Can I ask you a question, Savannah?" Coy was lifting the water bucket off its hook on the wall by the stall door when he spoke. The bucket was almost empty. Some hay had fallen into it from the net that hung beside it. "How come you don't have automatic watering bowls like I've seen advertised? Seems to me it'd make life a little easier."

"You're right," said Savannah, following Coy to the sink outside the barn's back door. "A bucket filled with water feels like a bag full of wet cement, I know. But," she said, raising her forefinger and shaking it for emphasis, "using a bucket means I can control the amount of water the horse drinks.

Which is very important. You don't want a hot horse just in from a rough workout to guzzle himself to death."

"I never thought of that," said Coy. He lifted the full, heavy bucket. His tennis-ball-sized biceps looked big against the thinness of the rest of his arm.

"The bucket also helps me check on whether the horse has slacked off on his water intake or not, which is another sign — remember? — that something's wrong."

Back at R.D.'s stall, Coy lifted the bucket onto its hook on the wall. Savannah then showed him how to fill the hay net and fix it to the tie-up ring next to the bucket. "Good job, Coy," she said, just a little out of breath from her wrestling match with the hay net. "I can see you're going to make my summer a lot more pleasant."

*

"Most working students I've come across," said Savannah, "don't want to do this part of the job. Which is too bad, because it's got to be done every day." She was referring to the process known as *mucking out.*

Mucking out a stall means that soiled straw and dung are separated from the clean portions of the horse's straw bedding with a pitchfork. The clean straw is heaped neatly at the back of the stall, to be used again. The soiled straw and dung are dumped into a wheelbarrow for removal to the manure pile outside the barn.

"What's the purpose of the bedding?" Savannah demanded suddenly.

Coy winced, as if the question were too simple to merit an answer. "Gives the horse something nice to lie on, I guess," he said, with a trace of hesitation.

Savannah laughed. "Horses sleep standing up. Oh, you're basically right, of course. It prevents him from getting injured by the cement floor beneath. But there's more to it than that. Bedding insulates the stall against drafts, for one thing. It also absorbs moisture, so the horse doesn't have to stand in his own urine. So, naturally, the bedding's got to be cleaned. Right?"

"Right."

"Hence," said Savannah, "the daily and seemingly never-ending task of mucking out stalls." She ceremoniously handed Coy her pitchfork.

When Coy had removed all the soiled straw and "buns" and had heaped the clean straw at the back of the stall, Savannah swept the floor clean of any remaining dirt and debris. All the while R.D. had been munching contentedly from his hay net, more than happy to move out of anyone's way when he had to.

"Okay," said Savannah. "Let's leave the floor bare for a while to air it out." They made their way to the next stall to begin the entire quartering and feeding and watering and mucking-out process once again.

When all ten horses had finally been catered to, Coy and Savannah returned to R.D.'s stall to finish the mucking-out process. They retrieved the clean straw from the back of the stall ("the daybed," Savannah called it) and spread the thin golden stalks so that they covered the entire floor of R.D.'s stall.

As Savannah led Coy to the next stall to lay another daybed, she continued with the young man's education. "Straw," she said, "is the best possible bedding material because . . ."

*

It had taken Coy and Savannah an hour and a half to check and quarter the horses and muck out the ten stalls. It was now seven-thirty, time for the first real feeding of the day. Savannah led Coy into her office, which contained the bins in which the concentrated feed was stored.

"The horses in this particular stable all work very hard. They exercise every day and compete most every weekend, from May through October," said Savannah. "So, besides hay,

they need additional food to keep them fit and hard-muscled."
She lifted the hinged plywood cover of one of the feed bins.
"I feed each horse a different amount of food and vitamins,
depending upon how much work he's going to do. It's like a
person — if a horse is active, he needs to eat more."

In her position as stable manager, one of Savannah's many
responsibilities is to provide the extra nutrition the horses
need by feeding them concentrated food. In a very real sense,
she's as much a dietitian as she is a nurse to the horses in
her care. "The best additive to anything I prepare for them,"
she explained, while measuring ingredients like some scientist
in her laboratory and then pouring the contents of the measuring cups into feed buckets, "is oats. Oats has no equal as
a natural, high-protein, high-energy food. But," she said, suddenly ceasing her routine and staring into Coy's ever-observ-
ing eyes, "be darned careful of the amount of oats you feed
these horses. They just might get so energetic they become
unmanageable." There was silence momentarily. Then she
grinned and continued with her measuring and pouring.

This particular morning she would also make a special
"pick-me-up" breakfast for Red Rover, who had been less than
a spitfire during his last two workouts, according to his rider.
"He's just a wee bit tired," said Savannah as she mixed two-
thirds of a bucket of bran — a cereal grain — with one-third
of a bucket of boiling water.

"What do you call that concoction?"

"Mash," Savannah said. She poured some molasses into the
steamy brew. Then she chopped some hay, added the short
stalks to the boiling brew, and mixed the whole recipe together
as though she were mixing a frosting for a cake.

"How do you know how much food to feed each horse?" Coy
asked.

Savannah continued pouring some corn oil into Yerk's feed
bucket. "There's no hard-and-fast guideline," she answered,
"as to the exact amounts of food each horse should be fed. It
all depends on the type and size of the horse, and ——"

"I know," Coy interrupted. "How much work the horse is going to do."

"Right you are. A ballpark figure to start with is to build on how much a typical horse would eat in the wild. Studies have been done which show that a horse standing fifteen-two hands will eat about twenty-six and a half pounds of grass a day. For every extra inch of height, figure on an additional pound of grass.

"The best guideline of all, though," she concluded, placing the final feed bucket in the wheelbarrow for the trip to the stalls, "is simple observation." She paused, put her hands on her hips, and added, "If a horse looks fat, he's eating too much — just like with people."

*

Sometimes during the hectic summer months, Savannah works fourteen consecutive days before she gets a couple of days off. Normally, though, she says, "Most stable management positions require that you work a six-day week, Tuesday through Sunday."

Including Coy, Savannah has four working students at various times at the stable. "They're working for riding lessons from my boss, Mr. McNicholas," says Savannah. "Or to learn about stable management from me. Plus they get free room and board for their horses — if they have them — which are stabled in another barn, next to the main one. Most of the working students are very dependable. They do what they're supposed to do, when they're supposed to do it. But having the four of them working under me doesn't make my working life any easier, really. If anything, it makes it more difficult — I don't tell them that, of course — because I've got to check to see that everything they do is done right.

"If they don't show up for some reason, their responsibilities still have to be met. I end up mucking out and grooming every day. Maybe not all ten horses, but I still have to do some. A stable manager just doesn't sit back in her office, put her feet up, and relax while the working students take control of the place. I'm paid to supervise and instruct the workers in proper stable management. I can't do all that that entails without getting my hands dirty, too."

*

"Mmmm. Goood coffee," Savannah declared. "Sure you won't have some, Coy?"

"No, thanks. It stunts your growth," he said, grinning from one cheek to the other.

"Ha, ha," Savannah replied. Coy's good-natured teasing was in obvious reference to his height superiority. But at four feet eleven, Savannah was well used to people towering over her. Like water off a pitched roof, Coy's ribbing rolled right off her. She smiled at him, and then let the last drop of coffee trickle down from her nearly upside-down cup. "Okay, Coy," she said, glancing at her wristwatch. "It's nine o'clock. The horses should be just about finished eating by now. Let's go back and ——"

"Morning, Savannah! Sorry I'm a little late!" squeaked Gage Hunt as she bolted into the office. She tossed her brown-bagged lunch onto Savannah's desk. "Flat tire. Honest," insisted the ponytailed teenager while slipping on a sweat shirt.

"Gage," said Savannah. "I want you to meet Coy Bacon. Coy, this is Gage Hunt. She's a working student, too."

"Hiya!" said Gage. Her sweat shirt was about three sizes too big for her. She had to pull about five inches of excess sleeve above her right hand in order to offer a greeting to Coy.

"Okay, gang. Let's get to work," said Savannah. The first stop for her and Coy was R.D.'s stall, while Gage headed toward the far end of the stable to Chopin's quarters.

"A lot of different types of clothing have been devised," said Savannah, "to keep horses warm." While she spoke from outside R.D.'s stall, Coy was inside pitchforking newly deposited manure into the wheelbarrow. "I'd say the best of all of them is this one here." She fingered R.D.'s bathrobe, draped over the leggy animal. She walked into the stall and removed the wool-lined rug, folded it twice, and draped it over the iron arm attached to the outside of the stall door.

"All set," said Coy. He leaned on his pitchfork at the rear of the stall.

"Great. Come on out here for a sec." Savannah led R.D. into the corridor once again and crosstied him as before. She proceeded to demonstrate how to unwrap the stable bandages from each of R.D.'s legs. They had been wrapped from the knee all the way down to the fetlock. "To keep them warm and protected," Savannah explained, "so they don't get stiff or scratched." She let Coy finish the task while she took a look outside at the source of the hubbub that been gradually building for the last half-hour.

She saw what looked like moving day at a college. All of Stonehenge Farm's riding students had arrived. They would be making a five-hour journey later in the morning to an important horse show. Several horses were parked in the lot, waiting to be loaded into a six-horse van. A half-dozen students were running in and out of the boarder's barn, making last-minute preparations. Savannah headed back to Coy. She would return to the confusion outside in a while. First, she had to show her new working student how to get R.D. ready for his workout this morning with Stonehenge's owner and chief riding instructor, Mr. McNicholas.

"All stabled horses need regular exercise," said Savannah, placing a saddle pad on R.D.'s back. "Not just for their physical well-being, either."

"What do you mean?"

"Well," Savannah replied, "a horse that's not ridden regularly becomes bored. When that happens, he'll develop bad habits to entertain himself, like chewing on his stall door or something like that."

"How can you tell how much exercise each horse should get?"

"Good question. You're going to do all right, Coy." Savannah lifted Mr. McNicholas's saddle onto the patient R.D. "It varies with the type and weight of the horse," she said, "and the work he'll ultimately be expected to do. A show horse, for example, or a hunter needs more exercise than just a hack." As with feeding, she said, there are a few basic rules she observes in overseeing the horses' exercise routines.

"The first," she explained, "is that I never schedule a horse for exercise until an hour after a light feed like this morning's." She pulled on the girth strap and secured the saddle. "The whole point is to get — and keep — a horse fit enough for the demands being made on him. You can tell when you've finally got him into shape. His muscles increase, and that heavy, lathery sweat he used to get after a workout disappears almost entirely." In her role as stable manager, Savannah has to be as much a *trainer,* then, as she is a nurse and a dietitian, inasmuch as she supervises the amount and kind of exercise each of the horses gets. "A horse," she added, "can't be conditioned by going right out and cantering him and galloping him every day. He needs slow, steady, regular work. Like ——"

"I know, don't tell me," said Coy. "Like people."

"Exactly. If you were forty years old, say, and you suddenly decided you wanted to get back into shape, you wouldn't go out that very day and run ten miles. If you did, you might kill yourself. It's the same with horses. A horse has to be brought along slowly, even if it means just a ten-minute walk at first, depending upon what kind of shape he's in when I get him. Then I see to it that the amount of exercise he gets is gradually increased until he's at the point where he should be. At a larger stable, there would probably be a full-time trainer to do that."

"Makes sense to me," said Coy.

"Good. Now why don't you go help out Gage while I help straighten out that confusion outside."

"What about R.D.?"

"Mr. McNicholas will be here any sec."

"Okeedokee."

*

"Listen up, gang! Toby and Tiki will be loaded first," Savannah announced. The show-bound group was spread out all over the parking lot, and she had to raise her voice in order to be heard above the din. Six horses were lined up alongside the van, like so many schoolchildren waiting in a bus line.

"Ready, Cody?" Savannah asked. The driver indicated that his mobile stable was ready for its passengers.

Although Savannah had only been outside for a short while, she had actually orchestrated the entire affair, having begun preparations several weeks ago. First she had to arrange for transportation for the horses and the riding students, as well as accommodations for them all for the duration of the horse show. Then, earlier in the week, she saw to it that the all-important preparations got underway. For example, she made sure each horse would have his own hay net for the trip in the van. In addition, she gave each student a checklist of things to pack — items such as rugs, bandages, grooming tools, a head collar, a water bucket, and a filled water container. "Very important," she had told all the students when she reviewed the packing list with them. "Five hours is a long time for a horse to go without water." She had also specified that each horse was to wear a rug while in transit and that traveling bandages would be necessary, as well as a tail bandage, knee caps, and hock boots.

Before she began supervising the loading of the horses into the van, Savannah had checked with each rider, making sure her instructions had been heeded. Lale, as usual, was the only one who had a problem. She couldn't manage to bandage Toby's tail properly.

"I'll give you a hand," Savannah told her when she came to check on her. First Savannah dampened Toby's tail hairs with a water brush. Next, she unrolled a short length of the bandage and placed it beneath the tail. "Close to the dock, like this," she said. Then, holding the end of the bandage against the underside of the tail with her left hand, she made one turn of the rest of the rolled bandage with her right. When the first wraparound was secure, Savannah continued wrapping the rest of the tail, stopping just short of the last tailbone.

"Now we take the remaining length of bandage," said Savannah, "and we bandage *up* the tail this time, like this." About one-third of the way up, there was no more bandage left. She fastened the whole kit and caboodle with tape. Lastly, she took the wrapped tail in both her hands and bent it slightly, as though she were bending a rubber hose. "Think you can do it next time, Lale?"

"I think so. Thanks an awful lot."

Now Lale was being asked to lead her horse into the van first. "Because he's the calmest of the bunch," Savannah explained. She was right. Toby went in without fanfare.

Rasputin was next. His hind legs had been wrapped in what looked like the leg pads a baseball catcher would wear. He too was loaded into the van without ado, as were Detour, Benvolio, and Sergeant Pepper. Burly, the sleekly muscular quarter horse/Thoroughbred combination, was last to be led aboard. He walked two noisy steps up the ramp and backed off immediately. His owner tugged at his lead shank, but Burly wouldn't budge. Even Big Bear — the always-half-asleep Newfoundland, who had situated himself in the shade next to the van — lifted an ear in anticipation of a battle.

"Wait a minute," said Savannah. "Don't fight him. I've got an idea." She ran into the boarders' barn and quickly returned with two armfuls of straw. "He might be afraid of the noise his hooves are making on that ramp," she said, laying the straw all over it. "This ought to deaden the sound a little."

It did. Burly walked up the ramp at the first tug.

Inside the van, the six horses had been backed into their stalls — three at one end, three at the other — and were immediately occupied with the hay that had been hung in front of them by Savannah. Assured that the animals were all snug, she then went outside to the back of the vehicle, to be certain the students had secured their suitcases, tack trunks, and extra bales of hay tightly to the tailgate. "I believe in a lot of rope," she said to no one in particular while adding one more length around the entire package.

All was ready now. The caravan, consisting of the six-horse van and several cars filled with students and parents, maneuvered in the parking lot.

"Good luck, people! Send me a postcard!" Savannah shouted, smiling, and thinking how quiet it would be around Stonehenge for the next three days. She waved goodbye to the entourage and then thrust both thumbs up in a final good-luck salute.

*

After lunch, the second stage of the grooming of the horses — *strapping* — commenced. Once again, Savannah and Coy began with R.D. Gage started at the far end of the stable, in the last stall, and would work her way toward them.

R.D. was crosstied in the corridor outside his stall. "Pick out his feet, Coy, will you please while ——"

"Again?"

"Again," said Savannah.

Facing in the direction of R.D.'s tail, Coy slid his hand down from the horse's shoulder to his fetlock, just as Savannah had taught him earlier in the day, thereby encouraging R.D. to move his weight to his other legs. Working from the frog to the toe, and concentrating on the edges of the hoof first, Coy used the point of the hoof pick to dig out all the foreign substances. "There's a million pebbles in here," he said.

"Ever get one of those in your shoe?" Savannah asked him.

"Once in a while."

"Hurts, doesn't it?"

"Yup."

"It hurts a horse, too, you know. Even worse. It can make him go lame."

"I s'pose that's why we've been picking out feet so much today. Right?"

"You bet. You're catching on awfully fast for a rookie." As she spoke, Savannah was using the hard-bristled *dandy brush* to remove the heavy dirt and sweat stains left by the girth and the saddle. She worked from the ears to the tail, first on the near side and then on the off. "This is a fairly hard brush," she advised. "You never use it on any tender areas. And always use it lightly."

Next, she again demonstrated the use of the body brush. Its shorter, denser bristles, she said, were designed to penetrate and clean the horse's coat. Starting with R.D.'s mane, she pushed the hairs to the wrong side so she could remove any dirt from its roots. Then she brushed his forelock.

All the while, Coy leaned against the corridor wall, arms folded. "Don't you ever get tired of the same routine all the time?"

"Not at all," said Savannah. She started brushing R.D.'s body, working from head to tail once again, and grooming the nearside first. She worked with a circular motion, always completing a stroke in the direction of the hairs and then flicking the brush outward to push away any dust from the body. "If I did," she added, "this wouldn't be the kind of job I should be doing, because *routine* is very much a part of any stable manager's job."

Next she showed Coy how to groom the tail. "A few hairs at a time," she said, "starting with the undermost ones." She removed all the mud and tangles, taking care not to break any hairs. After each one had been stroked, she brushed the whole tail into one lustrous shape. "What do you think, Coy?"

The young man whistled his approval. "He looks great to me, Savannah. You really know what you're doing."

"Thanks. But we're not done yet. Wring out one of those sponges in the bucket there, will you please?"

Savannah cleaned R.D.'s eyes first, wiping outward from their corners. Then she sponged over the muzzle, the lips, and the nostrils. The second sponge she used to wipe the tail area, washing first around the dock and then lifting the tail itself as high as it could go so that the skin beneath could be cleaned.

"Now," said Savannah, "we have to lay the mane." She dipped the tip of her water brush into the bucket. Then, keeping the brush flat, she made firm downward strokes through the mane, beginning at the roots. When she was finished, the hairs lay neat and slightly damp along R.D.'s long neck.

"That should do it — right, Savannah?"

Savannah dropped the brush into the bucket and put her hands to her hips. "I can see you're going to have to learn some patience, Coy. Look at him. Real close. You mean to tell me there's nothing else we can spruce up on him?"

Coy eyed the horse for at least a minute. "I give up," he said. "Honest. He looks great to me."

"Look at his feet."

"His feet? But I already picked them."

"I'm not talking about picking them," said Savannah. "I'm talking about brushing and oiling them."

Coy looked as though he'd just bitten into an apple with a worm in it. "Huh?"

Savannah demonstrated how to brush the outside of R.D.'s hooves, taking care not to get water into the hollow of the heel. When the hooves were dry, she brushed oil over the outside of each, as high as the coronary band. "To prevent hoof cracks," she told Coy as she applied the oil with what looked like an artist's paintbrush.

"I have to admit," said Coy. "That sure makes a difference. I mean his feet are actually shining!"

"Hold your horses, rookie. We're still not done yet." She folded a slightly damp cloth into a flat bundle and began rubbing R.D.'s body with it. "To remove any last traces of dust," she explained. When she had finished, R.D.'s coat shone like the hood of a brand-new Rolls-Royce. "Now. We're done."

Coy looked at his wristwatch. "That took almost half an hour," he said, in somewhat disbelief. "We've still got nine more to do!"

"You're forgetting Gage."

Coy turned around and saw his fellow working student enter her second stall.

"You and I have four more to do," said Savannah. "Gage pulls her weight around here. Come on. Let's put R.D. back in his stall and see how well you can do with Macomber."

*

"In a very real sense," says Savannah, "I am a teacher — in addition, of course, to all my other duties. For instance, when it's a bit slow — which is almost never — I'll give the working students a mini-clinic in, oh, braiding or clipping or dosing a horse. I love doing that sort of thing. I consider that an integral part of any stable manager's job.

"Also, I'm a natural organizer. I take a lot of pride in how my stable looks. To me, it's like a hotel around here, and I'm its manager. I have finicky guests staying with me that require an awful lot of special attention. It's a challenge just to get through a normal day because something unexpected almost always happens.

"But all those things aside, the greatest thing about my job is the fact that I'm constantly around horses. That means a lot to me — plus the fact that I'm considered the resident expert, and people tend to rely upon me. It's a good feeling when people respect you as a professional."

Savannah's typical day varies, although — as we've seen — the variety happens within a rather strict framework of regularity. In theory, she works from seven until five. "But I'm always on the job — by choice — by six, and many days I'm not out of here until six at night, or later. If you're a person who watches the clock, you're in the wrong business if you're working with horses.

"What makes my particular situation so enjoyable is the

people I work for. Mr. and Mrs. McNicholas trust me — my judgment and knowledge. They're not in here looking over my shoulder all the time. They know I can do the job, so they let me do it — my way."

How, though, did she reach such a level of competency concerning horses?

"Formal schooling," she says, "and then five years of hands-on experience in various related horse jobs before I ever even thought about accepting a stable manager's responsibility.

"By itself, schooling — I don't care how thorough the program is, whether it's six months or two years — just can't expose you to all the various emergencies that a couple or more years on the job will give you.

"And, in my opinion, just working your way up the stable ladder, with no formalized schooling, isn't the answer either, because then you've got to hope that someone at that stable is knowledgeable enough and a good enough teacher — as well as willing to give up his time — to give you all that you're going to need. That's asking an awful lot, don't you think?

"I recommend a combination of formal schooling and then hands-on, work-your-way-up-the-ladder experience before trying to tackle the stable manager's job."

Savannah's own route to the position followed such a path, although her interest in horses came relatively late in life. She was attending a junior college, studying liberal arts, and had never had anything to do with horses. By chance, the college offered a riding program to its students as an extracurricular activity.

"My roommate rode all the time," Savannah recalls. "Shy stabled her horse right at the college, competed in shows every other weekend — the whole bit. She was really into it. I suppose it was inevitable that I'd get hooked, too. I was nineteen at the time, but it was as if I were ten years old and seeing horses for the first time. Shy showed me all the ropes. Took me with her to shows, taught me how to ride."

When Savannah graduated from the two-year college, she worked initially as a secretary. "I absolutely couldn't stand the nine-to-five routine," she insists. "And I was still following Shy to horse shows every chance I could get. Finally, I realized that I not only enjoyed horses, I wanted to make them my life's work."

Shy recommended a school, and Savannah completed a one-year program in stable management. When she graduated, at twenty-two, she went looking for her first bona fide job in the horse industry.

"I started out as a groom," she says, "at the junior college I'd graduated from three years earlier. One hundred dollars a week. Fortunately I was still living with my parents, so the money was enough to get by on. The good thing, though, was that I got to practice most everything I had learned about stable management. And the stable manager was very helpful, always there to clarify or demonstrate something for me if I had a problem."

Eventually, Savannah left that position to take on an assistant's job at a racing stable. "For more money," she says. "And a different kind of horse experience."

Following the racing stable position, she chose to round off her on-the-job learning by working as an assistant to an equine practitioner.

"Her qualifications to manage my stable," says Reid McNicholas, "were outstanding. First of all, she had had that year of formal equine training at a fine school. Second, she had more than five years of varied work experience under her belt. She had conditioned horses, fed them, and cared for them. She was ready."

Savannah had earned a reputation for being not only knowledgeable, but reliable and cooperative as well. She didn't have to go looking for Stonehenge Farm's stable manager position. Reid McNicholas came looking for her.

"I wanted someone reliable, responsible," he says. "The schooling and work experience were fine, all right. But above all, I was most interested in her references. The most important attribute a stable manager can possess, you see, is reliability — total dedication to getting the job done well, day in and day out. Everyone Savannah had worked for vouched for her reliability. That was more than enough for me, given her schooling and so on."

Savannah's base salary at Stonehenge is $200 per week, $10,400 per year — some $4,100 per year less than the average stable manager earns. But with her particular job, there are fringe benefits which make her "real" salary more than the money she receives. For example, she gets her housing free. She lives on the McNicholases' property, in a furnished three-room apartment next to the stable. "That's worth about three thousand dollars right there," says Savannah, "which brings me up near the national average, salarywise, if Mr. Mc-Nicholas decided to pay me that money and then charge me rent. Plus I don't have to use a car to get to work. So most of my salary I keep. It doesn't go toward paying rent and gas. That makes a very big difference."

Moreover, there is ample opportunity for her to earn additional money beyond her base salary. "I'll braid a couple of the riding students' horses on the day of a show at thirty dollars each. Or, I'll travel with them to the show and be their groom for the day, at twenty dollars each, plus expenses.

"With all the extra ways I have of earning money, I pulled in about two hundred and fifty dollars a week on the average last year. The thing is, I know I'll never get rich in this business. But that's okay by me, because I have no need to. The most important thing in my life is doing what makes me happy. I happen to be most happy when I'm around horses and stables and horse people. It's as simple as that. And no one can put a monetary value on that for me. I'd do it for nothing — so two or three hundred dollars a week is like a godsend!"

*

Below is a sample of a formalized curriculum in stable management (sometimes referred to as "horse management"). This particular curriculum is designed to be completed in six months.

History of Various Breeds of Horses — Characteristics of the various horse breeds and their development, as well as a comparative evaluation of the performance of the breeds.

Horse Buildings and Facilities — A study of the functional requirements of housing as it relates to sanitation and protection from injury.

Care and Grooming — Development of skills and extensive practice in the daily care and grooming of horses.

Nutrition — A study of the nutritional needs of horses and the principles and practices involved in providing balanced rations of a variety of foodstuffs.

Pedigree Study and Genetics — Understanding pedigrees, heredity, mating systems, etc., to develop desired traits in horses.

Horse Breeding — A vet performs the key activities for viewing by students. Procedures include methods of checking heat, preparation of mares and stallions, foaling, etc.

Keeping Records — The basics of successful record-keeping, the keystone to profit or loss in horse management.

Diseases and Medication — The study of health and soundness in horses and the relationship to growth, performance, and reproduction.

Safety — A study of the principles of stable safety.

Training and Showing — A study of training horses for competition.

Business Principles — Analyzing profit and loss, establishing a budget, etc.

The Competitive Edge — A study of the methods and techniques of competition, the skills necessary in fitting and showing various classes of horses. Actual competition in shows is included.

Promotion — A study of the various ways to market horses via auctions, private sales, etc.

Law and Taxes — An analysis of the principles of law which pertain to horses. Special attention given to taxes relating to stable management.

Insurance — A practical study of how to insure horses, buildings, liabilities, etc.

Career Opportunities — An overview of where the jobs are and how to get them.

NINE

The Trainer

ACHILLES WAS ALMOST ANGRY. The air that whistled through his flaring nostrils sounded rough and harsh, even threatening. The snorts expressed the indignation he was feeling — the half scorn, half surprise aroused by the seemingly unnecessary, unjust predicament his new trainer was putting him in. Achilles hadn't known Bram Twain very long. He trusted him even less.

Bram held Achilles's lead shank in his left hand, a saddle blanket in his right. Aware that Achilles was suspicious of the blanket more than anything else, Bram let the horse examine it, holding it a foot in front of Achilles's noisy nostrils. As he did, the animal's ears dropped sideways and he looked as though he had horns growing out of the sides of his head. Ever so slowly, Achilles lowered his head and then cautiously pushed his nose toward the blanket. When he touched it, he snorted loudly and drew back his head quickly.

Bram continued to hold the blanket in place and followed Achilles as the horse kept stepping backward, making no attempt to restrain the frightened animal. In fact, Bram made certain to keep the lead shank slack.

By introducing the saddle blanket, Bram was officially

Photo by William Haggis

beginning Achilles's "basic training." His first strategy would be to teach the young horse to become accustomed to being touched and handled — by *sacking* him. The idea was for Bram to rub and rustle the saddle blanket around and over and under the inexperienced horse, until Achilles finally relaxed and accepted the blanket without fear. It was a lesson in trust as much as anything else. But as Achilles now backed into the paddock fence, the task of relaxing him looked like a tall order. Bram, however, was up to it.

"The lad's a smart trainer," observed a pug-nosed spectator from the far end of the paddock. He and another of Bram's new clients were leaning over the fence, watching their young trainer.

"Why do you say so?" the second spectator asked.

"Because he's avoiding a pulling contest with that horse, that's why. No way a small guy like Bram can come out on top. And I'll bet that horse has a heck of a long memory. They usually do." He stuffed a wad of chewing tobacco into his mouth.

Both men watched as Bram encouraged Achilles to examine the blanket once more. The horse could back up no farther — his rump was already pressing on the fence. It seemed to the two spectators that whenever Achilles relaxed even slightly, Bram would lower the blanket to his own side, wait a minute, then show it to the horse again. After a while Achilles understood that whenever he became still, Bram would withdraw the scary-looking object from his immediate space.

"See what the lad's doing," observed the pug-nosed spectator, jabbing the second man with an elbow. "He's letting the horse think that *he's* in control!"

The second man was fingering a gray sliver of fence that had sneaked its way into the synthetic fibers of his beige leisure suit. "I still can't understand," he mumbled absentmindedly, "why you call it 'sacking,' though. That's a blanket he's using, isn't it?"

"Yyyuuup," agreed the first man. "In the olden days they

used to use burlap sacks. Most likely that's where the term sacking came from."

As the second man pulled the troublesome splinter from his suit sleeve, he looked up and saw Bram move closer to Achilles, lift the blanket in a smooth and easy motion, and touch the horse with it on the side of his neck. Achilles appeared to stiffen immediately. His ears drew straight back and he tried to jerk himself away from Bram, who moved the blanket slowly and spoke soothingly to the uneasy colt. After a minute, he repeated the process, gradually reaching the point where he would let the blanket touch the horse for several seconds at a time before moving it away.

"What's he trying to accomplish by all of this?" asked the leisure-suited man. He dabbed at his half-bald head with a yellow handkerchief. The perspiration caused by the furnace of a sun soaked the soiled cloth quickly.

"He's learning about the horse's personality."

"Huh?"

"He's learning how far he can persist in getting his point across to the horse, before he has to back off."

The second man squinted as he continued watching Bram work. "The horse still looks scared to me."

"Of course. Sacking will make any young horse nervous at first. All Bram's doing is getting him to accept a little more touching and handling than he'd tolerate on his own."

"So what?"

"Be*cause*," the first man replied. "He has to figure out how much pressure he can put on the horse. When he learns the horse's limits, he can then work *within* them, so the horse can learn to trust him."

"Why's that important? That the horse trust him, I mean?"

"Because he'll be easier to train if he feels he can trust Bram."

"Oh," said the second man. He fingered a grease stain on the left sleeve of his suit, obviously embarrassed at annoying the pug-nosed stranger.

Meanwhile, Achilles continued to pull the lead shank taut whenever Bram touched him with the blanket. He was ready to flee from Bram in an instant. Bram would lighten the shank at those times, figuring that a tight hold would only trigger Achilles's instinctive fear of entrapment.

Eventually, though, the horse began to relax, gradually accepting the innocent feel of the blanket. His body would stiffen only briefly when the blanket touched him. At that point, Bram began rubbing his pupil's neck with the blanket — first in tiny circles, which grew steadily bigger until he was rubbing Achilles's entire shoulder. The long-legged youngster continued to be quiet, although not completely at ease. He still looked as though he had horns instead of ears on his head. After massaging Achilles for a minute, Bram would remove the blanket for another minute, then resume. Eventually, he worked on the horse's other shoulder, too. All the while, Achilles became noticeably calmer. Indeed, by the time Bram got around to rubbing the animal's other shoulder, Achilles had become so accustomed to the blanket that he actually appeared to be bored. That's when Bram figured it was time to wake his daydreaming pupil.

He began by gently slapping the colt on the shoulder with the blanket. Immediately, Achilles's ears cocked backward and his body stiffened once again. But he remained still. A dozen or so slaps later, he again realized the blanket was harmless, so he relaxed. Bram continued the light slapping, touching Achilles all over his bronze body. The more relaxed the horse became, the bolder Bram got. He'd swing the blanket over his head before touching it to Achilles, letting it rustle and flutter and make all sorts of strange noises.

Finally, Bram placed the blanket on Achilles's rump and worked it along the horse's back — rubbing and slapping, rubbing and slapping, very gently. He even touched the areas behind the colt's sensitive ears and under his jaw.

"Looks like he's bored again," observed the second spectator. As he spoke, Bram rubbed, rustled, and swung the blanket in seemingly any manner he could possibly invent. Nevertheless, Achilles remained a statue.

The successful sacking had taken forty-five minutes. Bram would repeat it tomorrow, to confirm that he had won Achilles's trust. If he had, he would promote his new student to the second stage of his elementary education.

*

No matter what kind of specialized training was in store for Achilles later in his life, he first had to learn the basics — to be obedient and well-mannered, steady in his paces, and comfortable and safe to ride. For the most part, Bram Twain works exclusively with young horses like Achilles, teaching them such basics.

"It doesn't matter to me," he insists, "whether the horse brought to me is a Thoroughbred, saddlebred, hunter type, or whatever. The approach I use is always the same as far as basic training is concerned."

Bram's primary responsibility is to teach young horses brought to his ranch how to be pleasure horses under saddle. "After that," he says, "they can be put into other types of specialized, more advanced training — like jumping, for example — if the owner wants me to. But the *basic* training is vital. If it's done properly, it'll increase the horse's chances of success in any advanced schooling he undergoes later on in his life. You can't learn algebra before you learn to add one plus one." plus one."

Of itself, basic training is usually exciting to a young horse, because he is naturally unsure of himself in his first-time role of carrying a rider. With Bram's professional help, Achilles would learn not only to accept a rider and to move forward, turn, and stop in response to signals but also to trust his rider's judgment, even above his own instincts. "And," adds Bram, "if he's trained properly, he'll learn to want to please, too. It's a tall order for any trainer to fill. Believe me."

Bram's county encompasses several breeding farms, ranches,

and backyard horse owners. It is from these operations and individuals that he gets his young horses to train. He is certainly capable of training older horses in more advanced routines, but, he insists, "I usually don't have the time for them. I only accept twenty horses at any one time at my ranch for training. I couldn't handle any more than that unless I got a bigger place and hired some more help. That's just not necessary. There are always enough horses in need of basic training for me to keep my stables full."

He charges $300 per month to feed, stable, and train a horse. In general, he doesn't accept a horse for basic training unless its owner agrees to let Bram work with the horse for a minimum of three months.

"I don't ever tell someone," he says, "that I can train his horse in one month, or three, or even six. Time schedules are pretty meaningless. Every horse is different. What's more important is to know and follow the sequence of steps necessary in basic training, and then allow as much time as necessary for the accomplishment of each one of those steps. Some horses learn some lessons quickly and other lessons slowly. Other horses learn all their lessons slowly. Trying to hold myself and the horse to a time schedule is just not realistic."

Bram must know what he's talking about. Consider that after expenses and taxes last year, he earned himself a tidy $38,000 for his considerable efforts. That's well above the average yearly income of $15,900 that the American Horse Council estimates the nation's 2,900 full-time trainers earn.

One reason for Bram's success, certainly, is his ability to explain what he wants to the horses he's training. That ability is what ultimately determines the rate of progress of the horses he's training. But there are many other factors, too, which make the length and difficulty of basic training different for every horse.

"For example," Bram explains, "if the horse has been hardly handled at all, he'll take a lot more time to train. Or if the owner has tried to train the horse himself and has let him get away with some bad habits, the length of time spent in teaching that horse the basics will have to be extended, too.

"You know," he adds, almost as a second thought, "most inexperienced horse owners don't realize it, but they're actually training their horses the first time they put their hands on them after they're born. Which is why I tell them no matter how young your colt or filly is, always treat it like it's a big *horse.*"

Many owners, he says, unknowingly ruin their horses by allowing them to develop bad habits that seemed cute when the horses were small but are absolutely intolerable when they weigh half a ton or more. "Whenever a colt does something you think is cute," says Bram, "imagine how that same behavior would seem if he were full-grown. Would you want a sixteen-hand horse to rear and paw at you? To bite you? Of course not. You'd want him to have good manners. But good manners have to be taught from the beginning."

If a colt, for example, is allowed to be frisky with people and isn't made to mind his manners, he grows into maturity believing that he can literally push people around — and get away with it. Obviously, a colt that grows up without learning to respect people is going to be more difficult to train than even a horse that's never been handled before.

"Which is why," says Bram, "I never promise how long it's going to take me to train someone else's horse."

*

What, exactly, is training?

"It's a two-part job," explains Bram. "On the one hand, it involves teaching a horse good habits, like loading into a trailer without trouble. On the other hand, it also entails an even greater challenge — seeing to it that the horse doesn't pick up any *bad* habits along the way. The best trainers are the ones who usually notice the first small signs of a problem developing and are quick — *real* quick — to take corrective measures."

Horses are born, says Bram, without any "habits" at all, either good or bad. In fact, they have no innate sense of right or wrong. They do, however, have a strong sense of self-preservation. "Which means they're primarily interested in their own well-being," says Bram. In the process of basic training, there are many times when horses will feel threatened or uncomfortable. "Like when they don't understand a new lesson," says Bram, "or when they're tired, or when a clumsy rider causes them grief." Consequently, it's natural for them to experiment with tactics that will relieve them of their fear or discomfort. "And if those experiments are successful," Bram says, "then the horse will obviously try them again. And again. That's how a bad habit starts."

Training, then, does not mean taming a horse. "If you tame a horse," says Bram, "all you do is teach him to accept the presence of humans. Just because the horse learns to be gentle doesn't mean he's automatically going to know everything that'll ultimately be expected of him. That's where training takes over. Training means that I teach that same horse to understand, and habitually obey, certain signals. Anybody can tame a spooky colt so that he comes running for a cube of sugar or a carrot when you appear at the pasture fence. Given enough time, that same individual might even be able to convince the colt to allow him to sit on his back without any fuss. But whether that same person can train that colt to work, to do willingly whatever he's asked to do, is another matter altogether."

A trainer's job, then, is first to "explain" to a horse what's expected of him, and then to get the horse to do it. Bram can teach a young horse many things within a relatively brief period of time. He's effective at communicating new ideas quickly during workouts, without subjecting his pupils to undue or prolonged periods of confusion. "If I do confuse them, they quickly get frustrated. If they stay frustrated, they resent me. I can't teach them anything then."

Patience on Bram's part is therefore a must. But an equally

important asset is his ability to see problems developing at their very outset. "The earlier it's recognized," he insists, "the easier it is to solve the problem." For example, Bram was immediately aware when he felt Teaticket deliberately freeze in place for a second before the horse complied with Bram's request to go forward. "I knew he was toying with the idea of balking," he says.

A less experienced rider might not have noticed Teaticket's subtle indiscretion. Bram did, though. He was quick to drive Teaticket forward with convincing authority. "Which meant a sound whack on his hind end," he says. The brief and slight unpleasantness quickly convinced Teaticket that balking at Bram's command to go forward was not a good idea. The horse moved — fast.

"If that particular problem hadn't been dealt with on the spot," Bram says, "Teaticket would have done it again sooner or later. And again, and again. Pretty soon, not only would he not go forward when I asked him, but he might buck or kick or rear when I finally decided to punish him. And why not? How would he know why he was being punished? I'd never treated him harshly before when he balked."

The ability to detect behavior problems early, then, is certainly one of the reasons Bram rarely has to resort to harsh measures when he trains young horses. "Of course," he says, "we trainers aren't perfect, you know. We get into difficulty once in a while. Thing is, we don't blame the horse. We figure out what *we* did wrong or what *we* failed to do, then look for a new approach to teach the horse what we wanted him to learn in the first place."

*

Achilles had been sacked successfully. Bram was certain, because the horse was accepting the grooming of his neck and body with no apparent anxiety. For the rest of his stay, daily grooming by Bram's assistant trainer, Bree Largo, would complete the task of gentling Achilles to a human's touch.

In the meantime, Bram's next responsibility would be to get Achilles to let people handle his legs. This was not a job he'd delegate to Bree until she had been with him a while longer. "Simply because it can be dangerous," Bram had explained to her, "until you've had more experience. Most young horses are a whole lot more than just uneasy at first about someone handling their lower legs. In fact, you'll find them especially nervous when you first try to pick up and hold one of their feet."

"How come?" Bree asked, in between chews of her bubble gum.

"Well," said Bram, "I suppose nature has warned the horse that his legs have to be protected at all times, so he can flee from danger at a moment's notice."

"Think Achilles will give us problems?"

"Maybe," Bram said. He had finished grooming Achilles all over, except for his legs. He had deliberately saved those for last. He wouldn't attempt to pick up the colt's feet until he willingly accepted his lower legs being groomed with the soft-bristled body brush.

"Watch me, now," Bram told Bree. Starting up high, near the horse's shoulder, and working his way down the horse's leg, Bram rubbed with smooth, sure strokes. It would not be necessary for him to get all the way down Achilles's leg today — or tomorrow — or even the next day. Bram would grant Achilles all the time he needed.

When the brush edged below the horse's knee for the first time, the colt jerked his foot off the ground as a warning for Bram to proceed no further. The trainer instantly glided the brush higher, but he didn't stop brushing altogether. When Achilles relaxed and put his foot down, Bram inched the brush down the leg again until he reached the knee. Then he quit and started the other foreleg. Achilles's reaction was the same there, too — jerking his foot up the instant Bram's brush licked his knee.

When Bram began working on a hind leg, he stood close alongside Achilles's hip, facing rearward as a farrier would. "It's dangerous," he explained to Bree, "and less than smart to face the horse from two feet directly behind him, stretch to reach his leg, and then brush it. I'd be a perfect target. If Achilles acted up, I'd have no choice but to jump back. What do you suppose he'd learn from that?"

Bree blew a good-sized bubble as she thought for a moment. "I know," she said. "That kicking people is a good way to keep them from bothering him."

"Very good," said Bram. "You're learning."

It was five days before Achilles would stand quietly for complete brushing of his legs. Once that was accomplished, however, Bram promoted the colt to "third grade," where he'd learn to lift his feet for Bram — or anyone else. Again, there would be no hurry. Achilles might spend two days or two weeks in this third phase. It was his choice.

He chose four days. Bram started the new lesson with a foreleg again, standing beside Achilles's shoulder and facing rearward. First, he gently ran his strong hands down behind the horse's leg to a point midway along the *cannon bone* (the long leg bone that connects the knee with the "ankle," or *fetlock*). With his thumb and forefinger, Bram pinched the back tendon. It was a sensation Achilles had never felt before. His leg lifted instantly. With his free hand, Bram cradled the raised hoof for just one moment, and then released it before Achilles snatched it away.

Bram then stood upright and stroked the horse's shoulder, all the while praising his well-behaved pupil. After repeating the brief lesson with the other foreleg, Bram declared that school was over for another day.

The following afternoon, he repeated the lesson with the forelegs, and this time applied it to the hind legs as well. The first hind leg presented no problem. With the second, however, Achilles let go with a heavyweight hoof-punch. Being a patient man, Bram was willing to make a few allowances for the fact that it is normal for a young horse to try kicking once or twice during early handling of his legs.

But when the kicking continued after Bram's fourth attempt at cradling the second hind foot, Bram was convinced that the misbehavior was deliberate. It would have to be stopped — with punishment.

Bree handed Bram the riding crop he requested. Again the trainer stood close alongside Achilles's hip and faced rearward. He ran his hand down behind the horse's knee, and when he reached the midway point of the cannon — before he could even pinch the tendon to try to raise Achilles's foot — the horse let loose once again. At that very instant, Bram struck the misbehaving colt sharply with the crop, just above the *hock* (the "elbow" of the hind leg). The blow was swift, like a bee's sting. Achilles swung his hind end away from the discomfort. He was wild-eyed and just a bit breathless at the unexpected result of his kick.

Bram waited until Achilles was again composed and then stroked him on the shoulder and spoke softly to him. "I want him to realize," he explained to Bree, "that I'm not angry with *him,* but with his kicking." Once the horse had relaxed, Bram repeated the procedure. Again Achilles kicked. Again Bram punished him with a quick sting. Again Bram began the lesson. On the third try, Achilles lifted his foot without further ado. He had learned.

*

Having learned during the span of two weeks to be gentle, Achilles was now ready to be promoted again.

Bram had devised a curriculum for the young horse. The subjects? Learning to be agreeable about being caught . . . to stand quietly when tethered for long periods . . . to behave well during clipping . . . not to be afraid of being sprayed and bathed . . . to lead correctly at halter.

For the first six weeks, then, Bram had concerned himself

with teaching the colt to allow himself to be handled for a variety of reasons. But he had not asked Achilles to do any work. Now that the horse had been promoted to the next level, the subjects would be much tougher. Achilles would now learn to be *longed* (pronounced "lunged").

In longeing, the colt would learn to respond to voice commands to perform certain maneuvers — stop, go, turn — for as long as Bram required. Longeing would lay the foundation for later work under saddle. On the first day of the seventh week with Achilles, Bram assembled his longeing equipment with some ceremony. First, he fitted Achilles with a leather halter that had metal rings attached where the cheekpieces joined the noseband. He snapped the longe line, a twenty-five-foot-long rope, to the left side of the noseband, rather than under the jaw. Then he brought out his longeing whip. Its black handle was five feet long, and its black lash an additional eight feet. It was the kind of whip you might see a lion tamer use.

Before the session commenced, Bram spent a few minutes acquainting Achilles with the whip. He showed it to him, rubbed him with it, and moved it about as if he were sacking him again. The whip would be an indispensable aid in longeing the horse. In effect, it would be an extension of Bram's arm. It would be used to help guide the horse, to urge him forward, and to stop him. The objective in the first longeing session would be to teach Achilles to move in a circle around Bram and to respond to voice commands to walk and halt. For this purpose, Bram escorted Achilles to the round pen.

He would have the horse move around him to the left first. He held the longe line in his left hand and the whip in his right, its lash trailing on the ground behind him. His biggest problem at the outset would be to make clear to Achilles what he must do.

Bram positioned Achilles facing in the direction in which he was to go, and then he moved to the center of the round pen. "Walk!" Bram shouted. As he gave the command, he extended the whip horizontally and lightly flicked the lash against Achilles's heels. The horse didn't budge. He simply turned his head to face Bram, as if to ask, "What am I supposed to do?" It was up to Bram to make his instructions more clear, since his pupil didn't understand the original command.

Bram shortened the longe line until he was within arm's length of the horse and stood facing Achilles's neck. Then, with his left arm held out to his left as a leading hand, Bram encouraged Achilles to move forward by shouting "Walk!" and moving with him. The horse began walking in the imaginary circle. Bram was sidestepping alongside, touching Achilles's hindquarters with the whip every few feet to keep the horse moving. As Achilles began to walk steadily, Bram gradually dropped back to the center of the pen, lengthening the longe line as he went. The horse quickly learned to maintain a true circle, staying as far from his trainer as the longe line permitted. In ten minutes, the lesson was concluded.

Bram knew immediately when his pupil had reached the limit of the physical work he could perform. The horse's body had become warm to the touch and slightly moist with sweat, so school was ended for the day. Bram was satisfied, though, because Achilles had now learned to move around him in a true circle — quite an accomplishment in just ten minutes.

Within four weeks, Achilles would learn to go forward, turn, and halt in response to voice commands. Furthermore, Bram would teach him, by a procedure known as *line driving,* to go anywhere, over anything, with little or no hesitation. During this part of the basic training, Achilles was still riderless. Bram continued to educate the young horse from the ground. After weeks of line-driving lessons, however, Bram promoted the horse once again. He would learn to be saddled and ridden for the first time.

*

A young horse being *broken* to ride needs all the help he can get. He won't get any of that help, though, from a beginning rider — who is, of necessity, primarily concerned with his own problems. The inexperienced rider usually tenses when trouble occurs, in natural fear for his own safety. That tenseness is upsetting to a young horse just learning the ropes himself.

"A trainer should be able to ride well enough," says Bram, "to stay physically relaxed and supple when he's in trouble on a horse. He can get away with being tense mentally if he doesn't let the horse feel it."

As part of his own education, then, the aspiring trainer who has little or no experience in riding should take lessons on horses already trained. "Go to the best riding instructor or school you can find," Bram advises. "It's a vital part of any trainer's education. It'll help you cultivate good habits with horses which will, in the long run, hasten your trainer's education. Self-assurance in riding gives any trainer a tremendous advantage in schooling horses. It makes his job a heck of a lot easier, because most training beyond the basic stage is done right from the horse's back. If you aren't comfortable and knowledgeable up there, you can't possibly be a good trainer. In other words, you can't be afraid of horses if you want to make a living at training them."

Anyone who wants to be a trainer must also, according to Bram, be able to accept the fact that a horse will not generously and diligently cooperate in learning his lessons solely out of affection for the trainer. Therefore, the horse must be taught discipline. A horse that has had little or no handling has absolutely no concept of the idea of pleasing or not pleasing his trainer — or anyone, for that matter. He is interested only in his own welfare and will, therefore, do what he thinks best for himself. He must learn that his own welfare is best served by trying to do whatever the trainer wants him to do.

*

A trainer who corrals an untamed young horse, throws a saddle on his back, and then climbs aboard is asking for trouble in the form of a bucking spree. That may prove he has nerve, says Bram, but it doesn't prove he is a horseman.

"Even if he's a good rider, he's exposing himself and the horse to a high risk of serious injury, because the horse will be frightened into a violent reaction and then may lose his footing or crash into a fence."

And, adds Bram, such a trainer takes the chance of allowing the horse to develop serious behavior problems. Whenever a young horse is alarmed into violence, there's always the chance that he will accidentally discover some means of dislodging his rider. If he does make such a discovery, the stage is then set for a terribly bad habit. The discovery may or may not involve bucking, because young, untrained saddle horses are not at all like rodeo broncs that can be depended upon to do nothing but jump up and down. A frightened colt may bolt, or he may rear or whirl wildly or even start backward and fall, before it occurs to him to try bucking.

The point is that any specific act that wins him relief — that is, that throws the rider — is sure to be repeated in the future. Even though later attempts to use the trick may not be as successful, the horse will cling to the memory of that initial experience, which is why the good trainers like Bram Twain try to remove the risks in horsebreaking well before the day they first mount their horses. They take time to handle the young horses before riding them, in order to allay the horses' instinctive fears and win their confidence and trust.

"Some of my clients find it hard to understand," says Bram, "why it takes three, four, or six months to break their horses. The reason's simple. I want to avoid a violent conflict with a horse being ridden for the very first time. Sometimes it takes a lot of weeks of learning ground manners before the horse trusts me enough. But in the long run, it's really the best thing for the horse."

It's easy to understand why it can be frightening to a young horse that is unaccustomed to human handling to be ridden for the first time. In a wild state, a horse can meet a threat from the ground, if necessary, by biting, striking, kicking, and trampling. But he is defenseless against an enemy on his back. If a beast of prey leaps on him from above, the horse's only chance for survival is to react with sufficient violence to dislodge the attacker. Small wonder that the horse will not accept a human rider calmly, *unless* he is conditioned beforehand to trust the rider.

Before putting a saddle on Achilles's back for the first time, Bram prepared him for the feeling of the *girth* — the broad strap attached to the saddle which, when strapped under the horse, keeps the saddle in place — by longeing Achilles with a *surcingle,* which serves as a girth, except that it's not attached to a saddle. It looks like an extra-big belt.

Bram fitted the surcingle on Achilles and drew it in just snug enough to hold it in place. After longeing the horse briefly to get him used to the idea of moving with a surcingle around his midsection, Bram then drew the strap a little tighter and longed him again.

After a few minutes, Bram removed the surcingle and spent a while reacquainting Achilles with the saddle blanket from his early sacking days. He rubbed him with it and rustled it over his back. Then he put the blanket on Achilles and quickly removed it, repeating this procedure several times. Achilles had no fear of it.

Next, even though he expected the horse to accept the saddle on his back just as calmly, Bram had Bree Largo hold the halter rope. If anything did startle the colt, Bram would need both hands free to handle the saddle. Allowing it to slip and fall off the colt when he suddenly moved would only make him saddle-shy.

Having folded the offside (right-side) stirrup back over the seat, Bram lifted the saddle onto Achilles's back in a gentle but confident manner. He took care not to allow the saddle to jar the horse, and he held the girth so that Achilles wouldn't be struck by a flying cinch buckle. Once the saddle was on Achilles's back, Bram lowered the stirrup to its proper place.

He kept his hands on the saddle, to prevent it from falling off, and rocked and jostled it a little to show Achilles it was harmless. The horse remained calm. Bram removed the saddle.

As he had done with the saddle blanket, Bram put the saddle on and took it off several times, giving Achilles a brief rest between times. Even though the horse was relaxed, Bram insisted on this step.

"When you introduce something new to a horse," he explained to Bree, "the horse worries about the possibility that you're building up to something that might hurt him. By repetitively putting the saddle on and taking it off, I'm reassuring him that nothing dangerous is going to happen."

The next step was for Bram to put the saddle on — *and* secure the girth, which would have to be drawn tight enough to keep the saddle in place, but not so tight that it would frighten the animal. The very second Bram secured the girth, he took the halter rope from Bree, attached the longe line to the halter, and began to lead the colt . . .

And then Achilles turned it on. He bucked . . . and bucked . . . and bucked some more. Bram played out the twenty-five-foot longe line and let the youngster buck his heart out, like a hugh marlin on the end of a fishing line, dancing above the ocean. After a tremendously long and tiring series of attempts, Achilles realized that he couldn't rid himself of the saddle, and he quit trying. Bram led him again. The pair took a long, leisurely stroll together, because Achilles was hot from the intense bucking spree and needed cooling off.

Before returning the horse to his stall and dismissing school for the day, Bram gave Achilles another light longeing lesson with the saddle still secure on his back. This time, there was no bucking. The youngster was simply too exhausted.

For three more days Bram continued to longe Achilles with the saddle on his back. Then it was time for him to introduce the horse to something else — a bit.

*

The primary goal in the basic training of a young horse under saddle, according to Bram, is to teach the horse to carry a rider and to respond obediently and calmly to signals to move at various gaits. When that stage of training is reached, Bram needs a means of turning, slowing, and halting the horse when he is on the horse's back. Thus, he needed to accustom the horse to a bit and bridle before he could hope to ride him. These were introduced to Achilles in two stages.

First, Bram inserted his thumb into the corner of Achilles's mouth and pressed the thumb downward on the bar of the jaw. The mouth opened instantly. He slipped the bit into place and put the crownpiece of the bridle over and behind the ears.

In this first stage of getting Achilles acquainted with the bit, Bram simply had the horse wear the gear for an hour or so daily in his stall. Initially the horse was somewhat puzzled by the presence of the steel in his mouth. In the beginning he chewed on it, trying to work it out of his mouth. By the fourth day, though, he ceased to worry about it. In the meantime the bridle never bothered him, because he had been wearing a halter for a couple of years.

When he was accustomed to the new oral sensations of the bit, the second-stage introduction — getting him used to the reason for the bit — began with Bram's line-driving Achilles from the ground. All work was at a walk, and during the first few sessions the turns and halts were gradual. Bram always forewarned Achilles of a halt, for example, by using a voice command before he pulled on the lines. His objective was to induce the horse to halt voluntarily, in response to a light signal from the reins. He never pulled the horse to a halt. Achilles's mouth was still tender and the bit could hurt him.

The first time Bram tried to stop Achilles, the youngster became frightened by the new sensation in his mouth. It didn't even occur to him that he was supposed to halt when he felt the steel tug on him. Bram didn't fight the horse. He relaxed the lines and let Achilles go on a few more steps. Then, he repeated the voice command (*"Whoa!"*) and the signal (a slight squeezing of the lines). He repeated the process four more times before Achilles realized he had nothing to fear from the sensation in his mouth. Soon, he was reducing his pace as soon as he felt the resistance in the lines.

Bram repeated the exercise for eight consecutive days. When he was certain Achilles had learned what he was supposed to learn, Bram was ready to mount the horse himself. It would be the first time anyone had ever done so.

The question was, how would Achilles react? Would the weeks and weeks of patience that Bram had demonstrated finally pay off for him?

*

The big day had arrived.

It was a particularly pleasant day. There was hardly a distracting breeze in the air, and the temperature was just high enough to make Achilles less than energetic.

Bram saddled and bridled the horse and gave him a settling-down workout on the longe line — just in case. Then Bree was summoned to hold Achilles. She would be a steadying influence, since the horse was accustomed to being controlled from the ground, not from his back.

After Bram checked to see that the girth was secure, all was ready. First he acquainted Achilles with the feeling of weight in the left stirrup by pressing down on it with the heel of his hand. Achilles stood still. Good, Bram thought.

Then Bram placed the toe of his foot in the stirrup and pressed down again — but only for a second. He removed his foot and brushed Achilles's mane for a minute or two. He then returned to the stirrup, put his toe in, and sprang gently up and down a few times, just high enough to allow the stirrup to catch a little weight. Another brief rest period followed, to reassure Achilles that Bram's intentions were harmless. So far, great, thought Bram. He smiled at Bree. She smiled back.

Bram repeated the stirrup procedure several more times. As soon as Achilles showed no concern at all when Bram sprang in and out of the stirrup, he went a little further. Facing the saddle — and taking great care not to dig his toe into Achilles's side — Bram stepped upward, smoothly and easily, and leaned his weight across the saddle. He was ready to kick his toe out of the stirrup and slide down if anything went wrong, because he was in no position to try to stay on the horse's back at that point. He was like a sack of potatoes slung over the saddle. After thirty seconds or so, he gave Achilles a pat and then slipped off the horse's back. Another rest period followed.

When Achilles seemed to accept Bram's weight across the saddle without demonstrating any fear of the new sensation, Bram made the decision to mount him. He kept his body low, bending over sharply in the saddle. He straightened up gradually, patting Achilles and talking to him. Sitting easily, he did not grip with his legs. In less than a minute, he bent forward again and quietly dismounted.

For four more days Bram practiced mounting and dismounting with Achilles. He was always certain to longe the horse first. "It eliminates his surplus energy," he told Bree, who would continue to hold Achilles with a halter rope during these training sessions. Gradually, Bram stayed for minutes at a time in the saddle.

On the fifth day, when Achilles was obviously accustomed to the mounting and dismounting, Bram started being deliberately "careless." He would allow his leg to brush across Achilles's hindquarters when he mounted, or rock around in the saddle and then lean over to dust a speck off one boot and then the other. He'd reach forward and scratch the horse's ears, or rub his legs along Achilles's side. He even practiced mounting and dismounting from the right side. "He's got to learn," Bram said, "not to be startled by unexpected gestures."

By the week's end, Bram was confident that Achilles was finally ready — not only to be mounted, but to be ridden, to be moved forward with a person on his back.

*

The sensation of carrying a living burden would feel strange to Achilles. And it would feel different to the horse at each of his *gaits,* too. Moreover, Achilles probably would get a little excited by his own fast gaits. Therefore, Bram explained to Bree, he would get Achilles accustomed to carrying a rider at a walk before he'd ask the horse to *trot,* and at a trot before he'd ask the horse to *canter.* More than likely, Bram figured he'd need to ride him at a walk for at least a week before Achilles would be able to trot.

Bram chose the small, enclosed paddock for the first riding lesson, so that Achilles wouldn't be tempted to try a brisk gallop before Bram's control was established.

At such an early stage of riding Achilles, Bram had no thought of punishing the horse for any erratic behavior. "Makes no sense to punish him for doing something wrong," he said, "when he doesn't even know what's right." He did, however, carry a riding crop — not as an instrument for punishment of misbehavior, but as an aid in conditioning the horse to go forward in response to a light squeeze of his legs. He carried the crop in his right hand, with the butt of the handle pointed approximately toward Achilles's left ear. The crop itself rested across Bram's thigh. He used it occasionally to reinforce signals from his legs.

Once in a while, Achilles failed to respond promptly to Bram's leg signals to go forward. When that happened, Bram did not increase the pressure from his legs, nor did he kick Achilles. Instead, he reached far back and tapped the horse on the rump, to help him understand that squeezing by the rider's legs meant the horse should go forward. Achilles got the idea quickly, too, because it was natural for him to want to escape the little attack from behind.

Within a week, Achilles was agreeable to going forward at a walk, turning, halting, and standing quietly. The next step was to teach him to carry Bram quietly and steadily at a trot — a slow jog. The up-and-down movement of Bram on his back at that gait would feel strange to Achilles at first. The new sensation, together with his own increase in speed, would probably excite the young horse. Bram's job, then, would be to try to minimize that excitement. "The best thing I can do," he told Bree, "is to let it seem like it just happens."

Instead of urging Achilles to lurch from a walk into a trot, Bram asked him to walk faster and faster, until the horse slipped into a slow jog by his own volition. At first, he trotted just a few steps, then dropped back to a walk. Bram didn't press him back into a trot immediately. Ceasing the demand was a reward for Achilles. After a while, though, Bram did ask him to trot again. Achilles remained calm, trotting for a short distance and then walking again. The first trotting lesson was concluded at that point.

During the second lesson, the next day, Bram asked Achilles to maintain the slow jog for longer distances. After three days, Achilles was taken out of the enclosed paddock for this work. He would now be educated in the large round pen.

Bram's next objective was to teach Achilles to maintain a steady rate of speed. He would have to find a rate that seemed natural and easy for Achilles. If he tried to make the horse trot too slowly, he'd have to get after him constantly to maintain the rate; that kind of nagging annoyance would only cause Achilles to start fighting Bram eventually.

Actually, though, Bram wasn't so concerned that Achilles might go too slowly as he was with preventing the horse from going too fast. "He might have a tendency to trot faster and faster until he breaks into a canter," said Bram.

"How fast is too fast?" Bree asked him.

"When he nears the breaking point of his gait," Bram said, "he'll become noticeably anxious."

"Like how?"

"His breathing will quicken and his stride will get hasty and uneven. My job will be to recognize those symptoms and control his pace so that he stays just below that level."

To control Achilles's rate of speed, Bram used turning movements rather than pulling back on the reins. He put the horse through *schooling figures,* riding him in circles, half-circles, and figure eights. The figures were large enough to be easy on Achilles, but tight enough to slow his pace. Whenever his trot quickened, Bram would ride him in the school figures. Over a period of four days, Achilles eventually learned to lock in to a steady rate of speed. He had learned to trot. His next lesson would be to learn how to canter.

To minimize Achilles's initial excitement in starting to canter for the first time, Bram waited until the end of a trotting session to ask for the faster gait, so that Achilles would not have a surplus of energy to expend.

As he did when he taught the horse to trot, Bram let the canter just happen. He eased Achilles into a faster and faster trot until the horse literally rolled into a canter. Achilles was a bit surprised at his new gait, but not frightened. He cantered only a few strides and quickly dropped back to a trot. Bram let him continue trotting for a while, making certain the horse was calm before asking him to canter once again.

The second time, Achilles held the gait much longer. Bram was quick to show his pupil he was pleased with him by ceasing work for the day.

In less than four weeks, Achilles had learned to walk, trot, and canter with a human on his back — something he'd never experienced before in his brief life. He was now ready for the final phase in his basic training: cross-country riding. There would be no better or more pleasant way to confirm those lessons than by taking Achilles on excursions across various kinds of terrain.

Within a few days, Bram would begin to see results. Achilles, he was certain, would accept riding as a matter of routine. It would be, perhaps, the most enjoyable part of the horse's education. Achilles would undertake his final lessons in the spirit of adventure as Bram showed him streams and bridges to cross, hills and valleys to explore. Perhaps the best thing about the final experiences would be the growing sense of partnership Bram and Achilles would foster, for it would be in the cross-country work that the young horse would learn to put all his faith in his rider.

By that time, although Achilles would not yet have been schooled in any specialties that required him to move like an athlete, he would be a pleasure to ride and handle — precisely what trainer Bram Twain had set out to accomplish.

TEN

Other Career Options

ALTHOUGH THE PREVIOUS NINE chapters have dealt with perhaps the most popular of the career possibilities for horse lovers, there are many other opportunities available — either working directly with horses, or working in a capacity that relates to or affects horses. This chapter outlines some of those career opportunities. It is by no means, however, intended to be an all-inclusive list.

The information on earnings given here is based on a 1977 survey of the horse industry by the American Horse Council.

I. The employment opportunities listed in this section involve either semiskilled or skilled work. These jobs are usually available to those with no formal education beyond the high school level.

Job Title	Duties	Average Annual Earnings
Paddock Judge	Supervises activities in the paddock area of a racetrack.	$13,100
Patrol Judge	Watches races from a tower to detect fouls.	$15,100
Race Starter	Supervises the loading of horses into the starting gate and then starts the race.	$17,400
Tack Salesman (Wholesale)	Sells tack to retailers and to professional horsemen.	$18,800

Photo by David O. Aronson

Job Title	Duties	Average Annual Earnings
Feed Salesman (Wholesale)	Sells feed to racetracks, horse shows, and/or feed stores.	$17,200
Horse Identifier	Confirms identification of horses in racetrack paddock area before a race.	$15,000
Packer/Guide	Leads trail rides into recreational areas, usually mountains.	$16,100
Announcer	Announces races or horse shows either over the PA system at the events or on TV or radio.	$13,100
Horse Show Secretary	In charge of entries, stall assignments, payment of fees, etc.	$ 9,300
Feed Store Manager	Operates retail feed store.	$16,600
Harness Driver	Drives horses in harness races.	$25,300
Horse Show Judge	Judges various horse show classes.	$ 7,700
Horse Show Steward	Enforces the rules at the show.	$ 8,000
Saddle Maker	Makes and repairs saddles, tack, and other leather goods.	$16,100
Harness Maker	Makes harness equipment and repairs leather goods.	$14,300
Veterinarian's Assistant	Helps vet in nontechnical aspects of his job.	$ 9,800
Horse Buyer	Buys horses for clients.	$12,800

II. The employment opportunities listed in this section are usually available to those with a high school diploma and at least one additional year of specialized training at either a college, a vocational school, or a specialty school.

Job Title	Duties	Average Annual Earnings
Lab Technician	Performs various laboratory tests such as blood analysis.	$14,300
Commercial Artist	Prepares artwork for advertisements, magazines, etc.	$16,900
Veterinary Technician	Aids vet in the technical aspects of his job.	$10,300
Transportation Specialist	Transports horses by van across country.	$19,000

III. The employment opportunities listed in this section are usually available to those who hold an associate's degree from a college or have had two years of vocational school or specialty school training beyond high school.

Job Title	Duties	Average Annual Earnings
Horse Show Manager	Manages the show and supervises all personnel.	$11,800
Teacher	Teaches equine science and agricultural courses in a vocational school.	$14,600
Artificial Inseminator	Under the direction of a vet, performs artificial insemination of mares.	$16,000

IV. The employment opportunities in this section are usually available to those with a baccalaureate degree from a college or a university.

Job Title	Duties	Average Annual Earnings
Racing Secretary	Arranges racing and stabling activities at a racetrack.	$25,000
Handicapper	Determines the weight that horses will carry in handicap races.	$24,700
Director of Public Relations	Supervises the public relations staff at a racetrack.	$28,500
Bloodstock Agent	Buys and/or sells horses for others; arranges breeding contracts; etc.	$19,900
Rehabilitation Specialist	Under direction of a vet, operates equipment (e.g., hydrotherapy) to benefit ill or injured horses.	$20,000
Editor	In charge of all editorial content in a magazine.	$22,600

V. The employment opportunities listed in this section are usually available to those with at least a master's degree from a college or a university.

Job Title	Duties	Average Annual Earnings
Racing Chemist	At a racetrack or a horse show, analyzes blood, urine, and saliva samples to determine if a horse has been illegally drugged.	$22,700
Trail Engineer	Designs and supervises the construction of riding trails.	$23,500
Agricultural Researcher	Performs various kinds of agricultural research (e.g., in genetics or nutrition).	$27,500
College Professor	Teaches horse science and other agricultural courses.	$23,100
Architect	Designs stable buildings, racetracks, horse show arenas, etc., and supervises construction.	$23,500
Pedigree Analyst	Analyzes horse pedigrees to determine the advisability of breeding mares to particular stallions.	$20,000

VI. The employment opportunities listed in this section are usually available to those holding a Ph.D. or professional degree (e.g., "DVM" — Doctor of Veterinary Medicine) from a university.

Job Title	Duties	Average Annual Earnings
Extension Horse Specialist	Employed by the state, advises and instructs on horse matters within and occasionally outside the state.	$24,800
Geneticist	Performs research on horse genetics; often teaches the subject at the college level.	$22,400
Horse Feed Developer	Tests various kinds of feed; observes the horses fed this feed and makes recommendations to the manufacturer; etc.	$22,700
Animal Nutritionist	Performs nutrition research; often teaches courses and delivers public lectures on horse nutrition.	$25,100

VII. For further information about some of the careers presented here, you should write directly to the following organizations and associations.

Racing

Paddock Judge
Patrol Judge
Race Starter
Horse Identifier
Racing Secretary
Handicapper

Thoroughbred Racing Association
5 Dakota Drive
New Hyde Park, NY 11040

Harness Driver

U.S. Trotting Association
750 Michigan Avenue
Columbus, OH 43215

Horse Shows

Judge
Steward
Manager
Secretary

American Horse Shows Association
598 Madison Avenue
New York, NY 10022

Specialists

Extension Specialist

National 4–H Service Committee
150 North Wacker Drive
Chicago, IL 60605

Racing Chemist

Association of Official Racing
    Chemists
148–07 Hillside Avenue
Jamaica, NY 11435

Merchandising

Tack Salesman
Tack Shop Manager
Saddle Maker
Harness Maker

Western Apparel and Equipment
    Manufacturers Association
415 East 85th Avenue
Denver, CO 80216

Western/English Retailers of
    America
390 National Press Building
Washington, D.C. 20045

Western and English
    Manufacturers Association
789 Sherman Street, Suite 380
Denver, CO 80203

Merchandising

Feed Salesman

Feed Store Manager

Future Farmers of America

National FFA Center

Box 15160

Alexandria, VA 22309

Miscellaneous

Pedigree Analyst

See the breed associations listed in Appendix IV.

Trail Engineer

National Trails Council

7120 Ridge Road

Frederick, MD 21701

Packer/Guide

Trail Riders Association International Ltd.

Route 2, Box 443A

Cornelius, OR 97113

Many of the career opportunities discussed in this book involve going into business on your own — being "self-employed," in other words. Self-employment involves not only knowing about horses and, say, teaching riding, but it also involves knowing about how to run a business.

To help you get your business started, the federal government has published *Starting and Managing a Small Business of Your Own,* a 95-page comprehensive guide to financing and managing a business, any kind of business. The principles in the book apply to a business of training horses as well as of making pottery. The book explores such topics as how to establish a business, tax and insurance information, recordkeeping, and other key aspects of self-employment. It also includes a checklist for starting your own business.

To obtain a copy of the book, send a check or money order for $3.50 to: Superintendent of Documents, Washington, D.C. 20402. Allow six weeks for delivery.

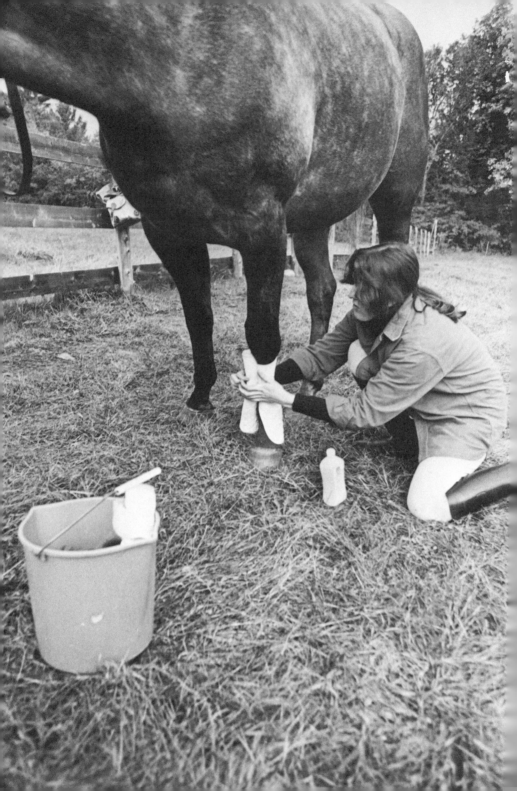

ELEVEN

How to Get Experience Working with Horses

THE FIRST THING DAR DeMORGAN had to do was find out who owned horses in his immediate area. His mother had suggested the Yellow Pages of the telephone directory. Dar decided he'd take her advice, although he was apprehensive about going to a public stable to get his initial experience working with horses. He figured that the public stables would be less likely to be short of help, and therefore less likely to let a kid onto the premises even if he was willing to volunteer his services. Anyway, he'd try his mother's technique.

"The Yellow Pages," Mrs. DeMorgan reminded him, "list all the businesses in the community alphabetically, by categories." She opened to the middle of the directory as she spoke. "See," she said. "All the hairdressers are listed together." She turned a chunk of pages. "All the shoe stores are ——"

"I get it, ma," said Dar. "I get it already. That means all the stables around here will be listed on one page, too. Right?"

"Should be. Let's see," said Mrs. DeMorgan, thumbing through the pages rapidly.

"There it is!" said Dar, slapping his hand on top of his mother's as she was about to turn the page. "One, two, three of them!"

Photo by David O. Aronson

"You'd think there'd be more than that under the *Stables* category, wouldn't you?"

Her words went unnoticed by Dar. His tongue poking out the side of his mouth as it always did when he wrote, he diligently recorded the names, addresses, and telephone numbers of the three stables into his notebook.

"There'll probably be some others listed under another category," said Mrs. DeMorgan. "Why don't you look under *Horses?*"

Dar did. There was nothing.

Mrs. DeMorgan suggested that he look for a category entitled *Stables.* It was a good suggestion, because Dar found a listing there.

"Now try *Riding Lessons,*" his mother advised.

Dar did. There was no such listing, but under *Riding Academies,* he discovered six more stables. He recorded all seven of the new listings into his notebook, with the other three.

His mother had secured for him a street map of their county. Working from his list of ten stables, Dar located each on the map. He quickly realized that four of the stables would be relatively easy for him to get to, either by bicycle or by public transportation. The other six would necessitate his getting dropped off and picked up by one of his parents, so he eliminated those stables from his immediate consideration.

Four stables to call on didn't seem like a whole lot to Dar. Mrs. DeMorgan suggested that he call one of the tack shops they had seen listed in the Yellow Pages under *Riding Apparel and Equipment.* "If those places sell equipment like saddles and whatnot," Mrs. DeMorgan theorized, "they might be able to tell you of some private stables around here, too." She was right. There would be three times as many private stables in the area as public facilities — private farms, ranches, and stables not listed in the Yellow Pages, but still places where horses were quartered, raised, and cared for. Which meant there was work to be done for which Dar could volunteer, and thereby gain experience working with horses.

Mrs. DeMorgan agreed with her son that he should probably try out the privately owned places first, since they were more likely to be short on help. "And have less money coming in to pay for it anyway," she told him. "They might relish the idea of getting a hard worker for free — even if he doesn't know *cannon bones* from *withers*," she said, smiling and playfully punching Dar in the arm.

"How do you know about cannon bones and withers?" Dar asked, somewhat surprised at his mother's equine vocabulary.

"Oh," she said, still smiling, "I get around, you know."

"I guess," said Dar, tossing his notebook on the coffee table. "Now what?"

His mother again suggested that he try calling the tack shop in the next town.

Dar told her he would pursue that course of action only if push came to shove. He didn't want to resort to that tactic because he wasn't sure that the tack shop's proprietor would feel good about giving out the names and addresses of his customers to a complete stranger, even if his story sounded legitimate.

"I think you're being a bit negative," said his mother. "I think the tack shop would be perfectly willing to help you out."

Dar was stubborn, though. He insisted that he had a better idea that he wanted to try first. His business teacher — with whom Dar frequently discussed his horse fantasies, since Mr. Kennerly himself was most interested in horses, albeit the kind that carry little people wearing silks and win money for their fanciers — had previously advised Dar to check out his town hall.

"A lot of local governments," Mr. Kennerly had told Dar, "tax people who own horses. Which means they're likely to keep records of where those horses are stabled."

Recalling Mr. Kennerly's remarks, Dar had already decided what his next move would be.

"Be back by five, please!" shouted Mrs. DeMorgan. Her

announcement was too late. Dar was already out the door and halfway down the driveway.

*

"Do you tax horses?"

The tall, fiftyish gentleman to whom the question was addressed put down his pencil and tilted his nearly bald head downward, so that he could peer over his half-moon spectacles at the young visitor who had just walked into his office. "I beg your pardon, young man?"

"I said, do you tax horses?"

"That seems like a rather strange question, doesn't it? Especially coming from someone your age. You shouldn't have to be worrying about taxes for several years yet, at least."

"You're right, sir." Dar folded his hands on the counter top that separated him from the tax collector. "I'm working on a summer project," he continued. "I'm trying to locate places where horses are stabled around here. My business teacher told me that this office probably collects taxes on horses, and so maybe you'd have the addresses of all the private stables around here."

The tax collector got up from his desk and moved slowly toward the counter. "Well, young man. I s'pose I could make up a list like that for you. 'Course, that means extra work for me, you know. Might take me a couple days or more, dependin' on how busy it gets around here. Don't keep records like that at my fingertips, you understand." He took a handkerchief from his pocket, removed his spectacles, and began wiping them clean. "What's your teacher's name?"

"Mr. Kennerly. Know him?"

"Beard and glasses?" asked the tax collector, wiping the second lens.

"Yes, sir."

"I know 'im, all right. Good man, that Mr. Kennerly." The tax collector put his spectacles back on and then stared at Dar for just a moment. "Come back tomorrow," he said. "I'll have that list for you."

"Thanks an awful lot, mister!" said Dar. He shook the tax collector's freckled hand.

"What's your name, son?"

"Dar. DeMorgan."

The tax collector bowed. "Glad to make your acquaintance. What did you say you wanted this list for?" He leaned down onto the counter top and toward Dar, as if the boy was about to impart some tremendous secret.

"Well, sir, it's like this. I've been sorta fascinated by horses all my life, but I've never really been around them much. A few rides here and there at summer camps. That's all."

"I see," said the tax collector. "But those few times you speak of were just enough to hook you. Right?"

"Yes, sir."

"So now you want to find out if you really like horses well enough to want to work with 'em. Right?"

"Yes, sir."

"You're a smart young man, Dar. I like your attitude. Be here at ten tomorrow morning. That list'll be ready and waitin' for you." He shook Dar's hand, again.

"Thanks a lot, Mr. —?"

"Kennerly." The tax collector smiled. And then he laughed a loud belly laugh.

"Are you related to my teacher?"

"You might say so," replied the tax collector. "He's my son."

*

As promised, the tax collector supplied the names and addresses of all the privately owned stables in and around town — twenty-two in all. Dar circled their locations with a red pen on his map of the county and then recorded the names and addresses of the stables next to their circles. Five of them were close enough for him to get to on his own. In all, he now had nine stables to call on out of the thirty-two public and private stables located in his county. That was plenty, he was sure.

"What's your next step, Dar?" his father asked.

"Go visit every one of them until somebody lets me go to work for him."

"Do you have any idea what you're up against, son?"

"What do you mean?"

"I mean," said his father, sighing pleasant-smelling pipe-tobacco clouds from his mouth as he spoke, "that there are a lot of kids older than you trying to get jobs at stables. Some of them have probably gone to special schools to learn about horses, or have worked with horses before. Don't you think they'd be more apt to be hired before you?"

"Sure, dad." Dar's matter-of-factness surprised his father. Mr. DeMorgan had expected an argument. "But I won't be looking for a job. I'm going to volunteer my services."

Mr. DeMorgan was obviously puzzled. "Why," he asked, "do you want to work for free? No red-blooded American boy I know of ever wanted to work . . . for *free!*" Dar knew his father was interested in his decision — really interested — because Mr. DeMorgan had stopped reading the evening paper for the first time since their discussion began.

"I know what I'm doing, dad. Look. Without any experience behind me, nobody will hire me. Right?"

His father nodded.

"Okay. If nobody will hire me, I can't get any experience. Right?"

His father nodded.

"Okay. So how do I get the experience needed so somebody will hire me, if he won't hire me in the first place because I have no experience?" Dar paused. "In a *roundabout* way!" he exclaimed. "First I'll just get my foot in the door by offering to do whatever's got to be done."

"For free?"

"For free."

Mr. DeMorgan sat way back in his easy chair and put his slippered feet on the hassock in front of him. He folded his dark-haired hands on his belly and thought for several moments. "You know," he said, "you just might have something there."

"Does that surprise you?"

"Not one bit," said his father. "Not one bit."

"I've been doing a lot of reading," said Dar. "There are a ton of jobs that need doing around a stable. But they seldom get done. The regular workers are usually too busy doing the really important chores."

"Like what, might I ask?"

"Like feeding the horses, and training them, and exercising them, and ——"

"Okay, okay, Dar. I get the point. I'm behind you a hundred percent. Where will you go first?"

"A place called Mad Cap Stable. It's over by . . ."

*

"Hi! My name's Dar DeMorgan. Could you please tell me where I can find the manager or the owner?"

"You're speaking to both of them," said Mr. Crabtree. He stopped pitchforking manure into his wheelbarrow just long enough to glance once at Dar. Then he quickly continued about his business.

"I'm looking to get some experience around horses, sir."

"So?" The wheelbarrow was nearly full. Dar figured he'd have to talk fast, before the old man sped away with his brown heap.

"I don't know a lot, sir . . . about horses, I mean. I mean, I do know a lot about horses. From reading books. I've read a lot of books and ——"

"Get to the point, boy!" The old man stopped pitchforking and leaned on his three-fingered tool. "You either know a lot about horses or you don't. Which is it?"

Dar looked down at the ground and pretended to be interested in the rock underneath the toe of his sneaker. When he realized he was being shy, he looked directly into the old man's eyes. "I know a lot about horses from books, sir. What I need now is some practical experience around them. I'd like to volunteer my services to you."

"What services?" asked the old man. "You just told me you have no experience around horses."

Dar wanted to turn around and run away and never come back. He hadn't planned on meeting such a difficult character. He had thought everyone he would meet would be ecstatic to take on the free help of a hard worker. To his credit, he rejected the urge to flee. "I could sweep floors," he said, again looking down at the ground. He looked up at the old man's eyes. They seemed to have changed a little, seemed to be just a little more interested in hearing him continue. This encouraged Dar.

"Is that all?" the old man asked. He resumed his attack on the manure.

"No, sir. I could fill water buckets and clean the saddles and things like that, sir. I could do what you're doing right now."

The old man stopped forking and stared at Dar for several uncomfortable seconds. "What would you want in return?" he asked, turning his head slightly so that only one eye focused on Dar.

"Three free rides a week on one of your horses," said Dar. He paused for a reaction to his request.

"That's it?"

"And one free riding lesson each week."

The old man leaned his pitchfork against a stall. He took out a plug of chewing tobacco and stuffed a gob of the brownish threads into his mouth. After he had sufficiently moistened the tobacco with his chewing, he spoke. "You'll have to come here every day, boy. What time can you be here?"

"Well, sir, I have a paper route ——"

"Ha! I should have known better!" shouted the old man.

"Just when do you plan on doing all of this wonderful work you've offered to do for me?"

"After my paper route," Dar replied, obvious disappointment reverberating in his unsteady voice.

"That's an easy promise for you to make to me now, boy. But what'll happen in September when school starts up again? I suppose you'll disappear until the time comes when you want to try to talk me out of some more free rides and lessons. You young kids today are all alike, aren't you? You all want something for nothing. *Don't you?*"

"No, sir!" Dar shouted. Even he was surprised at the defiance in his voice. It was as if he'd been pushed against a wall and had decided to push back. "I'm a hard worker," he continued, his voice lower. "And when school starts again, I could possibly convince my parents I should give up the paper route because I was learning more here. They only wanted me to do it in the first place so I could learn some responsibility. They'd be behind me here if they knew I was serious about it."

The old man was impressed with Dar, but he didn't want to let him know it. Not now, anyway. "All right," he mumbled. "I'll give you a try. But no crying in your milk, boy, if I let you go in a week. You're going to have to work hard, harder than you've probably ever worked before. Three hours of work for every hour of free rides. Got that? And six hours of work for every free lesson? Agreed?"

"Yes, sir!" shouted Dar. "When can I start?"

*

Despite the fact that Mr. Crabtree had him doing all sorts of jobs around the stable and the property, Dar actually saw very little of the horses. However, he did get to ride regularly. And, after all, that was one of the reasons he had accepted the job in the first place, so he was content. He performed all tasks as best he could. When he wasn't certain his performance was good enough, he was never afraid to ask questions. In addition, he took every available opportunity to ask the grooms what they were doing and why. In short, Dar learned something new every day.

Toward summer's end, the grooms were assigning him more and more important tasks to do. They taught him, for example, how to muck out a stall, clean the tack, roll bandages, and do other vital stable chores. Dar was well aware that the grooms were allowing him to perform those chores because he was in fact doing their work for them. It didn't bother him, though. True, they were getting paid for the work he was doing for free. But they were checking his work, so he knew he was doing it right. He kept reminding himself that he was learning skills that someday somebody would pay *him* to do.

For example, he learned how to clean a saddle pad, the cloth cushion placed on a horse's back underneath the saddle. Dar was told that the pad absorbs the sweat and hair from the horse, which quickly makes the pad stiff and caked. "If it's not cleaned periodically," warned Mr. Crabtree, "it can cause a sore back for the horse." Dar learned to clean the Mad Cap saddle pads by using a curry comb first and then a dandy brush.

There were other jobs, of course. He had to periodically scour the water buckets, because the minerals and chemicals in the water would build up a deposit of slime on the inside. Dar had to remove the pails from the stalls, empty them, scrub their insides with a stiff brush, and rinse them clean before he refilled them with fresh water. The scrubbing was tough work, as Dar could not use any soap or detergent to help loosen the slime from the buckets.

Like the water buckets, the feed tubs — in which the horses' grain was placed for consumption — needed periodic cleaning, too. The buildup of grain particles, glued together with the horses' saliva, had to be removed, or the animal's health could suffer. Again, no soap or detergent could be used to make the job a little easier on Dar's developing muscles. But he never complained. After all, he reasoned, he'd asked for it.

There was one job, though, that — although he never complained about it — he hated, nonetheless.

Like all other living creatures on this planet, flies eat. After their food is digested, they expel their waste products. Unfortunately and inevitably, practically every stable has thousands of flies around during the warm summer months. And, even more unfortunately, the flies deposit their brown wastes in every nook and cranny in a stable — on walls, doors, windows, ceilings, everywhere. Because it is dirty and unhealthy, Mr. Crabtree wanted it cleaned off the walls and the windows and wherever else "human contact is likely," he said to Dar. So, once every week or so, Dar would pour a cupful of ammonia into a bucket of hot water and start scrubbing the whole stable with a stiff brush. Afterward, he would rinse all the scrubbed areas with clean water and wipe them dry with a towel.

Washing off the fly waste was really the only task he disliked. He did it just the same, expending nearly as much energy as he did in cleaning the stable windows, raking and cleaning the area in front of the main entrance to the stable, rolling bandages, polishing riding boots, removing manure from the paddock, washing trailers, and tidying the tack room.

Then came the turning point in Dar's budding horse career. The weekend before school was to reopen, Mr. Crabtree had planned to sponsor a small horse show at his stable for the students and other customers who regularly rode there. Dar, having ridden regularly all summer long as payment for his work, wanted to ride in the show, too, to see for himself just how much progress he'd made. However, Mr. Crabtree — in his typically grumpy voice — informed Dar that he was not a paying student. "You're a stable hand, boy, and if you don't hurry up and finish mucking out these stalls, you just might not even be that!" The old man's veins protruded out of his forehead as he spoke. "What in the world do you think I'm running here, anyway? I need you to *work* at that show, not to strut around with a horse that doesn't even belong to you!"

Dar said nothing. But he was deeply hurt. He went back to forking manure into the wheelbarrow. And then, suddenly, it happened — he began feeling sorry for himself. Why, he thought, should I put up with old Crabtree's guff? He threw the pitchfork into the straw. I don't have to take this, he thought. I don't have to work hard like this and not even be appreciated — never mind, paid! He stormed out of the stall and headed for the door.

"Where do you think you're running off to?" roared a voice from the back of the stable.

"Home!" shouted Dar. "You can keep this lousy job!"

Mr. Crabtree ran-walked-ran after Dar. Grabbing him by the shoulder, the old man spun the boy around. "You're a quitter, just like I figured you. Like all you kids are. Everybody wants something for nothing these days. And now you're running off like some kicked puppy, just because you don't get your own way."

Dar tried to speak, but it was futile.

"So. You think you've been getting a raw deal around here I suppose. If you had to pay for what I've let you learn around here you'd be working for somebody else for the next ten years!" The old man paused a moment to catch his breath. "So what am I supposed to do about Saturday? Why wasn't I supposed to count on your help? What's so different about this Saturday than the other nine you've worked? I was even going to *pay* you for working at the show. And I'll tell you something, boy — I've *never* done that before, for any kid. You've been doing a good job around here, and that was gonna be my way of thanking you."

Dar remained speechless. Now, though, he was overwhelmed with joy.

"Well, boy? Speak up!"

Dar cleared his throat before he spoke. "Well, sir." He gulped. He was so scared-happy that it was hard for him to even swallow, never mind talk. "I was going home because I figured you weren't too happy with me."

"Oh yeah? Well you figured wrong, boy," said Mr. Crabtree, his tone of voice a little softer now. "Let me do the figuring for myself. You hear? Now why don't you just get yourself back to the stall. I want this place to sparkle by Saturday." He winked at Dar. And then he did something Dar had never seen him do. Mr. Crabtree smiled!

Dar went back to the stall and his pitchfork and his wheelbarrow. When Saturday came, he worked at Mr. Crabtree's show doing different kinds of odd jobs like getting trophies and ribbons to the ringmaster, bringing coffee and sandwiches to the judges, shining boots, selling programs, and walking hot horses. He got paid rather well, too, for his considerable efforts.

After the show, Dar sat on the paddock fence and counted his earnings over and over again. It was the first money he'd ever earned in the horse world, and it made him feel very good — mostly because it convinced him that there were opportunities in his chosen career, after all.

He thought about what he had learned this summer — about himself as well as horses. He'd learned that his suspicion that he would like to make a career out of working with horses was correct. Not only had he learned invaluable skills, not only had he learned to ride, but he had also been able to see the horse world from the ground up. It wasn't all glamour, he now realized. But it still didn't lessen his desire to become more involved with horses. School would start in a few days. Somehow, some way, he would earn enough money to buy his own horse. He knew now what that would involve, and he was ready to accept that responsibility. With the skills he had acquired over the summer, he would now stand a better chance of securing a paying job next time around and thereby increase his chances of realizing his dream of owning a horse. Maybe Mr. Crabtree would even consider *hiring* him next summer.

Dar thought of the old man and smiled. Perhaps he wasn't a bad sort, after all.

TWELVE

How to Find Money for Your Education

IT's GETTING MORE AND MORE DIFFICULT to stem the rising tide of escalating educational costs. In 1980, for example, college tuition fees were up twelve percent over 1979 — and in the last two decades, overall costs at public colleges and universities have surged ahead by a whopping three hundred percent!

Don't despair, however. There is help available, although not many people know about it. Which is why, in the period from 1977 through 1979, a sizable fortune in grant and scholarship monies — $135 million or so — went unclaimed. No one even applied for it.

Why not?

There are two reasons, primarily — both involving misconceptions about the very nature of scholarships. One is that they are awarded exclusively on the basis of academic achievement. The other is that an applicant's family has to be living below the poverty level in order to qualify for any money. The fact is, however, that scholarship money is given away for all kinds of reasons — and not for merely an abundance of brains

Photo by David O. Aronson

or a lack of cash. You just have to know where and how to look for it.

There are three basic kinds of financial aid available: grants, loans, and scholarships. A grant is an outright gift of money which does not have to be repaid and has no strings attached to it. A scholarship is a gift, too, but usually some academic standards must be met if it is to be renewed another year. A loan, of course, is repayable.

The lion's share of grants and loans is handled by the federal government. If you wish information about federal grants and loans, there are two ways to obtain it. One is by dialing this toll-free number: 800–638–6700 (if you live in Maryland, the number is 800–492–6602). The second way is to consult the *Student Consumer's Guide: Six Federal Financial Aid Programs,* a comprehensive booklet which explains the loan, grant, and work-study programs offered by the Bureau of Student Financial Aid. For a free copy, send a postcard to the bureau at Box 84, Washington, DC 20044 (allow six weeks for delivery).

Although the federal government is by far the biggest spender, financial aid for postsecondary educational expenses also comes from many other sources. For example, most states have aid programs; individual colleges sponsor assistance programs; and literally thousands of local, religious, civic, business, and other kinds of private groups offer financial aid programs.

The publications below contain information about these other aid sources. They can be found in most high school guidance offices, college financial aid offices, or even local public libraries:

Financial Aids for Higher Education, by Oreon Keeslar. William C. Brown Co. Publishers, Dubuque, Iowa.

"Need A Lift?" American Legion Education and Scholarship Programs, Indianapolis, Indiana.

The College Bluebook: Scholarships, Fellowships, Grants, and Loans. Macmillan, New York, N.Y.

Financial Aid for College, by Donald R. Moore. Barron's Educational Series, Woodbury Inc., New York, N.Y.

Scholarships, Fellowships and Loans, by S. Norman Feingold. Chronicle Guidance Publications, Inc., Moravia, N.Y.

Student Aid Manual. Chronicle Guidance Publications, Inc., Moravia, N.Y.

The key to getting financial aid of any kind is to start looking early. High school students, for example, should be checking out potential aid sources by their junior year at the latest.

To apply for federal financial aid, there are usually two forms to complete, one for the government, and one for the school you plan to attend. The government's form, known as the "Financial Aid Form," can be obtained by writing the Bureau of Student Financial Aid at the address given above. In addition, most postsecondary educational institutions also require the student to complete their own financial aid application.

Unfortunately, many students mistakenly think that they cannot submit a school's financial aid application until they've actually been accepted for admission to the school. They're wrong. The admissions and financial aid application processes are entirely separate. In fact, most schools want the student to apply for financial aid well before the school accepts or rejects him or her.

Again, it is important to start inquiring early.

Most financial aid awards are based on the applicant's financial need, which is equal to the difference between his or her total estimated educational expenses and the amount the applicant's family can pay toward those expenses.

How can you estimate what your educational expenses will be?

You can get help from the College Scholarship Service's Early Financial Aid Planning Service. By completing a form and sending it to the College Scholarship Service (along with a small fee) in the student's junior year of high school, the family receives a planning guide and a report of probable eligibility for financial aid from several different sources. For further information write: Early Financial Aid Planning Service, c/o College Scholarship Service, Box 2843, Princeton, NJ 08541.

Above all, remember: don't automatically dismiss the possibility of seeking financial aid just because you think your parents' income is too high. Go ahead and apply anyway. You may be eligible under the terms of the Middle Income Assistance Act, passed by Congress in 1979. It enables families with incomes in excess of $25,000 per year to qualify for federal grants of up to $1,800 per year. You can learn more about the act by calling the toll-free number listed above, or by writing the Bureau of Student Financial Aid.

In addition, higher-income families may also be eligible for federal aid if they have more than one child in college at one time.

The point is, don't overestimate your family's situation. You never know what you can get until you actually ask for it.

Another source of financial aid information is the research service of Scholarship Search, an organization with a nationwide data bank of donor awards and scholarship sources. Using a computer, they match student eligibility with donor requirements and will supply you with an individually tailored printout list of the potential sources of financial aid for which you are eligible to apply. For further information, write Scholarship Search, 1775 Broadway, Suite G627, New York, NY 10019. They ask that you enclose one dollar for postage and handling of the information they'll be sending you.

Even if you find out that your family does in fact have too large an income to qualify for financial assistance from the government, *you* may still be eligible if you are financially independent of your parents. To be able to apply for federal assistance as a financially independent student, you (1) should not have lived with your parents for more than six consecutive weeks during the year preceding your application; (2) should not have received parental support in excess of $750 during the year preceding application; and (3) should not have been claimed as a dependent on your parents' previous two income tax forms.

Regardless of your situation, start looking around early and give some of the programs a shot at helping you. Don't let another $135 million in eligible financial assistance go untapped again.

Besides, what have you got to lose?

Appendices

Veterinary Schools

Alabama

School of Veterinary Medicine
Auburn University
Auburn 36830

School of Veterinary Medicine
Tuskegee Institute
Tuskegee Institute 36088

California

School of Veterinary Medicine
University of California
Davis 95616

Colorado

College of Veterinary Medicine and
  Biomedical Sciences
Colorado State University
Fort Collins 80523

Florida

College of Veterinary Medicine
University of Florida
Gainesville 32601

Georgia

College of Veterinary Medicine
University of Georgia
Athens 30601

Illinois

College of Veterinary Medicine
University of Illinois
Urbana 61801

Indiana

School of Veterinary Medicine
Purdue University
West Lafayette 47907

Iowa

College of Veterinary Medicine
Iowa State University
Ames 50011

Kansas

College of Veterinary Medicine
Kansas State University
Manhattan 66502

Louisiana

College of Veterinary Medicine
Louisiana State University
Baton Rouge 70803

Massachusetts

School of Veterinary Medicine
Tufts University
Medford 02155

Michigan

College of Veterinary Medicine
Michigan State University
East Lansing 48824

Minnesota

College of Veterinary Medicine
University of Minnesota
Saint Paul 55108

Mississippi

College of Veterinary Medicine
Mississippi State University
Mississippi State 39762

Missouri

College of Veterinary Medicine
University of Missouri
Columbia 65201

New York

New York State College of
   Veterinary Medicine
Cornell University
Ithaca 14853

Ohio

College of Veterinary Medicine
Ohio State University
Columbus 43210

Oklahoma

College of Veterinary Medicine
Oklahoma State University
Stillwater 74074

Pennsylvania

School of Veterinary Medicine
University of Pennsylvania
Philadelphia 19104

Tennessee

College of Veterinary Medicine
University of Tennessee
Knoxville 37901

Texas

College of Veterinary Medicine
Texas A & M University
College Station 77843

Virginia

College of Veterinary Medicine
Virginia Polytechnic Institute
Blacksburg 24061

Washington

College of Veterinary Medicine
Washington State University
Pullman 99163

Major U.S. Quarter Horse, Standardbred, and Thoroughbred Racetracks

Arizona

Thoroughbred and Quarter Horse

Arizona Downs
Phoenix 85068

Prescott Downs
Prescott 86301

California

Thoroughbred

Hollywood Park
Inglewood 90306

Santa Anita Park
Arcadia 91006

Standardbred and Quarter Horse

Bay Meadows
San Mateo 94402

Los Alamitos Race Course
Los Alamitos 90720

Colorado

Thoroughbred

Centennial Turf
Littleton 80120

Quarter Horse

Uranium Downs
Grand Junction 81501

Delaware

Thoroughbred and Standardbred

Dover Downs
Dover 19901

Florida

Thoroughbred

Hialeah Park
Hialeah 33011

Quarter Horse and Standardbred

Gator Downs
Pompano 33060

Idaho

Thoroughbred and Quarter Horse

Pocatello Downs
Pocatello 83201

Illinois

Thoroughbred and Standardbred

Balmoral
Crete 60417

Kentucky

Thoroughbred

Churchill Downs
Louisville 40208

Keeneland
Lexington 40592

Standardbred

Louisville Downs
Louisville 40213

Louisiana

Thoroughbred and Quarter Horse

Delta Downs
Vinton 70668

Maryland

Thoroughbred and Standardbred

Laurel Race Course
Laurel 20810

Massachusetts

Thoroughbred

Suffolk Downs
East Boston 02128

Standardbred

Bay State Raceway
Foxboro 02035

Michigan

Thoroughbred and Standardbred

Hazel Park Raceway
Hazel Park 48030

Montana

Thoroughbred and Quarter Horse

Chouteau County Fairgrounds
Fort Benton 59442

Western Mountain Fair and
Race Meet
Missoula 59801

Nebraska

Thoroughbred

Columbus Races
Columbus 68601

Ak-Sar-Ben Raceway
Omaha 68106

Nevada

Thoroughbred and Quarter Horse

Elko County Fairgrounds
Elko 89801

New Hampshire

Standardbred

Hinsdale Raceway
Hinsdale 03451

New Jersey

Thoroughbred

Monmouth Park
Oceanport 07757

New Mexico

Thoroughbred and Quarter Horse

Ruidoso Downs
Ruidoso Downs 88346

Sunland Park
Sunland Park 88063

New York

Thoroughbred

Aqueduct
Jamaica 11417

Saratoga
Saratoga Springs 12866

Standardbred

Buffalo Raceway
Hamburg 14075

Batavia Downs
Batavia 14020

Yonkers Raceway
Yonkers 10704

Ohio

Thoroughbred and Quarter Horse

Beulah Park
Grove City 43123

Standardbred

Scioto Downs
Columbus 43207

Oregon

Thoroughbred and Quarter Horse

Portland Meadows
Portland 97217

Pennsylvania

Thoroughbred

Keystone Race Track
Cornwells Heights 19020

Standardbred

The Meadows
Meadow Lands 15347

South Dakota

Thoroughbred and Quarter Horse

Jefferson Park
Jefferson 57038

Vermont

Thoroughbred and Standardbred

Green Mountain Raceway
Pownal 05261

Washington

Thoroughbred

Playfair Race Course
Spokane 99220

Quarter Horse

Rimrock Meadows
Ephrata 98823

Thoroughbred and Quarter Horse

Yakima Meadows
Yakima 98907

West Virginia

Thoroughbred

Shenandoah Downs
Charles Town 25414

Waterford Park
Chester 26034

Standardbred

Wheeling Downs
Wheeling 26003

Wyoming

Thoroughbred and Quarter Horse

Central Wyoming Fair Race Meet
Casper 82601

For a complete list of racetracks in the U.S., write to the National Association of State Racing Commissioners, P.O. Box 4216, Lexington, KY 40504.

Breed Magazines

The American Trakehner
2100 Hassell Road, #201
Hoffman Estates, IL 60172

Appaloosa News
P.O. Box 8403
Moscow, ID 83843

Arabian Horse Times
819 East Elm Avenue
Waseca, MN 56093

Arabian Horse World
2650 East Bayshore
Palo Alto, CA 94303

The Arabians
P.O. Box 3
31776 Cowan Road
Westland, MI 48185

The Arizona Quarter Horse
7702 West Greenway Road
Peoria, AZ 85345

The Blood Horse
c/o Thoroughbred Owners and
   Breeders Association
P.O. Box 4038
Lexington, KY 40504

The Bluegrass Horseman
P.O. Box 389
Lexington, KY 40501

Buckskin World News
P.O. Box 357
Saint John, IN 46373

Cal-Western Appaloosa
P.O. Box 185
Clovis, CA 93613

Connemara News
HoshieKon Farm
R.D. 1
Goshen, CT 06756

*Eastern/Western Quarter Horse
   Journal*
P.O. Drawer 690
Middleboro, MA 02346

The Hackney Journal
P.O. Box 4333
New Windsor, NY 12550

The Harness Horse
P.O. Box 1831
Harrisburg, PA 17105

Indiana Quarter Horse Journal
6304 South 450 East
Lafayette, IN 47905

The Intermountain Quarter Horse
Journal
P.O. Box 0
Sandy, UT 84070

Michigan Thoroughbred
Breeder & Owner
1110 Catalpa Drive
Royal Oak, MI 48067

Midwest Appaloosa Spotlite
P.O. Box 441
N89 W16342 Main Street
Menomonee Falls, WI 53051

The Missouri Fox Trotter
P.O. Box 191
West Plains, NY 65775

The Morgan Horse Magazine
P.O. Box 1
Westmoreland, NY 13490

New York Thoroughbred Breeder
575 Lexington Avenue
Room 1650
New York, NY 10022

Ohio Quarter Horse Association News
P.O. Box 101
Minster, OH 45865

The Oregon Horse
Oregon Thoroughbred Breeders
Association
P.O. Box 17248
Portland, OR 97217

Paint Digest & Racing News
P.O. Box 278
Raymore, MO 64083

Paint Horse Journal
P.O. Box 18519
Fort Worth, TX 76118

Palomino Horses
P.O. Box 249
Mineral Wells, TX 76067

The Palomino Parade
P.O. Box 324
Jefferson City, MO 65102

Peruvian Horse Review
P.O. Box 816
Guerneville, CA 95446

Peruvian Horse World
P.O. Box 2035
California City, CA 93505

The Pinto Horse
7525 Mission Gorge Road
Suite C
San Diego, CA 92120

Pony of the Americas
P.O. Box 1442
1452 N. Federal
Mason City, IA 50401

The Pony Journal
P.O. Box 435
Fowler, IN 47944

Quarter Horse Digest
Rte. 2, Box 14
Gann Valley, SD 53741

The Quarter Horse Journal
P.O. Box 9105
Amarillo, TX 79105

Quarter Horse of the Pacific Coast
P.O. Box 254822
Sacramento, CA 95825

Quarter Horse World
P.O. Box 1035
Daytona Beach, FL 32019

Rocky Mountain Quarter Horse
Rush, CO 80833

Saddle Horse Report
1211 East Lane Street
P.O. Box 1007
Shelbyville, TN 37160

The Spanish Barb Quarterly
P.O. Box 7479
Colorado Springs, CO 80907

Spotted Horse
P.O. Box 3045
Wenatchee, WA 98801

Voice of the Tennessee Walking Horse
Ellington Parkway
P.O. Box 286
Lewisburg, TN 37091

Walking Horse Report
1211 East Lane Street
P.O. Box 1007
Shelbyville, TN 31760

The Yearling
Illinois Quarter Horse Association
2513 E. Higgins Road
Elk Grove, IL 60007

APPENDIX IV

Breed Associations

Andalusian Horse Registry
Box 1290
Silver City, NM 88061

The Appaloosa Horse Club
P.O. Box 8403
Moscow, ID 83843

Arabian Horse Registry
3435 South Yosemite Street
Denver, CO 80231

American Buckskin Registry
P.O. Box 1125
Anderson, CA 96007

Clydesdale Breeders of the United
States
Route 1, Box 131
Pecatonica, IL 61063

Royal International Lipizzaner Club
of America
Route 7
Columbia, TN 38401

The American Morgan Horse
Association
P.O. Box 1
Westmoreland, NY 13490

American Paint Horse Association
P.O. Box 18519
Fort Worth, TX 76118

Palomino Horse Breeders of
America
P.O. Box 249
Mineral Wells, TX 76067

Paso Fino Owners and Breeders
Association
P.O. Box 1579
Tryon, NC 28782

The Pinto Horse Association of
America
7525 Mission Gorge Road
Suite C
San Diego, CA 92120

Pony of the Americas Club
P.O. Box 1447
Mason City, IA 50401

American Quarter Horse
Association
2736 West Tenth Street
Amarillo, TX 79168

American Saddle Horse Breeders
  Association
South Fourth Street
Louisville, KY 40203

Spanish Barb Breeders Association
P.O. Box 7479
Colorado Springs, CO 80907

United States Trotting Association
  (Standardbred)
750 Michigan Avenue
Columbus, OH 43215

Tennessee Walking Horse Breeders
  and Exhibitors Association
P.O. Box 286
Lewisburg, TN 37091

The Jockey Club (Thoroughbred)
300 Park Avenue
New York, NY 10022

American Trakehner Association
P.O. Box 268
Norman, OK 73070

Vocational Training

Please note that the last line of each institution's listing contains one or more of the following abbreviations:

RI	Riding Instructor
T	Trainer
BFM	Breeding Farm Manager
SM	Stable Manager

These represent the career orientation of the institution's particular training.

California

Lassen College
Admissions Office
Susanville 96130
Horsemastership courses
RI, SM

Merced College
3600 M Street
Merced 95340
1-year certificate program in Horse
  Management
RI, T, SM

Pacific Horse Center
P.O. Box L
Elk Grove 95624
36-week certificate program in
  Horsemastership
RI, T, BFM, SM

Delaware

Delaware Technical and
  Community College
Stanton Campus
400 Stanton-Christiana
Newark 19702
10-week course
SM

Illinois

Black Hawk College
East Campus
P.O. Box 489
Kewanee 61443
1-year certificate program in Horse
  Science Technology
BFM, SM

Parkland College
2400 W. Bradley Ave.
Champaign 61820
1-year certificate.
Equine Training and Management
T, BFM, SM

Maryland

Goucher College
Admissions Office
Towson 21204
Courses in riding, schooling, and
  managing horses
T, SM

Potomac Horse Center
14211 Quince Orchard
Gaithersburg 20760
16-week certificate programs
RI, T, SM

Massachusetts

Fulmer International School of
  Equitation
Prescott Street
Pepperell 01463
7-month certificate,
  Horsemastership
RI, SM

Mount Ida Junior College
777 Dedham Street
Newton Center 02159
15-week courses
RI, SM

Newbury Junior College
Holliston Campus
100 Summer Street
Holliston 01746
1-year certificate program in
  Horsemanship
RI, SM

Michigan

Black Forest Farm
Bester Road

Harbor Springs 49740
Various short courses
RI, T, BFM, SM

Cheff Center for the Handicapped
R.R. 1, Box 171
Augusta 49012
4-week certificate program
RI, SM

Flintlock Equestrian Center
P.O. Box 396
Ontonagon 49953
40-week certificate program,
  Professional Equestrian
RI, T, SM

Missouri

University of Missouri
Department of Animal Husbandry
Room 125, Mumford Hall
Columbia 65211
12-week program in Horse Science
BFM, SM

New Hampshire

New England College
Admissions Office
Henniker 03242
1-year program in Horsemanship
RI, BFM, SM

New York

Saint Lawrence University
Office of Admissions
Canton 13617
Courses in Horsemanship
RI, SM

Ohio

Devan Technical Institute
Wilmot 44689
6-month diploma program in Horse
  Management
T, BFM, SM

Pennsylvania

Chesterfield Farms
Pine Creek Road
Chester Springs 19425
11-month certificate program,
 Horsemastership
RI, T, BFM, SM

Pen-Y-Byrn Equestrian
 Center, Ltd.
Seven Oaks Road
Chester Springs 19425
9-month program
RI, SM

Pleasant Hollow Farms
Box 481, RD 1
Coopersburg 18036
12-month certificate program, Horse
 Management
RI, T, SM

Wonderland Farms
RD #5
West Chester 19380
9-month Working Student program
BFM, SM

Tennessee

Huntlea
Leatherwood Creek Road
Pulaski 38478
30-week certificate program
RI, T, BFM, SM

Virginia

Hollins College for Women
Office of Admissions
Hollins 24019
15-week courses
SM

Lord Fairfax Community College
U.S. Route 11
Middletown 22645
1-year certificate program in Horses
 and Livestock Management
BFM, SM

Morven Park International
 Equestrian Institute
Route 2, Box 8
Leesburg 22075
9½-month certificate program
RI, T, SM

West Virginia

Meredith Manor
Route 1
Waverly 26184
Various certificate programs
RI, T, BFM, SM

Whiting's Neck Equestrian Center
Rte. 3, Box 105D
Martinsburg 25401

Two-Year Degree Programs in Equine Education

Please note the following degree abbreviations:

A.A.S. Associate in Applied Science
A.A.   Associate in Arts
A.S.   Associate in Science

Please note further that the last line of the listing for each institution contains one or more of the following abbreviations:

RI   Riding Instructor
T   Trainer
BFM Breeding Farm Manager
SM   Stable Manager

These abbreviations represent the career orientation of the institution's particular training.

Arizona

Northland Pioneer College
Admissions Office
1200 East Hermosa Street
Holbrook 86025
A.A.S. in Agriculture
BFM, SM

Scottsdale Community College
P.O. Box Y
Scottsdale 85253
A.A. in Equine Training and
  Management
T, BFM, SM

California

Merced Community College
Agriculture Division
3600 M Street
Merced 95340
A.S. in Horse Management
RI, T, BFM, SM

Connecticut

Post College
800 Country Club Road
Waterbury 06708
A.A.S. in Horsemanship
RI, T, SM

Florida

Santa Fe Community College
3000 N.W. 83rd Street
Gainesville 32601
A.S. in Farm Management
BFM, SM

Idaho

Ricks College
Office of Admissions
Rexburg 83440
A.S. in Horsemanship and Stable
  Management
RI, T, BFM, SM

Illinois

Black Hawk College
East Campus
P.O. Box 489
Kewanee 61443
A.A.S. in Horse Science Technology
BFM, SM

Parkland College
2400 W. Bradley Avenue
Champaign 61820
A.A.S. in Stable Management
T, BFM, SM

Iowa

Kirkwood Community College
6301 Kirkwood Blvd., S.W.
Cedar Rapids 52406
A.A.S. in Horse Science Technology
RI, T, BFM, SM

Kansas

Colby Community College
1255 South Range
Colby 67701
A.S. in Horse Production and
  Stable Management
BFM, SM

Massachusetts

Newbury Junior College
Holliston Campus
100 Summer Street
Holliston 01746
A.A.S. in Equestrian Studies
RI, SM

Minnesota

Saint John's University
College of Saint Benedict
Collegeville 56321
A.A. in Horse Management
RI, T, SM

University of Minnesota Technical
  College
Admissions Office
Crookston 56717
A.A.S. in Animal Science
  Technology
RI, T, BFM, SM

University of Minnesota Technical
  College
Admissions Office
Waseca 56093
A.A.S. in Agricultural Production
RI, T, BFM, SM

New Jersey

Centenary College
400 Jefferson Street
Hackettstown 07840
A.S. in Horsemanship
RI, SM

New York

Cazenovia Women's College
Admissions Office
Cazenovia 13035
A.A.S. in Stable and Farm
  Management
A.A.S. in Horsemanship
RI, BFM, SM

State University of New York,
Canton Campus
Agricultural and Technical College
Canton 13617
A.A.S. in Animal Husbandry
BFM, SM

State University of New York,
Cobleskill Campus
Agricultural and Technical College
Cobleskill 12043
A.A.S. in Animal Husbandry
BFM, SM

State University of New York,
Delhi Campus
Agricultural and Technical College
Delhi 13753
A.A.S. in Animal Husbandry
BFM, SM

Ohio

Findlay College
Office of Admissions
Findlay 45840
A.A. in Equestrian Studies
T, SM

Ohio State University/Agricultural
Technical Institute
Admissions Office
Third Floor Lincoln Tower
1800 Cannon Drive
Columbus 43210
A.A.S. in Horse Production and
Management
RI, T, BFM, SM

Oregon

Rogue Community College
3345 Redwood Highway
Grants Pass 97526
A.S. in Horse Industries
BFM, SM

Pennsylvania

Wilson College for Women
Chambersburg 17201
A.A. or A.S. in Equine Studies
RI, SM

Rhode Island

Johnson and Wales College
Abbott Park Place
Providence 02903
A.S. in Equine Studies
RI, SM

South Carolina

Tri-County Technical College
Highway 76, Box 587
Pendleton 29670
A.S. in Animal Industry
BFM, SM

Washington

Spokane Community College
N1810 Greene Street
Spokane 99207
A.A.S. in Animal Science
BFM, SM

Wyoming

Northwest Community College
Admissions Office
Powell 82435
A.A.S. in Equestrian Studies
RI, T, BFM, SM

Sheridan College
Admissions Office
Sheridan 82801
A.A.S. in Livestock Production
BFM

Four-Year Degree Programs in Equine Education

Please note the following degree abbreviations:

B.A.   Bachelor of Arts
B.S.   Bachelor of Science

Please note further that the last line of the listing for each institution contains one or more of the following abbreviations:

RI   Riding Instructor
T   Trainer
BFM   Breeding Farm Manager
SM   Stable Manager

These represent the career orientation of the institution's particular training.

Arkansas

University of Arkansas
Office of Admissions
222 Administration Building
Fayetteville 72701
B.S. in Agriculture
BFM, SM

California

California Polytechnic State
    University

Animal Science Department
San Luis Obispo 93407
B.S. in Animal Science
T, BFM, SM

California State Polytechnic
    University
Admissions Office
3801 West Temple Avenue
Pomona 91765
B.S. in Animal Science
T, BFM, SM

California State University
School of Agriculture
Fresno 93740
B.S. in Animal Science
T, BFM, SM

University of California
Office of Admissions
Mrak Hall 175
Davis 95616
B.S. in Animal Science
BFM, SM

Colorado

Colorado State University
Office of Admissions
Fort Collins 80523
B.S. in Animal Science
RI, T, BFM, SM

Connecticut

University of Connecticut
Department of Animal Industries
Storrs 06268
B.S. in Animal Science
RI, T, BFM, SM

Delaware

University of Delaware
Admissions Office
Newark 19711
B.S. in Animal Science
BFM, SM

Florida

University of Florida
Office of the Registrar
Tigert Hall
Gainesville 32611
B.S. in Animal Science
BFM, SM

Idaho

University of Idaho
Office of Publications
Moscow 83843
B.S. in Animal Science
BFM, SM

Illinois

University of Illinois
Office of Admissions
10 Administration Building
Urbana 61801
B.S. in Animal Science
BFM, SM

Kentucky

Morehead State University
Department of Agriculture
UPO 702
Morehead 40351
B.S. in Agriculture
RI, T, BFM, SM

Murray State University
Office of Admissions
Murray 42071
B.S. in Agriculture
RI, T, BFM, SM

University of Kentucky
Admissions Office
Lexington 40506
B.S. in Agriculture
BFM, SM

Western Kentucky University
Department of Agriculture
Bowling Green 42101
B.S. in Agriculture
T, BFM, SM

Louisiana

Louisiana Tech University
College of Life Sciences

Ruston 71272
B.S. in Animal Science
BFM, SM

Northwestern State University of
Louisiana
Admissions Office
Natchitoches 71457
B.S. in Equine Science
BFM, SM

Massachusetts

University of Massachusetts
College of Food and Natural
Resources
Department of Veterinary and
Animal Sciences
Amherst 01003
B.S. in Animal Science
RI, BFM, SM

Mississippi

Mississippi State University
Department of Animal Science
P.O. Drawer 5228
Mississippi State 39762
B.S. in Animal Science
BFM, SM

Missouri

The Lindenwood Colleges
Admissions Office
Saint Charles 63301
B.A. in Horsemanship
RI, T, SM

Stephens College
Office of Public Information
Columbia 65201
B.A. in Equestrian Science
RI, T, SM

William Woods College
Admissions Office
Fulton 65251

B.S. in Equestrian Science
RI, T, BFM, SM

Montana

Montana State University
Office of Admissions
Bozeman 59717
B.S. in Agriculture
BFM, SM

New Hampshire

University of New Hampshire
Admissions Office
Thompson Hall
Durham 03824
B.S. in Animal Science
RI, BFM, SM

New Jersey

Centenary College
400 Jefferson Street
Hackettstown 07840
B.S. in Equine Studies
RI, T, BFM, SM

Rutgers University
Cook College
Office of Resident Instruction
P.O. Box 231
New Brunswick 08903
B.S. in Animal Science
BFM, SM

New York

Cornell University
Building 7, Research Park
Ithaca 14850
B.S. in Animal Science
BFM, SM

Skidmore College
Admissions Office
Saratoga Springs 12866
B.S. in Physical Education
RI, T, SM

Ohio

Findlay College
Admissions Office
Findlay 45840
B.A. in Equestrian Studies
RI, T, BFM, SM

Otterbein College
Admissions Office
Westerville 43081
B.A. in Equine Science
T, BFM, SM

Oklahoma

Panhandle State University
Animal Science Department
Goodwell 73939
B.S. in Animal Science
T, BFM, SM

Rhode Island

University of Rhode Island
Admissions Office
Kingston 02881
B.S. in Animal Science
BFM, SM

South Carolina

Clemson University
Undergraduate Admissions
Sikes Hall
Clemson 29631
B.S. in Animal Industries
BFM, SM

South Dakota

South Dakota State University
Admissions Office
Administration 200
Brookings 57007
B.S. in Animal Science
BFM, SM

Tennessee

Middle Tennessee State University
Office of Admissions
Murfreesboro 37132
B.S. in Animal Science
T, BFM, SM

University of Tennessee
Institute of Agriculture
Department of Animal Science
P.O. Box 1071
Knoxville 37901
B.S. in Animal Science
BFM, SM

Texas

Sul Ross State University
Department of Range Animal
  Science
Box C–110
Alpine 79830
B.S. in Range Animal Science
BFM, SM

Tarleton State University
Department of Agriculture
Stephenville 76402
B.S. in Agriculture
T, BFM, SM

Texas A & M University
College of Agriculture
Department of Animal Science
College Station 77843
B.S. in Animal Science
RI, T, BFM, SM

West Texas State University
Office of Admissions
Canyon 79016
B.S. in Animal Science
RI, BFM, SM

Utah

Brigham Young University
College of Biological and
  Agricultural Sciences

380 Widstoe Building
Provo 84602
B.S. in Animal Science
BFM, SM

Vermont

University of Vermont
Office of Admissions
Clement House
194 South Prospect Street
Burlington 05405
B.S. in Animal Science
BFM, SM

Virginia

Averett College
Office of Admissions
Danville 24541
B.S. in Physical Education
RI, T, SM

Ferrum College
Office of Admissions
Ferrum 24088
B.S. in Leisure Studies
RI, SM

Sweet Briar College
Office of Admissions
Sweet Briar 24595
B.S. in Physical Education
RI, T, SM

Virginia Intermont College
Director of Admissions
Bristol 24201
B.A. in Horsemanship
RI, T, SM

Virginia Polytechnic Institute and
State University
Department of Animal Science
Blacksburg 24061
B.S. in Animal Science
BFM, SM

Washington

Washington State University
Office of Admissions
Pullman 99164
B.S. in Animal Science
BFM, SM

West Virginia

Salem College
Director of Admissions
Salem 26426
B.S. in Equestrian Studies
RI, T, BFM, SM

Wisconsin

University of Wisconsin
College of Agriculture
River Falls 54022
RI, T, BFM, SM

Colleges and Universities That Offer Degrees in Writing

Listed here are some of the U.S. colleges and universities that offer degree programs in writing. Although these institutions share common goals, criteria, and characteristics, their writing programs are many and diverse. Therefore, prospective students of writing should write directly to the institutions of their choice for more specific information about the courses and/or degrees offered.

At the undergraduate level, degrees listed include the Bachelor of Arts (B.A. or A.B.) and the Bachelor of Fine Arts (B.F.A.). Two-year institutions in this list offer the Associate of Arts (A.A.) degree. A few of the institutions offer a writing component with the Bachelor of Science (B.S.) degree.

Some of the institutions listed here do not offer a formal major in writing, but do offer a major in English or the humanities with, variously, a "concentration," a "track," or an "emphasis" in writing. For example, a B.A. in English with a Creative Writing Emphasis (or Track, Concentration, etc.) usually requires the completion of standard literature and composition courses for a major in English, in addition to specific courses in creative writing.

Alabama

University of South Alabama
Creative Writing Program
Department of English
Mobile 36688
B.A. in English with Concentration
in Creative Writing

Arizona

University of Arizona
Creative Writing Program
Department of English
Tucson 85721
B.A. in Creative Writing

Arkansas

Arkansas Tech. University
Writing Program Director
English Department
Russellville 72801
B.F.A. in Creative Writing

University of Arkansas
Director of Creative Writing
English Department
Little Rock 72204
B.A. in English with Creative
Writing Emphasis

California

Pomona College
Writing Program Director
Department of English
Claremont 91711
B.A. in Writing

San Diego State University
Writing Program Director
Department of English
San Diego 92182
B.A. in English with Emphasis in
Creative Writing

San Francisco State University
Secretary, Creative
Writing Department
1600 Holloway Avenue
San Francisco 94132
B.A. in English with
Concentration in
Creative Writing

Sonoma State University
Chairman, English Department
Rohnert Park 94928
B.A. in Independent Study
with Writing Major

Stanford University
Creative Writing Director
Stanford 94305
A.B. in English with
Concentration in Writing

University of California
English Department Chairman
114 Sproul Hall
Davis 95616
B.A. in English with
Writing Emphasis

University of California
The Writing Program
English Department
Irvine 92717
B.A. in English with
Creative Writing Emphasis

University of California
English Department Chairman
405 Hilgard Avenue
Los Angeles 90024
B.A. in English with
Creative Writing Track

University of California
Writing Program Coordinator
English Department
San Diego 92093
B.A. in Writing

University of California
Chairman, Writing Caucus
c/o Literature Board
Santa Cruz 95054
B.A. in Creative Writing

University of Redlands
Writing Program Director
Department of English
Redlands 92373
B.A. in English with
Concentration in Writing

Colorado

Colorado State University
Chairman, Creative
Writing Committee
Department of English
Fort Collins 80523
B.A. in English with
Creative Writing Concentration

Metropolitan State College
Chairman, English Department
Denver 80204
B.A. in English with
  Creative Writing Concentration

University of Colorado
Writing Program Director
Department of English
Boulder 80309
B.A. in English with
  Creative Writing Emphasis

University of Colorado
Writing Program Director
1100 14th Street
Denver 80202
B.A. in English with
  Writing Concentration

University of Denver
Writing Program Director
Department of English
Denver 80210
B.A. in English with
  Writing Concentration

Connecticut

Central Connecticut State College
Composition Committee Chairman
English Department
1615 Stanley Street
New Britain 06050
B.A. in English with
  Concentration in Writing

Southern Connecticut State College
Writing Program Director
English Department
New Haven 06515
B.A. in English with
  Creative Writing Specialization

University of Bridgeport
Creative Writing Director
Department of English
Bridgeport 06602
B.A. or B.S. in English
  and Writing

Florida

Eckerd College
Writing Program Director
Department of English
B.A. in Creative Writing

Florida International University
Chairman, English Department
Miami 33144
B.A. in English with
  Creative Writing Track

Florida State University
Chairman, English Department
Tallahassee 32306
B.A. in English with
  Writing Concentration

University of Miami
Director of Admissions
Coral Gables 33124
B.A. in Creative Writing
B.A. in English with
  Creative Writing Concentration

University of Tampa
Chairman, English Department
Tampa 33606
B.A. in Writing

Georgia

Mercer University
Chairman, English Department
Macon 31207
B.A. in English with
  Creative Writing Track

Hawaii

University of Hawaii
Director, Creative Writing
Department of English
1733 Donaghho Road
Honolulu 96822
B.A. in English with
  Creative Writing Concentration

Illinois

Columbia College
Chairman, Writing Department
Chicago 60605
B.A. in Creative Writing

Knox College
English Department Writing
   Program
Galesburg 61401
B.A. in Creative Writing

Lake Forest College
Writing Program Director
Department of English
Lake Forest 60045
B.A. in English with
   Writing Concentration

Northwestern University
Writing Program Director
Evanston 60201
B.A. in English with
   Writing Major

Rosary College
Writing Program Director
7900 West Division Street
River Forest 60305
B.A. in English with
   Writing Concentration

Southern Illinois University
Director, Undergraduate
   Programs in English
Carbondale 62901
B.A. in English with
   Specialization in
   Creative Writing

University of Illinois
Writing Program Director
Department of English
Champaign 61820
A.B. in English with
   Writing Concentration

Indiana

Indiana State University
Coordinator, Creative
   Writing
Terre Haute 47809
B.A. in English with
   Creative Writing Major

Indiana University
Chairman, English Department
1825 Northside Blvd.
South Bend 46615
B.A. in English with
   Writing Concentration

Iowa

Drake University
Des Moines 50311
B.A. in English with Major
   in Creative Writing

Loras College
Writing Program
Dubuque 52001
B.A. in English with
   Specialization in Writing

Morningside College
Chairman, English Department
Sioux City 51106
B.A. in English with Writing
   Emphasis

Kansas

Emporia State University
Chairman, English Department
Emporia 66801
B.S. in English with
   Concentration in Creative
   Writing

Kansas State University
Writing Program Director
Department of English
Manhattan 66506
B.A. in English with Creative
   Writing Emphasis

University of Kansas
Writing Program
c/o English Department
Lawrence 66045
B.A. in Creative Writing

Wichita State University
Coordinator of Creative
Writing
Department of English, Box 14
Wichita 67208
B.A. in English with Major
in Creative Writing

Kentucky

Murray State University
Writing Program Director
Murray 42071
B.A. in English with
Creative Writing Emphasis

Louisiana

Louisiana State University
Writing Program Director
Department of English
Baton Rouge 70806
B.A. in English with
Concentration in
Creative Writing

Maryland

Johns Hopkins University
Baltimore 21218
B.A. in Writing

University of Baltimore
Baltimore 21201
B.A. in English with
Concentration in
Creative Writing

University of Maryland
Writing Program Director

Department of English
College Park 20742
B.A. in English with
Writing Concentration

Western Maryland College
Chairman, English Department
Westminster 21157
B.A. in English with
Concentration in Writing

Massachusetts

Brandeis University
Chairman, English Department
Waltham 02154
B.A. in English with
Writing Track

Emerson College
Chairman, English Department
148 Beacon Street
Boston 02116
B.F.A. in Creative Writing

Harvard College
Writing Program Director
Department of English
Cambridge 02138
B.A. in English and American
Literature with Emphasis
in Writing

Michigan

Michigan State University
Writing Program Director
Department of English
East Lansing 48824
B.A. in English with
Concentration in
Creative Writing

Western Michigan University
Chairman, English Department
Kalamazoo 49008
B.A. in English with
Writing Emphasis

Minnesota

Bemidji State University
Chairman, English Department
Bemidji 56601
B.A. or B.S. in English
    with Concentration in
    Creative Writing

Macalester College
Chairman, English Department
Saint Paul 55105
B.A. in English with
    Concentration in Creative
    Writing

Mankato State University
Office of Admissions
Mankato 56001
B.A. or B.S. in English
    with Concentration in
    Writing

Moorhead State University
Chairman, English Department
Moorhead 56560
B.A. in English with
    Concentration in Creative
    Writing

Missouri

Southwest Missouri State
Chairman, English Department
Springfield 65802
B.A. in English with
    Writing Major

Stephens College
Writing Program Director
Department of English
Columbia 65201
B.F.A. in Creative Writing

University of Missouri
Director, Creative Writing
Department of English
Columbia 65211
B.A. in English with
    Concentration in
    Creative Writing

Westminster College
Writing Program Director
Department of English
Fulton 65251
B.A. in English with
    Writing Concentration

Montana

University of Montana
Chairman, English Department
Missoula 59801
B.A. in English with
    Creative Writing Track

Nebraska

University of Nebraska
Lincoln 68588
B.A. in English with
    Writing Emphasis

University of Nebraska
Omaha 08101
B.F.A. in Creative Writing

New Jersey

Farleigh Dickinson University
Writing Program Director
Department of English
Madison 07940
B.A. in English with
    Concentration in Creative
    Writing

Princeton University
Writing Program Director
185 Nassau Street
Princeton 08540
B.A. in English with
    Concentration in Creative
    Writing

New Mexico

New Mexico State University
Writing Program Director
Department of English
Las Cruces 88003
B.A. in English with Creative
Writing Concentration

University of New Mexico
Creative Writing Director
Department of English
Albuquerque 87131
B.A. in Creative Writing

New York

Brooklyn College
City University of New York
Department of English
New York 11210
B.A. in English with Concentration
in Writing

Dowling College
Oakdale 11769
B.A. in English with Certificate in
Writing

Dutchess Community College
Chairman, English Department
Poughkeepsie 12601
A.A. in English with Writing
Emphasis

Hamilton College
Writing Program Director
Department of English
Clinton 13323
B.A. in English with Concentration
in Writing

Hofstra University
Writing Program Director
Hempstead 11550
B.A. in English with Concentration
in Creative Writing

Keuka College
Chairman, English Department
Keuka Park 14478
B.A. in English with Writing
Emphasis

Herbert Lehman College
City University of New York
Chairman, English Department
Bronx 10468
B.A. in English with Specialization
in Creative Writing

Saint Lawrence University
Chairman, English Department
Canton 13617
B.A. in English with Major in
Writing

Sarah Lawrence College
Admissions Office
Bronxville 10708
B.A. in English with Writing
Emphasis

Skidmore College
Writing Program Director
Department of English
Saratoga Springs 12866
B.A. in English with Concentration
in Creative Writing

Southampton College
Chairman, English Department
Southampton 11968
B.A. in Writing and Literature

State University of New York
Writing Program Director
Department of English
Binghamton 13901
B.A. in English with Specialization
in Creative Writing

State University of New York
Chairman, English Department
Brockport 14420
B.A. in English with Concentration
in Writing

State University of New York
Director, Program in Writing Arts
Oswego 13126
B.A. in English with Concentration
in Writing Arts

North Carolina

East Carolina University
English Department
Greenville 27834
B.A. in English with Concentration
in Writing

North Carolina State University
Writing-Editing Chairman
School of Humanities
Raleigh 27650
B.A. in English with Writing-
Editing Option

Saint Andrews Presbyterian
Writers' Program Director
Laurinburg 28352
B.A. in English with Concentration
in Writing

North Dakota

University of North Dakota
Chairman, English Department
Grand Forks 58202
B.A. and B.S. in English with
Concentration in Creative
Writing

Ohio

Antioch University
Dean, Antioch International
Writing Program
Yellow Springs 45387
B.A. in Creative Writing

Bowling Green State University
Bowling Green 43403
B.F.A. in Creative Writing

Case Western Reserve University
Chairman, English Department
Cleveland 44106
B.A. in English with Concentration
in Writing

College of Wooster
Writing Program
Department of English
Wooster 44691
B.A. in English with Writing
Emphasis

Denison University
Director, Writing Program
Granville 43023
B.A. in English with Major in
Writing

Kent State University
Writing Program Director
Department of English
Kent 44242
Certificate in Creative and
Expository Writing

Miami University
Writing Program Director
Department of English
Oxford 45056
B.A. in English with Creative
Writing Concentration

Oberlin College
Director, The Creative Writing
Program
Rice Hall
Oberlin 44074
B.A. in Creative Writing

Ohio University
Athens 45701
B.A. in English with Concentration
in Creative Writing

Otterbein College
Chairman, English Department
Westerville 43081
B.A. in English with Concentration
in Writing and Language

University of Cincinnati
Cincinnati 45221
B.A. in English with Writing
Certificate

Oklahoma

University of Oklahoma
Chairman, English Department
Norman 73069
B.A. in English with Emphasis in
Creative Writing

University of Tulsa
Chairman, Rhetoric and Writing
Department
Tulsa 74104
B.A. in Rhetoric and Writing

Pennsylvania

Carnegie-Mellon University
Writing Program Director
Department of English
Pittsburgh 15213
B.A. in Creative Writing

Juniata College
Chairman, English Department
Huntingdon 16652
B.A. in English with Writing
Emphasis

King's College
Chairman, English Department
Wilkes-Barre 18711
B.A. in English with Concentration
in Writing

La Salle College
Philadelphia 19141
B.A. in English with Concentration
in Writing

Lock Haven State College
Writing Program Director
Lock Haven 17745
B.A. and B.S. in English with

Concentration in Creative
Writing

University of Pennsylvania
Writing Program Director
Department of English
Philadelphia 19104
B.A. in English with Concentration
in Writing

University of Pittsburgh
Chairman, English Department
Pittsburgh 15260
B.A. in English with
Concentrations in Fiction,
Newspaper, or Magazine Writing

University of Pittsburgh
Chairman, English Department
Johnstown 15504
B.A. in Creative Writing

West Chester State College
Chairman, Creative Writing
Department of English
West Chester 19380
B.A. in English with Concentration
in Creative Writing

Westminster College
Writing Program Director
Department of English
New Wilmington 16142
B.A. in English with Concentration
in Writing

Rhode Island

Brown University
Writing Program Director
Department of English
Providence 02912
A.B. in English with Creative
Writing Emphasis

Roger Williams College
c/o Creative Writing Program
Division of Fine Arts
Bristol 02809
B.F.A. in Creative Writing

South Carolina

Columbia College
Director, Center for the Writing
Arts
Department of English
Columbia 29203
B.A. in English with Writing
Emphasis

South Dakota

University of South Dakota
Writing Program Director
Department of English
Vermillion 57069
B.A. or B.S. in English with
Creative Writing Emphasis

Tennessee

University of Tennessee
Writing Program Director
Department of English
Chattanooga 37401
B.A. in English with Concentration
in Writing

University of Tennessee
Director, Creative Writing
English Department
Knoxville 37916
B.A. in Creative Writing

Vanderbilt University
Director, Creative Writing
Department of English
Nashville 37235
B.A. in English with Creative
Writing Track

Texas

McMurray College
Chairman, Department of English
Abilene 79605
B.A. in English and Writing

Saint Edwards University
Chairman, Humanities Department
Austin 78704
B.A. in English with Writing
Emphasis

Southern Methodist University
Writing Program Director
Department of English
Dallas 75275
B.A. in English with Concentration
in Writing

University of Texas
Chairman, English Department
Austin 78712
B.A. in English with Concentration
in Creative Writing

University of Texas
c/o Writing Program
School of Arts and Humanities
Richardson 75080
B.A. in English with Concentration
in Writing

Utah

Brigham Young University
Provo 84602
B.A. in English with Writing
Emphasis

Vermont

Bennington College
Writing Program Director
Department of Languages and
Literature
Bennington 05201
B.A. in English with Creative
Writing Concentration

Johnson State College
Director, Humanities Division
Johnson 05656
B.F.A. in Writing

Virginia

Emory and Henry College
Chairman, English Department
Emory 24327
B.A. in English with Writing Track

George Mason University
Fairfax 22030
B.A. in English with Major in
Writing

Hollins College for Women
Hollins 24020
B.A. in English with Concentration
in Creative Writing

Mary Washington College
Fredericksburg 22401
B.A. in English with Concentration
in Writing

Old Dominion University
Chairman, English Department
Norfolk 23508
B.A. in English with Writing
Concentration

Radford University
Chairman, English Department
Radford 24142
B.A. or B.S. in English with
Writing Concentration

Sweet Briar College
Creative Writing Program
Sweet Briar 24595
B.A. in English and Creative
Writing

University of Virginia
Writing Program Director
Department of English
Charlottesville 22903
B.A. in English with Concentration
in Creative Writing

Washington

Central Washington University
Chairman, English Department
Ellenburg 98926
B.A. in English with Concentration
in Creative Writing

Eastern Washington University
Cheney 99004
B.A. in English with Concentration
in Creative Writing

Western Washington University
Director of Creative Writing
Department of English
Bellingham 98225
B.A. in English with Concentration
in Writing

West Virginia

Alderson-Broaddus College
Writing Program Director
Department of English
Philippi 26416
B.A. in Humanities with
Concentration in Creative
Writing

Wisconsin

University of Wisconsin
Chairman, English Department
Green Bay 54302
B.A. in English with Creative
Writing Track

University of Wisconsin
Director of Creative Writing
Department of English
Helen C. White Hall
600 North Park Street
Madison 53706
B.A. in English with Creative
Writing Emphasis

Institutions That Offer Degrees in Photography

For an explanation of degrees abbreviated below, see the introductory note to Appendix VIII.

Alabama

John C. Calhoun State
  Community College
Art Department
P.O. Box 2216
Decatur 35602
A.A. in Photography

Arizona

Arizona State University
Art Department
Tempe 85281
B.F.A. in Photography

Northern Arizona University
Journalism Department
C.U. Box 6001
Flagstaff 86011
B.A. in Photography

Northland Pioneer College
Photography Department
P.O. Drawer Y

Show Low 85901
A.A. in Photography

Scottsdale Community College
9000 East Chaparral
Scottsdale 85252
A.A. in Photography

University of Arizona
Fine Arts Department
Tucson 85721
B.F.A. in Photography

California

Bakersfield College
Art Department
1801 Panorama Drive
Bakersfield 93305
A.A. in Photography

Brooks Institute
2190 Alston Road
Santa Barbara 93108
A.A. and B.A. in Photography

California College of Arts
and Crafts
Film Arts Department
5212 Broadway
Oakland 94618
B.F.A. in Photography

California Institute of the Arts
School of Art and Design
24700 McBean Parkway
Valencia 91355
B.F.A. in Photography

California State University
Art Department
Shaw and Maple Streets
Fresno 93710
B.A. in Photography

California State University
Art Department
800 N. State College Blvd.
Fullerton 92634
B.A. in Photography

California State University
Industrial Education Department
Long Beach 90840
B.A. in Photography

California State University
Art Department
18111 Nordhoff Street
Northridge 91324
B.A. in Photography

Chaffey College
Creative Arts Department
5885 Haven Avenue
Alta Loma 91701
A.A. in Photography

City College of San Francisco
Photography Department
50 Phelan Avenue
San Francisco 94112
A.A. in Photography

College of the Redwoods
Art Department

Tomkins Hill Road
Eureka 95501
A.A. in Photography

Cypress College
Photography Department
9200 Valley View
Cypress 90630
A.A. in Photography

De Anza College
Photography Department
21250 Stevens Creek
Cupertino 95014
A.A. in Photography

Foothill College
Fine Arts Department
Los Altos 94022
A.A. in Photography

Lone Mountain College
Art Department
2800 Turk Blvd.
San Francisco 94118
B.F.A. in Photography

Long Beach City College
Photography Department
1305 P.C.H.
Long Beach 90806
A.A. in Photography

Modesto Junior College
Art and Photography Department
College Ave.
Modesto 95355
A.A. in Photography

Mount San Antonio College
1100 N. Grand Avenue
Walnut 91789
A.A. in Photography

Mount San Jacinto College
Photography Department
21400 Highway 79
San Jacinto 92383
A.A. in Photography

Palomar College
Communication Department
San Marcos 92069
A.A. in Photography

Pasadena City College
Art Department
1570 E. Colorado Blvd.
Pasadena 91106
A.A. in Photography

Rio Hondo College
Fine Arts Department
3600 Workman Hill Road
Whittier 90601
A.A. in Photography

Riverside City College
4800 Magnolia
Riverside 92506
A.A. in Photography

San Francisco Art Institute
Photography Department
800 Chestnut Street
San Francisco 94133
B.F.A. in Photography

San Jose State University
Photography Department
125 S. 11th Street
San Jose 95192
B.A. in Photography

Taft College
Fine Arts Department
29 Emmons Park Drive
Taft 93268
A.A. in Photography

University of California
Art Department
Davis 95616
B.A. in Photography

University of California
Art Department
Riverside 92502
B.A. in Photography

Ventura College
Photography Department
4667 Telegraph Road
Ventura 93003
A.A. in Photography

Colorado

Colorado Mountain College
Photography Department
West Campus
Glenwood Springs 81601
A.A. in Photography

Metropolitan State
Art Department
1006 11th Street
Denver 80204
B.A. in Photography

University of Colorado
Fine Arts Department
Boulder 80309
B.A. in Photography

Connecticut

University of Bridgeport
Art Department
Bridgeport 06602
A.A., B.A., and B.F.A. in
Photography

Wesleyan University
Art Department
Middletown 06457
B.A. in Photography

Western Connecticut Community
College
Audiovisual Department
181 White Street
Danbury 06801
B.A. in Photography

District of Columbia

George Washington University
Art Department

2013 G Street
Washington, DC 20006
B.A. in Photography

Florida

Art Institute of Fort Lauderdale
Photography Department
3000 E. Las Olas Blvd.
Fort Lauderdale 33316
A.A. in Photography

Barry College
Fine Arts Department
11300 N.E. Second Ave.
Miami Shores 33161
B.F.A. in Photography

Brevard Community College
Clear Lake Road
Cocoa 32922
A.A. in Photography

Daytona Beach Community College
Photography Department
P.O. Box 1111
Daytona Beach 32015
A.A. in Photography

Florida Atlantic University
Art Department
Boca Raton 33431
B.A. and B.F.A. in Photography

Florida Technological University
P.O. Box 25000
Alafaya Trail
Orlando 32816
B.A. and B.F.A. in Photography

University of Southern Florida
Fowler Avenue
Tampa 33620
B.A. in Photography

Georgia

Art Institute of Atlanta
Photography Department
3376 Peachtree Rd., N.E.

Atlanta 30326
A.A. in Photography

University of Georgia
Art Department
Athens 30602
B.F.A. in Photography

Hawaii

University of Hawaii
Art Department
253 The Mall
Honolulu 96822
B.F.A. in Photography

Idaho

University of Idaho
Photography Department
Moscow 83843
B.F.A. in Photography

Illinois

Belleville Area College
Photography Department
Belleville 62221
A.A. in Photography

Bradley University
Journalism Department
Peoria 61265
B.A. in Photography

College of Du Page
Photography Department
Glen Ellyn 60137
A.A. in Photography

Governors State University
Park Forest South 60466
B.A. in Photography

Illinois Institute of Technology
Design Department
3300 South Federal Street
Chicago 60616
B.A. in Photography

Prairie State College
197th and Halsted
Chicago Heights 60411
A.A. in Photography

Southern Illinois University
Photography Department
Carbondale 62901
B.A. in Photography

Stuart-Rodgers School of
Photography
2504 Greenbay Road
Evanston 60201
A.A. in Photography

Triton College
2000 Fifth Avenue
River Grove 60171
A.A. in Photography

Indiana

Ball State University
Art Department
Muncie 47306
B.A. in Photography

Indiana State University
Art Department
6th and Chestnut
Terre Haute 47809
B.A. and B.F.A. in Photography

Indiana University
Fine Arts Department
Bloomington 47401
B.A. and B.F.A. in Photography

Iowa

Grandview College
1200 Grandview Avenue
Des Moines 50316
A.A. in Photography

Hawkeye Institute of Technology
Box 8015

Waterloo 50704
A.A. in Photography

University of Iowa
Art Department
Iowa City 52240
B.F.A. in Photography

University of North Iowa
Art Department
Cedar Falls 50613
B.A. in Photography

Kentucky

Brescia College
Art Department
120 West 7th
Owensboro 42301
A.A. and B.A. in Photography

North Kentucky University
Fine Arts Department
Munn Drive
Highland Heights 41075
B.A. and B.F.A. in Photography

University of Louisville
Fine Arts Department
Louisville 40208
B.A. in Photography

Western Kentucky University
Journalism Department
Bowling Green 42101
B.A. in Photography

Louisiana

Louisiana Tech University
Art Department
Ruston 71270
B.F.A. in Photography

Northeast Louisiana University
Art Department
700 University Avenue
Monroe 71203
B.F.A. in Photography

Maine

Portland School of Art
97 Spring Street
Portland 04101
B.F.A. in Photography

Maryland

Catonsville Community College
Applied Arts Department
800 S. Rolling Road
Catonsville 21228
A.A. in Photography

Cecil Community College
Photography Department
Bay View
Northeast 21901
A.A. in Photography

College of Notre Dame
Photography Department
4701 N. Charles Street
Baltimore 21210
B.A. in Photography

Essex Community College
Art Department
7201 Rossville Blvd.
Baltimore 21237
A.A. in Photography

Loyola College
Communication Arts Department
4501 N. Charles Street
Baltimore 21212
B.A. in Photography

Maryland Institute College of Art
Photography Department
Mt. Royal Avenue
Baltimore 21217
B.F.A. in Photography

University of Maryland
Visual Arts Department
5401 Wilkins Avenue
Baltimore 21228
B.A. in Photography

Massachusetts

Boston University
Fine Arts Department
725 Commonwealth Avenue
Boston 02215
B.A. in Photography

Endicott College
Photography Department
Hale Street
Beverly 01915
A.A. in Photography

Fitchburg State College
Communications Department
Pearl Street
Fitchburg 01420
B.A. in Photography

School of the Museum of Fine Arts
Photography Department
230 Fenway
Boston 02115
B.A. and B.F.A. in Photography

Michigan

Alma College
Art Department
614 West Superior
Alma 48801
B.A. and B.F.A. in Photography

Center for Creative Studies
Photography Department
245 East Kirby
Detroit 48202
B.F.A. in Photography

Central Michigan University
Applied and Fine Arts Department
Mount Pleasant 48859
B.A. and B.F.A. in Photography

Ferris State College
Graphic Arts Department
901 South State
Big Rapids 49307
A.A. and B.A. in Photography

Lansing Community College
Media Department
419 North Capitol
Lansing 48914
A.A. in Photography

Northern Michigan University
Art Department
Marquette 49855
B.A. and B.F.A. in Photography

University of Michigan
Art Department
2000 Bonisteel Blvd.
Ann Arbor 48109
B.F.A. in Photography

Washtenaw Community College
Photography Department
4800 East Huron River Drive
Ann Arbor 48106
A.A. in Photography

Western Michigan University
Art Department
Kalamazoo 49001
B.F.A. in Photography

William James College
Art and Media Department
Allendale 49401
B.A. in Photography

Minnesota

Bemidji State University
Communications Media Department
14th and Birchmont Drive
Bemidji 56601
B.A. in Photography

Mankato State University
Art Department
Mankato 56001
B.A. and B.F.A. in Photography

Saint Cloud State University
Photography Department
Saint Cloud 56301
B.F.A. in Photography

University of Minnesota
Studio Arts Department
Minneapolis 55455
B.F.A. in Photography

Mississippi

University of Southern Mississippi
Journalism Department
Box 5344
Hattiesburg 39401
B.A. in Photography

Missouri

Kansas City Art Institute
Photography Department
4415 Warwick Blvd.
Kansas City 64111
B.F.A. in Photography

The Lindenwood Colleges
Studio and Performing Arts
    Department
Saint Charles 63301
B.A. and B.F.A. in Photography

Northeast Missouri State
Practical Arts Department
Kirksville 63501
B.A. in Photography

University of Missouri
Photojournalism Department
100 Neff Hall
Columbia 65201
B.A. in Photography

Webster College
Media Department
470 E. Lockwood
Saint Louis 63119
B.F.A. in Photography

Montana

Montana State University
Bozeman 59715
B.A. in Photography

Nebraska

University of Nebraska
Art Department
Lincoln 68588
B.F.A. in Photography

New Jersey

Mercer County Community College
Visual Arts Department
Box B
Trenton 08690
A.A. in Photography

Ocean County College
Fine Arts Department
College Drive
Toms River 08753
A.A. in Photography

Stockton State College
Media Department
Pomona 08240
B.A. in Photography

New Mexico

University of New Mexico
Art Department
Albuquerque 87131
B.A. and B.F.A. in Photography

New York

Cornell University
Art Department
Ithaca 14853
B.F.A. in Photography

Fashion Institute of Technology
Photography Department
227 West 27th Street

New York 10804
A.A.S. in Photography

Hartwick College
Art Department
Orion Hill
Oneonta 13820
B.A. in Photography

Marymount College
Art Department
Tarrytown 10591
B.A. in Photography

National Technical Institute for the
    Deaf
Visual Communications
    Department
1 Lomb Memorial Drive
Rochester 14623
A.A.S. in Photography

New School for Social Research
Photography Department
66 West 12th Street
New York 10011
B.F.A. in Photography

Pratt Institute
Photography Department
215 Ryerson Street
Brooklyn 11205
B.F.A. in Photography

Rochester Institute of Technology
Photography Department
1 Lomb Memorial Drive
Rochester 14623
A.A.S., B.A., and B.F.A. in
    Photography

School of Visual Arts
Photography Department
300 East 46th Street
New York 10010
B.F.A. in Photography

State University of New York
Studio Art Department
New Paltz 12561
B.A. and B.F.A. in Photography

State University of New York
Art Department
Oswego 13126
B.A. in Photography

State University of New York
Agricultural and Technical
  College
Farmingdale 11735
A.A. in Photography

Syracuse University
Photography Department
Syracuse 13210
B.A. in Photography

North Carolina

Chowan College
Photography Department
Jones Drive
Murfreesboro 27855
A.A. in Photography

Randolph Technical Institute
Photography Department
629 Industrial Park Avenue
Asheboro 27203
A.A. in Photography

Ohio

Antioch College
Art Department
Yellow Springs 45387
B.A. and B.F.A. in Photography

Bowling Green State
Industrial Education Department
Bowling Green 43402
B.A. in Photography

Kent State University
Journalism Department
Kent 44242
B.A. in Photography

Ohio State University
Photography Department
128 N. Ovall Mall
Columbus 43210
B.A. and B.F.A. in Photography

Ohio University
Art Department
Athens 45701
B.F.A. in Photography

University of Dayton
300 College Park Avenue
Dayton 45469
B.A. in Photography

Pennsylvania

Bucks City Community College
Photography Department
Swamp Rd.
Newtown 18940
A.A. in Photography

Community College of Philadelphia
Photography Department
34 S. 11th Street
Philadelphia 19107
A.A. in Photography

Edinboro State College
Art Department
Edinboro 16444
B.F.A. in Photography

Moore College of Art
Photography Department
20th and Race Streets
Philadelphia 19103
B.F.A. in Photography

Slippery Rock State College
Art Department
Slippery Rock 16057
B.A. in Photography

Rhode Island

University of Rhode Island
Art Department

Kingston 02881
B.F.A. in Photography

South Dakota

University of South Dakota
Art Department
Vermillion 57069
B.F.A. in Photography

Tennessee

Cleveland State Community College
Adkisson Way
Cleveland 37311
A.A. in Photography

Memphis Academy of the Arts
Photography Department
Overton Park
Memphis 38112
A.A. and B.F.A. in Photography

Memphis State University
Journalism Department
Memphis 38152
B.A. in Photography

Texas

Austin Community College
Photography Department
205 E. Fifth Street
Austin 78701
A.A. in Photography

East Texas State University
Box D, E. Texas Station
Commerce 75428
B.A. in Photography

Kilgore College
Photography Department
1101 Broadway
Kilgore 75662
A.A. in Photography

Odessa College
Photography Department

Andrewa and 27th Streets
Odessa 79760
A.A. in Photography

Sam Houston State University
Photography Department
Huntsville 77340
B.A. in Photography

Stephen F. Austin State University
Box 6073
Nacogdoches 75962
B.A. in Photography

Texas State Technical Institute
Media Department
Waco 76705
A.A. in Photography

Texas Technical University
Lubbock 79409
B.A. in Photography

Texas Women's University
Art Department
Box 22995
Denton 76201
B.A. in Photography

Utah

Brigham Young University
Communication Department
Provo 84601
B.A. and B.F.A. in Photography

University of Utah
Communication Department
Salt Lake City 84112
A.A. in Photography

Utah State University
Art Department
Logan 84322
B.A. and B.F.A. in Photography

Webber State College
Photography Department
3850 Harrison Blvd.
Ogden 84408
B.A. in Photography

Virginia

Madison College
Art Department
Harrisonburg 22801
B.F.A. in Photography

Northern Virginia Commonwealth
College
Visual Arts Department
3001 N. Beauregard Street
Alexandria 22311
A.A. in Photography

Northern Virginia Community
College
1000 Harry F. Byrd Highway
Sterling 22170
A.A. in Photography

Thomas Nelson Community College
Art Department
99 Thomas Nelson Drive
Hampton 23670
A.A. in Photography

Washington

Central Washington State
Ellenburg 98926
B.A. in Photography

Wisconsin

Madison Area Technical College
Art Department

211 N. Carroll Street
Madison 53703
A.A. in Photography

Milwaukee Area Technical College
1015 N. 6th Street
Milwaukee 53203
A.A. in Photography

Milwaukee Center for Photography
207 E. Buffalo Street
Milwaukee 53202
A.A. and B.F.A. in Photography

University of Wisconsin
Communication Department
Green Bay 54302
B.A. in Photography

University of Wisconsin
Art Department
Milwaukee 53201
B.F.A. in Photography

University of Wisconsin
Communication Department
Main Street
Platteville 53818
B.A. in Photography

University of Wisconsin
Art Department
Superior 54880
B.A. and B.F.A. in Photography

Stock-Photo Agencies
That Handle Animal Photos

California

American Stock Photos
6842 Sunset Blvd.
Hollywood 90028

Georgia

Associated Picture Service
Northside Station
Box 52881
Atlanta 30355

Illinois

Candida Photos
4711 W. Byron Street
Chicago 60641

Massachusetts

Image Photos
Main Street
Stockbridge 01262

New Hampshire

Franklin Photo Agency
39 Woodcrest Avenue
Hudson 03501

New York

Alpha Photo Associates
251 Park Avenue
New York 10010

Animals Animals Enterprises
203 West 81st Street
New York 10024

Authenticated News International
170 Fifth Avenue
New York 10010

Black Star Publishing Co.
450 Park Avenue South
New York 10016

Camera Clix, Inc.
404 Park Avenue South
New York 10016

Bruce Coleman, Inc.
15 E. 36th Street
New York 10016

A. Devaney, Inc.
40 E. 49th Street
New York 10017

Freelance Photographers'
  Guild
251 Park Avenue South
New York 10010

Louis Mercier
342 Madison Avenue
New York 10017

Stock Photos
  Unlimited
100 W. 57th Street
New York 10019

Taurus Photos
118 E. 28th Street
New York 10016

Note: Consult *The Photographer's Market* for specific magazines, book publishers, etc., to whom you might try to sell your photos directly.

Farrier Schools

Alabama

Auburn University
School of Veterinary Medicine
Auburn 36830

Arizona

Mohave Community College
4165 North Skylark
Kingman 86401

Northland Pioneer College
1200 East Hermosa Drive
Holbrook 86025

Scottsdale Community College
P.O. Box Y
Scottsdale 85253

Tucson School of Horseshoeing
4680 South Stewart
Tucson 85714

Western School of Horseshoeing
2801 West Maryland Avenue
Phoenix 85017

California

California Polytechnic State
University
Horseshoeing Unit
San Luis Obispo 93407

California Polytechnic State
University
Horseshoeing Unit
Pomona 91768

College of the Siskiyous
P.O. Box 518
Etna 96027

Denton Horseshoeing School
Route 1, P.O. Box 243
Gerber 96035

Farrier College of California
P.O. Box 651
El Centro 92243

Fresno Metropolitan R.O.P.
11 South Teilman
Fresno 93706

Gavilan College
10941 Lone Tree Road
Hollister 95023

Grossmont Unified School District
338 North Magnolia
El Cajon 92020

La Puente Valley Adult Schools
320 North Willow
La Puente 91746

Lassen College
Route 3, P.O. Box 101-C
Susanville 96130

Marysville Unified School District
172 Circle Drive
Oroville 95901

Merced College
Agriculture Division
3600 M Street
Merced 95340

Porterville Horseshoeing School
P.O. Box 1632
Porterville 93258

Sacramento County R.O.P.
6248 Main Avenue
Orangevale 95662

Santa Cruz Horseshoeing School
722 Buena Vista Drive
Watsonville 95076

Shasta Community College
1065 North Old Oregon Trail
Redding 96001

The Thacher School
Horse Program
5025 Thacher Road
Ojai 93023

Valley Vocational Center
15359 East Proctor Avenue
City of Industry 91744

Colorado

Colorado Mountain College
School of Horseshoeing
P.O. Box 9010
Steamboat Springs 80477

Colorado State University
7-C Animal Science Building
Fort Collins 80523

Lamar Community College
2400 South Main Street
Lamar 81052

Pikes Peak Community College
1528 Turner Road
Colorado Springs 80918

Delaware

Warrington's School of
Horseshoeing
R.D. 2
Townsend 19734

Georgia

Southeastern School of
Horseshoeing
Route 5, Union Hill
Canton 30114

Illinois

Bast Horseshoeing School
P.O. Box 351
Tallula 62688

Equine Educational Services
P.O. Box 413, Dept. HS
O'Fallon 62269

Midwest Horseshoeing School
R.R. 3
Macomb 61455

Iowa

Tri-State Farrier's College
Highway 60
Sibley 51249

Kansas

Colby Community College
1255 South Range
Colby 67701

Dodge City Community College
Horse Science Department
Dodge City 67801

Kansas Horseshoeing School
Route 1, P.O. Box 33
Girard 66743

Kentucky

Kentucky Horseshoeing School
P.O. Box 120
Mount Eden 40046

Murray State University
Department of Agriculture
P.O. Box 2847, University Station
Murray 42071

Louisiana

Northwestern State University
Admissions Office
Natchitoches 71457

Michigan

Michigan School of Horseshoeing
P.O. Box 423
Belleville 48111

Mott Community College
1401 East Court
Flint 48503

Wolverine Farrier School
7690 Wiggins Road
Howell 48843

Minnesota

Anoka Vocational Technical
    Institute
P.O. Box 191
Anoka 55303

Minnesota School of Horseshoeing
6260 Highway 10, N.W.
Anoka 55303

Mississippi

Mid-South Academy of
    Horseshoeing
568 Laughter Road
Hernando 38632

Montana

Montana State University
Horseshoeing School
Bozeman 59715

New Jersey

South Jersey School of
    Horseshoeing
R.D. Box 126
Mullica Hill 08062

New Mexico

New Mexico State University
P.O. Box 3051
Las Cruces 88003

New York

Cornell University
Department of Clinical Sciences
Ithaca 14850

Eastern States Farrier School
R.D. 1, P.O. Box 49
Phoenix 13135

North Carolina

North Carolina School of
    Horseshoeing
Route 1, P.O. Box 343
Pleasant Garden 27313

Ohio

Great Oaks Joint Vocational School
    District
6930 Blue Rock Road
Cincinnati 45239

Ohio Horseshoeing School
2545 State Route 235
Xenia 45385

Otterbein College
Equine Science Program
Westerville 43081

Oklahoma

Eastern Oklahoma State College
Horseshoeing Program
Wilburton 74578

Oklahoma Farriers' College
Route 2, P.O. Box 88
Sperry 74073

Oklahoma Horseshoeing School
R.R. 4, P.O. Box 370
Oklahoma City 73111

Oklahoma State Horseshoeing
School
Route 1, P.O. Box 28-B
Ardmore 73401

Panhandle State University
Animal Science Department
Goodwell 73939

Superior Horseshoeing School
Route 2
Marietta 73448

Oregon

Clackamas Community College
P.O. Box 40
Beaver Creek 97004

Lane Community College
40093 Little Fall Creek Road
Fall Creek 97438

Linn-Benton Community College
Farrier School
630 N.W. Seventh
Corvallis 97330

Pennsylvania

Pennsylvania School of
Horseshoeing
R.D. 2, P.O. Box 20
New Holland 17557

Pennsylvania State University
324 Animal Industries Bldg.
University Park 16802

University of Pennsylvania
New Bolton Center
Kennett Square 19348

Texas

Hyatt School of Horseshoeing
Route 1, P.O. Box 232-A
Pottsboro 75076

North Texas Farriers' College
P.O. Box 666
Mineral Wells 76067

North Texas Horseshoeing Institute
821 East Southlake Boulevard
Grapevine 76051

Sul Ross State University
Animal Science Program
P.O. Box C-110
Alpine 79830

Tennessee

Middle Tennessee State University
Route 1, P.O. Box 295
Charleston 37310

Utah

Weston Blacksmithing School
P.O. Box 11161
Salt Lake City 84147

Virginia

Eastern School of Farriery
P.O. Box 1368
Martinsville 24112

Washington

Olympia Tech. Community College
P.O. Box 1905
Olympia 98507

Spokane Falls Community College
P.O. Box 141032
Spokane 99214

Walla Walla Community College
500 Tausick Way
Walla Walla 99362

West Virginia

Meredith Manor
Route 1, P.O. Box 76
Waverly 26184

Wisconsin

Blackhawk Vocational Technical
School
Route 3, Prairie Road
Janesville 53545

University of Wisconsin
Department of Animal Science
River Falls 54022

Gateway Technical Institute
East Centralia St. and Hwy. H
Elkhorn 53121

Wyoming

Central Wyoming College
Life and Physical Science Division
Riverton 82501

Northwest Community College
Horse Management Program
Powell 82435

All-Breed Magazines

American Horseman
257 Park Avenue South
New York, NY 10010

Bridle & Bit
Star Route 2, Box 680
Cave Creek, AZ 85331

Chronicle of the Horse
Middleburg, VA 22117

Equus
656 Quince Orchard Road
Gaithersburg, MD 20760

Grand Prix
P.O. Box 640
Chestertown, MD 21620

Horse & Horseman
P.O. Box HH
Capistrano Beach, CA 92624

Horse & Rider
41919 Moreno Road
Temecula, CA 92390

Horse Illustrated
31110 Riverside Drive, Box A
Lake Elsinore, CA 92330

Horse Lover's National Magazine
P.O. Box 3003
Menlo Park, CA 94025

Horse of Course
Temple, NH 03084

Horse Play
443 N. Frederick Avenue
Box 545
Gaithersburg, MD 20760

*Horseman, The Magazine of
Western Riding*
5314 Bingle Road
Houston, TX 77092

Practical Horseman
225 S. Church Street
West Chester, PA 19380

Spur
Delaplane, VA 22025

Trail Rider
Rte. 1, Box 387
Chatsworth, GA 30705

The Western Horseman
P.O. Box 7980
Colorado Springs, CO 80933

Horse Industry Associations

American Association of Equine
 Practitioners
Route 5
22363 Hillcrest Circle
Golden, CO 80401

American Farriers Association
P.O. Box 695
Albuquerque, NM 87103

American Horse Council
1700 K Street, N.W.

Suite 300
Washington, D.C. 20006

American Horse Shows Association
598 Madison Avenue
New York, NY 10022

National 4-H Service Committee
150 North Wacker Drive
Chicago, IL 60605